INTRODUCING RDA

ALA Editions purchases fund advocacy, awareness, and
accreditation programs for library professionals worldwide.

ALA Editions • **SPECIAL REPORTS**

INTRODUCING RDA

A Guide to the Basics after 3R

Second Edition

CHRIS OLIVER

CHICAGO 2021

CHRIS OLIVER is the head of Metadata and Processing at the University of Ottawa Library. She has been a cataloging manager in academic libraries for over twenty-five years and has participated in the development of cataloging standards for over twenty years. She has a long history of involvement with RDA, beginning with her years as chair of the Canadian Committee on Cataloguing, one of the bodies that contributed to the development of RDA. Then, in 2016, she changed her involvement from RDA development to RDA governance, becoming a member of the RDA Board as the representative of the Canadian Federation of Library Associations. She was chair of the IFLA Bibliographic Conceptual Models Review Group (formerly the FRBR Review Group) from 2013 to 2019. She continues to serve on the Review Group and is also a member of the IFLA Standing Committee on Subject Analysis and Access. She has been invited to give numerous presentations and training sessions on RDA in North America and around the world.

© 2021 by Chris Oliver

Extensive effort has gone into ensuring the reliability of the information in this book; however, the publisher makes no warranty, express or implied, with respect to the material contained herein.

ISBNs
978-0-8389-1908-8 (paper)
978-0-8389-4888-0 (PDF)
978-0-8389-4861-3 (ePub)

Library of Congress Cataloging-in-Publication Data

Names: Oliver, Chris, 1951– author.
Title: Introducing RDA : a guide to the basics after 3R / Chris Oliver.
Description: Second edition. | Chicago : ALA Editions, 2021. | Series: ALA editions special report | Includes bibliographical references and index. | Summary: "Reflecting the changes to RDA: Resource Description and Access after the completion of the 3R Project, Oliver brings her Special Report up to date. This essential primer provides an overview of the latest developments, focusing on the impact of the 3R Project, the results of aligning RDA with IFLA's Library Reference Model (LRM), and the outcomes of internationalization"—Provided by publisher.
Identifiers: LCCN 2020030015 (print) | LCCN 2020030016 (ebook) |
  ISBN 9780838919088 (paperback) | ISBN 9780838948613 (epub) |
  ISBN 9780838948880 (pdf)
Subjects: LCSH: Resource description & access. | Descriptive cataloging—Standards. | Cataloging—Standards.
Classification: LCC Z694.15.R47 O45 2021 (print) | LCC Z694.15.R47 (ebook) |
  DDC 025.3/2—dc23
LC record available at https://lccn.loc.gov/2020030015
LC ebook record available at https://lccn.loc.gov/2020030016

Series cover design by Casey Bayer. Series text design in Palatino Linotype and Interstate by Karen Sheets de Gracia.

♾ This paper meets the requirements of ANSI/NISO Z39.48-1992 (Permanence of Paper).

Printed in the United States of America
25 24 23 22   5 4 3 2

CONTENTS

Preface vii
Acknowledgments ix
List of Abbreviations xi

1 What Is RDA? 1
    1.1 The 3R Project 1
    1.2 Based on a Theoretical Framework 3
    1.3 Designed for the Digital Environment 4
    1.4 A Global Standard Appropriate for Use in Many Contexts 9
    1.5 Impact 11

2 RDA: An International Standard 15
    2.1 Alignment with International Principles, Models, and Standards 15
    2.2 Capacity for Use in an International Context 19
    2.3 Integration of Translations and the Translation Workflow 24
    2.4 Shared Governance 26

3 The IFLA Bibliographic Conceptual Models 33
    3.1 Overview of FRBR, FRAD, and FRSAD 34
    3.2 IFLA Library Reference Model 49
    3.3 Role of the Models 67

4 RDA's Background: Evolution from AACR2 into RDA 73
    4.1 Building on the Foundations of AACR 73
    4.2 Deconstruction of AACR2 74
    4.3 Continuity with AACR2 79
    4.4 Moving away from AACR2 87

5 RDA: Some Key Aspects 93
    5.1 Focus on the User 93
    5.2 Structure of RDA 95

5.3 Content and Carrier   103
   5.4 RDA Elements   109
   5.5 Aggregates   121
   5.6 Shortcuts   125
   5.7 Nomen   127
   5.8 New Ways of Thinking about Resource Description   131
   5.9 Summary   141

6 **Using RDA   145**
   6.1 Navigation in the RDA Toolkit   145
   6.2 Recording Methods   155
   6.3 Element Reference   159
   6.4 Condition/Option   163
   6.5 Encoding Schemes: Vocabulary Encoding Schemes and String Encoding Schemes   166
   6.6 Policy Statements and Application Profiles   171
   6.7 Data Provenance   175
   6.8 Examples   180
   6.9 Glossary   185

7 **RDA after the 3R Project   189**

Sources for Further Information   195
Index   197

PREFACE

The first edition of *Introducing RDA* was published in 2010. Ten years have passed and there have been changes to RDA, the standard, and to the RDA Toolkit. This edition of *Introducing RDA* is a guide to the basics "after 3R," that is, after the 3R Project.

The 3R Project is a short way of referring to the RDA Toolkit Restructure and Redesign Project. The project quickly became known as 3R: RDA, Restructure, Redesign. RDA has a different look and feel due to this restructure and redesign.

The 3R Project began in 2017 and took several years to complete. When I refer to RDA after 3R, the reference is not to RDA at a single point in time, but rather to the start of a new phase of RDA—RDA as it appears in the restructured RDA Toolkit. A beginning point for this phase is when the bulk of the major changes were completed with the stabilization of the English text in April 2019. "RDA after 3R" refers to RDA as it appears in the new RDA Toolkit after April 2019. When first released, it was called the "beta Toolkit." As of December 15, 2020, it is the regular, official RDA Toolkit. In this book, it is called the "new RDA Toolkit" to distinguish it from the original RDA Toolkit.

RDA after the 3R Project is not considered a new edition of RDA. RDA is an online integrating resource that is updated several times a year. RDA is developing all the time. RDA in the original RDA Toolkit and in the new RDA Toolkit is fundamentally the same. It is developed following the same objectives and principles. There are new aspects, but it also continues to support the same ways of working as in the original RDA Toolkit.

This edition of *Introducing RDA* is a complete revision of the first edition. Most of the original text was condensed and revised or removed to allow space for focusing on RDA in the new RDA Toolkit. This edition includes an overview of the major developments since the publication of RDA in 2010, focusing especially on developments that occurred during the 3R Project: the impact of the 3R Project itself, the results of aligning RDA with IFLA's Library Reference Model (IFLA LRM), and the outcomes of internationalization. This edition updates references to RDA text to match the wording and placement of those texts in the new RDA Toolkit (RDA September 2020). Images are from the December 2020 release of RDA Toolkit.

ACKNOWLEDGMENTS

I would like to acknowledge those who generously offered advice and comments while I was writing this edition. With much appreciation, thank you to Kate James, Pat Riva, Bill Leonard, Christian Aliverti, Laura May, Alexandre Fortier, David Oliver, and Jenny Wright.

ABBREVIATIONS

AACR	*Anglo-American Cataloguing Rules*
AACR2	*Anglo-American Cataloguing Rules*, 2nd edition
BIBFRAME	Bibliographic Framework
FRAD	Functional Requirements for Authority Data
FRBR	Functional Requirements for Bibliographic Records
FRSAD	Functional Requirements for Subject Authority Data
ICP	Statement on International Cataloguing Principles
IFLA	International Federation of Library Associations and Institutions
IFLA LRM	IFLA Library Reference Model
IRI	Internationalized Resource Identifier
ISBD	International Standard Bibliographic Description
MARC 21	MARC = Machine Readable Cataloging
	MARC 21 = a harmonized MARC format used in many countries
ONIX	Online Information eXchange
RSC	RDA Steering Committee
RDF	Resource Description Framework

1
WHAT IS RDA?

RDA, Resource Description and Access, is an international metadata standard designed to enable the discovery of library and cultural heritage resources in both traditional and linked data environments. It evolved out of the *Anglo-American Cataloguing Rules*, 2nd edition (AACR2), but RDA is quite different. It presents a new way of thinking about bibliographic data. It is based on a theoretical framework, it is designed as a standard for the digital environment, and it is developed as a global standard appropriate for use in many contexts. This chapter will give a brief overview of the key aspects that define RDA. These aspects are then explored in more detail in the following chapters. Before looking at these aspects, the chapter begins with a quick summary of the 3R Project to set the stage for the current edition of this book.

1.1 The 3R Project

1.2 Based on a Theoretical Framework

1.3 Designed for the Digital Environment

1.4 A Global Standard Appropriate for Use in Many Contexts

1.5 Impact

1.1   THE 3R PROJECT

For the cataloging community, the publication of RDA in 2010 marked a new approach to the recording of bibliographic data but it also introduced a new way of using the standard. RDA was designed to be used as an online tool. The content of the standard was published as part of an online web-based tool, RDA Toolkit.[1] The text of RDA had been prepared as a series of documents and these were then transferred into specially designed software in 2010.

As an online standard, it was straightforward to implement a process of regular updates and revisions to the content of RDA. This process began in 2011, with new amendments integrated into RDA beginning in April 2012. The yearly amendments to RDA instructions were the result of development work carried out through consultation and community input. There were also small "fast track" changes periodically throughout the year to correct minor problems such as typographical errors or incorrect links. This pattern of revision continued until 2017, when the original RDA Toolkit was frozen and work began on the 3R Project.

In an online environment, the pace of change is fast. Provision had been made to update the text of RDA regularly, but the software also needed to be updated. By 2016, it was becoming evident that the RDA Toolkit site needed some renewal and reorganization. It was labor-intensive and cumbersome to revise the standard. For example, the original structure and instruction numbering were inflexible, making it difficult to move instructions to more logical places and to expand the content. The interface was becoming dated, and the site did not meet international accessibility standards. The outcomes of the 2016 annual meetings of both the RDA Board and the RDA Steering Committee note plans for a "Toolkit reorganization" project.[2]

The 3R Project was announced in October 2016 and began in 2017.[3] The full name of the project was the RDA Toolkit Restructure and Redesign Project, but it was quickly nicknamed the 3R Project: RDA, Restructure, Redesign. The project covered changes in both the software and the content. On the technological side, there were changes to the way RDA instructions were stored; a thorough updating of the software; new efficiencies in design to streamline the editing and translating process; compliance with current accessibility standards; and modernizing the user interface. On the content side, RDA needed to be aligned with the most recent bibliographic conceptual model, the IFLA Library Reference Model (IFLA LRM).[4]

RDA after the 3R Project is still the same standard. The user interface in the new RDA Toolkit is very different, and the text of the standard is no longer presented as a linear e-book with a beginning, middle, and end. Much of the content is reorganized and appears in different places. There are areas that were expanded to make the standard more flexible and modular, taking into consideration both current requirements and expected future needs. Some wording was adjusted for consistency and to enable efficiencies for those who write, edit, and translate RDA text. The "guidelines" part of the standard was reorganized and expanded to support the new structure.

Although some elements are renamed, some instructions have different wording, and the organization of the content has been significantly altered, people who used RDA in the original RDA Toolkit will be able to continue to use RDA basically in the same way. For example, when recording data about a print book, one still records the date of publication, such as "2020." It is a discrete and precise data element, an element that describes the manifestation. Originally, it was treated as a descriptive characteristic, an attribute. Now *date of publication* is understood to be a relationship between a *manifestation* and a *timespan*. The data recorded in this element is a value of *timespan*.[5] However, as a cataloger, I am still recording "2020." There may be an updated way of thinking about the data element, but I am still recording the same recognizable data.

The RDA Toolkit has undergone dramatic changes. RDA is an online integrating resource with updates seamlessly integrated into the text. RDA in the new RDA Toolkit is still the same standard. It is not considered a new edition of RDA, nor is it RDA 2.0.[6]

The standard does not prescribe one single way of doing things but offers choices so that different communities can apply RDA in ways that fit with their needs. But even with the variances created by following different options, at the root, the metadata shares the same element set, uses the same controlled vocabularies, and is aligned with the same conceptual model. Thus, there is a fundamental consistency that supports data interoperability.

1.2   BASED ON A THEORETICAL FRAMEWORK

The purpose of RDA as defined in the Introduction:

> *Resource Description and Access* is a package of data elements, guidelines, and instructions for creating library and cultural heritage metadata that are well-formed according to international models.[7]

The defining feature of RDA is that it is based on a theoretical framework that shapes the structure and content of the standard and this framework comes from IFLA's bibliographic conceptual models.[8] The key to understanding RDA is its alignment with IFLA's bibliographic conceptual models.

IFLA's bibliographic conceptual models are a way of understanding the bibliographic universe. They make explicit what is implicitly understood about bibliographic data; their purpose is "to reveal the commonalities and underlying structure of bibliographic resources."[9] They identify the types of bibliographic data[10] and functionality needed by users to support successful resource discovery. The models provide a theoretical and logically coherent basis on which to build an improved resource discovery experience for the user.

In 2010, when RDA was first published, it was aligned with the first two of IFLA's conceptual models, Functional Requirements for Bibliographic Records (FRBR)[11] and Functional Requirements for Authority Data (FRAD).[12] In 2015, some additions were made to RDA so that it also aligned with Functional Requirements for Subject Authority Data (FRSAD).[13] FRAD and FRSAD were extensions of the FRBR model. Thus, as of 2015, RDA was essentially aligned with all three IFLA models that were in force at that time.[14]

In 2017, those three models became obsolete with the approval and publication of IFLA's new bibliographic conceptual model: IFLA Library Reference Model (IFLA LRM). Part of the 3R Project was to make the changes required to maintain alignment with the new model, IFLA LRM. The new model introduced changes that were difficult to integrate within the 2010 structure of RDA, such as introducing new entities.[15] The 3R Project provided an opportunity to extend the restructuring to include the revisions to RDA's structure required for alignment with IFLA LRM.

IFLA's models focus on the perspective and needs of the end user and this focus is expressed through the user tasks. The table below presents an excerpt from IFLA LRM table 3.1.

User Tasks Summary
Find
Identify
Select
Obtain
Explore

RDA adopts this same focus on the user. RDA references these same user tasks as a means to ensure that metadata will meet user needs. When RDA was originally published, the relationship between RDA elements and user tasks was explicitly mentioned throughout the instructions because it was a new approach. This perspective continues to shape the content of RDA in the new RDA Toolkit. However, many data elements can be used in different ways and almost all can be seen to support more than one user task. It was more efficient to summarize the user tasks in a "Guidance" section rather than explicitly noting relationships to user tasks throughout the text.

RDA, since its beginning, takes as its starting point the theoretical framework expressed in IFLA's bibliographic conceptual models. The practical instructions are organized according to this framework and the content of the instructions is shaped by the perspective of user needs and user tasks. When RDA was first published in 2010, this alignment with a theoretical framework was a new way of thinking about bibliographic data. It is no longer novel, but it continues to be a defining feature of RDA.

1.3 DESIGNED FOR THE DIGITAL ENVIRONMENT

The phrase "designed for the digital environment" was used to describe the purpose of RDA at a very early stage, in the Strategic Plan for RDA, 2005–2009.[16] The changes in the cataloging environment between the 1960s and 2000s were enormous, not only because of the rapid proliferation of new types of publications, new forms of content, and new carriers for content, but also because of the move into a highly networked online environment. This new environment qualitatively changed the way libraries and their users went about their work. Our understanding of the digital environment has continued to evolve into a more precise and nuanced understanding of the types of intellectual and artistic creations that can be produced and disseminated through the use of computers, and of new ways that machine processing and artificial intelligence can be applied to complex data with satisfactory results.

1.3.1 Bibliographic Information as Data

RDA's purpose is to support the production of robust or well-formed data[17] that can be managed using both current and upcoming technologies. Well-formed data has a consistent structure that is recognizable both by humans and by computers. It is well-defined and unambiguous data.

RDA answers the question: what data should I record and how should I record it? RDA defines the elements required for description and access and gives instructions on formulating the data that is recorded in each element. Where AACR2 led the cataloger to produce strings of characters, RDA leads the cataloger or metadata creator to produce data that is parsed or segmented into clearly defined elements that can be interpreted by humans and machines. Humans can easily decipher long strings of information and resolve ambiguity. But computers cannot. Machine processing requires bibliographic information that is recorded as distinct and precise data elements. RDA elements may seem choppy after the paragraph style of ISBD (International Standard Bibliographic Description)[18] and AACR2, but each element is unambiguously defined and contains one and only one particular kind of data. This way of recording data in a set of elements means that RDA data can be processed by computers in an effective way. It also means that RDA is not tied to a single encoding scheme or presentation style.

This does not mean that one can only use RDA in a high-tech environment. RDA offers different options for recording data according to the technological environment in which a metadata creator or cataloger operates.[19] Thus, RDA is optimized for machine processing, but RDA data can also be recorded in ways that are compatible with simpler technological environments.

RDA was designed to make bibliographical information usable as data. It was not designed for one particular encoding scheme; the intention is that RDA data should be suitable for use with a range of different encoding schemes. RDA is intended to be the basis for a metadata element set that will make data visible and usable in library catalogs, on the World Wide Web or in a Semantic Web environment.

Some schemas are better suited for encoding RDA than others, but it is possible to encode RDA data using existing schema, such as MARC 21, and it is also possible to use more web-friendly encoding schemes such as RDF (Resource Description Framework).[20] RDA will be encoded using new schema such as BIBFRAME (Bibliographic Framework)[21] and future schema as well.

1.3.2 Extensibility

RDA provides an extensible framework for the description of all types of resources. It provides the principles and instructions to record data about resources that are currently known and resources that have yet to be developed. This was a key point in the original strategic plan for RDA: RDA was designed to "provide a consistent, flexible, and extensible framework for both the technical and content description of all types of resources and all types of content."[22]

This extensible framework was an important feature in the development of RDA because it addressed a major stumbling block in its predecessor, AACR2. AACR2 did not have a structure that supported the description of new types of resources. AACR2 was originally developed as a cataloging code for print and paper-based documents. While rules for other media were grafted into the code, there was never a cohesive and logically consistent approach to the description of content, media, and carrier. This limitation made it difficult to extend AACR2 rules for the description of new types of resources, notably electronic resources.

RDA defines an extensive set of elements that can be used in many different combinations according to the needs of a metadata community. The move from long strings of bibliographic information to elements also makes it possible for other data communities to use all or parts of RDA's element set (as well as its controlled vocabularies).[23] Even as early as 2012, there were several examples where RDA elements were being used in linked data projects, such as projects at the British Library and the Deutsche Nationalbibliothek, along with data elements from other standards.[24] RDA is designed to be compatible with the structure of other metadata standards, particularly other standards optimized for Semantic Web use. This extends the usability of RDA and supports interoperability with data recorded according to other standards that share similar principles.

1.3.3 The Standard Delivered as a Web Tool

When RDA was published in 2010, the definitive version of the standard was the text within RDA Toolkit. The standard was delivered within RDA Toolkit along with tools and other resources to facilitate use of the standard in daily work. The standard was presented in an e-book format enabled with linking functionality for ease of use and exploration. The RDA Toolkit included mappings that indicated how to encode RDA elements with different encoding schema. Libraries and other institutions were able to share workflows and mappings, customize them, incorporate their local policies and procedures, and store them as part of RDA Toolkit, often also making them accessible to the larger community of RDA users.

After the 3R Project, RDA Toolkit continues to include the authoritative text of the standard; it also continues to include tools that support the efficient integration of RDA into the daily work of metadata creation. The redesign of RDA Toolkit changed the presentation of RDA from a linear text displayed as an e-book to a web tool organized as a collection of data elements. The new structure of RDA Toolkit removes the conventions of a beginning, a middle, and an end, and supports a more web-like approach of jumping into the standard where one needs to be. The new RDA Toolkit has a more efficient software design. For example, it builds on the infrastructure changes first implemented in 2016,[25] whereby the definitions throughout the RDA text were all linked to the definitions in the RDA Registry.[26] A change in the Registry definition pushes the change to all the places in RDA where that definition may appear. The new RDA Toolkit maintains and amplifies this original functionality, providing the basis for efficient workflows and streamlined maintenance of RDA.[27]

1.3.4 Optimized for the Linked Data Environment

One of the goals in creating RDA was to develop a metadata standard optimized for the linked data environment. Those involved in the original development of RDA were aware that libraries should be ready to take advantage of emerging technologies, not just for the web in general but also for the linked data environment of the Semantic Web.

Tim Berners-Lee and his colleagues provided a simple definition of the Semantic Web in 2001 when envisioning this new form of web content:

> The Semantic Web is not a separate Web but an extension of the current one, in which information is given well-defined meaning, better enabling computers and people to work in cooperation . . . For the Semantic Web to function, computers must have access to structured collections of information and sets of inference rules that they can use to conduct automated reasoning.[28]

RDA is designed to support the production of well-formed data that has a consistent structure, recognizable both by humans and by computers. The data should not just be structured but should also indicate relationships between data. This is the essence of linked data, the relationships that link data and that are machine-readable (using uniform resource identifiers or internationalized resource identifiers).[29] Linked data can join together data from different domains. Data within the Semantic Web can be used and reused in different and new ways that build knowledge and support exploration.

From the start, there was an intention to design RDA so that the data produced would be well-formed and interconnected, data that could be used as linked data.[30] There were initiatives related specifically to the preparedness for linked data, beginning with a 2007 meeting hosted by the British Library to discuss the relationship between RDA and data models used by other metadata communities. The focus was on metadata models from communities that were intending to create metadata compatible with the Semantic Web.[31] One of the anticipated benefits for the library community was "a metadata standard that is compatible with the Web Architecture and that is fully interoperable with other Semantic Web initiatives."[32] Compatibility with the Semantic Web's framework enables library-created metadata to be used and reused across the web, integrated with the data of other communities, aggregated with data from other sources and manipulated accurately by computers. Computers can query and draw inferences from this data, use the relationships to integrate data from diverse sources and enable global data discovery.[33] Metadata from the library community has the reputation of being reliable data that can be trusted. Pushing this data to the Semantic Web contributes to the discovery of new relationships, the development of new knowledge, and the enhancement of exploration.

Coming out of the 2007 meeting, the developers of RDA aimed to focus on two goals or outcomes:

1. Definition of an RDA Element Vocabulary
2. Disclosure on the public web of RDA Value Vocabularies using RDF/RDFS/SKOS technologies [34]

The idea was to go beyond definitions of terms that were accessible only to humans but to transform these parts of RDA, the elements and the controlled vocabularies, into terminology written for the web using Resource Description Framework (RDF), identifiable by unique resource identifiers (Internationalized Resource Identifiers, or IRIs) and accessible for data applications and automated processing.

Work to achieve these outcomes began in 2007. The process required a certain amount of infrastructure work—representing the elements and controlled vocabularies using RDF, the development of the RDA namespace, called the RDA Registry, and mapping to other linked data namespaces. The namespace known as the RDA Registry (http://rdaregistry.info) is considered the official RDA namespace.[35] It was first populated in January 2014 with the RDA elements and controlled vocabularies (definitions, scope notes, and translations), sometimes called collectively RDA Reference.[36] With the redesign of the RDA Toolkit infrastructure, the RDA Registry is not considered a parallel and separate development but is now integrated into the dataflow so that RDA Reference data is made available through a synchronized workflow both for Semantic Web applications and for human use in the RDA standard within RDA Toolkit. RDA is now intrinsically linked to its namespace.[37]

The intention of designing RDA for the digital environment has now advanced further as a result of the 3R Project.

1.4 A GLOBAL STANDARD APPROPRIATE FOR USE IN MANY CONTEXTS

RDA was designed by the library community for its use, but one of the goals was that RDA should also "be capable of adaptation to meet the specific needs of other communities."[38] This expanded scope applies both to cataloging and other metadata communities around the globe and to metadata communities outside the library.

1.4.1 An International Standard

RDA was designed for use in an international context. The predecessor standard, AACR2, was the product of international cooperation between four author countries: Australia, Canada, Great Britain and the United States. It had been translated into many languages and used in many countries beyond the four author countries. But it had a distinctively "Anglo-American" perspective, and its development was controlled by the four author countries.

RDA, as published in 2010, was also primarily the product of international cooperation between the four author countries: Australia, Canada, Great Britain, and the United States. However, RDA explicitly stated that the standard was "designed for use in an international context" (RDA 0.11.1). The inclusion of this statement underlines that RDA was being developed with recognition of its probable use by many countries around the world. RDA purposely aimed to shed the Anglo-American perspective of AACR2. The process of internationalization had begun with instructions adjusted so that they could be applied by communities that use different languages, scripts, numbering systems, calendars or measurement units. Also, during the original development process, the Joint Steering Committee for Development of RDA, the body responsible for the content of the standard, invited comments from international organizations and the national libraries and national cataloging committees of other countries; countries that had used AACR2; and also countries that had their own national cataloging codes.

The dialogue at the international level continued and increased after 2010. There was recognition that many "Anglo-American" viewpoints still remained entrenched in the text. The goal had started with the intention of making RDA usable in an international context. It has now broadened to making RDA a global standard enabling discovery of content.[39] RDA in the new RDA Toolkit has a new objective added to the four original ones: internationalization. Internationalization becomes a declared objective governing the design of RDA.[40]

During the 3R Project, the structure of the standard changed. One of the impacts of the change in structure was to demonstrate that RDA could be used in different ways by different communities. RDA defines a large set of data elements, and it also presents multiple options for recording data for each element. The shared element set supports data interoperability and data harmonization, but data can be recorded in up to four different ways. Elements can also be further extended or refined with local subtyping to fit local needs. The phrases "accommodating local cataloging traditions" and "accommodating local practices" began to appear in RSC presentations during 2018.[41] This capacity to accommodate diverse practices opens the door for broader use by communities around the world.

In 2015, work began on developing a governance structure appropriate for an international standard.[42] This was a development in parallel with the 3R Project but not directly related to it. However, it was also a sign of the ways in which the standard and its infrastructure were changing to accommodate a broad range of metadata communities. The new governance model explicitly aimed to expand representation in the decision-making bodies that controlled the standard.[43] At the same time, there was also a formalization of the relationship with communities that were translating RDA so that they would have a mechanism to provide input and feedback through the Translations Working Group. The increased reliance on working groups also provided additional avenues for input from more communities than previously.[44]

The intention is now that RDA should accommodate the needs of different communities around the globe and that it should also be a standard developed through decisions made by representatives from every part of the globe. The changes in the standard to accommodate diverse practices and the changes in governance have moved RDA closer to achieving the goal of being a global standard.

1.4.2 Not Just for Libraries

One of the features noted above was the flexible and extensible framework that allows for the description of all types of resources, whether traditional library resources or resources from other cultural heritage communities, such as archives, museums, digital repositories, publishers, etc. RDA was also designed so that it would not be tied to one encoding standard. This makes it possible to use RDA in a broad range of contexts, in different implementation scenarios, and not just in traditional library management systems.

Though it comes out of the library milieu, RDA was designed with an awareness of other metadata communities and their resource description standards. The boundaries between metadata communities are meaningless to a user who searches in a networked, online environment. Data produced following the RDA standard can be stored and transmitted using a variety of encoding schema, including schemas in use within other metadata communities. Likewise, by staying away from instructions about the presentation of the data, the door is opened to a potentially wider community of users, using RDA elements in new and different applications. In a linked data environment, library data can be used and reused with the data from other domains, such as museums or publishers. The greater the compatibility of data between metadata communities, the greater the benefits for the user.

1.5 IMPACT

RDA is a key step in the improvement of resource discovery because it guides the recording of data. The production of well-formed data is a vital piece of the infrastructure to support search and retrieval. RDA data alone will not improve navigation and display because the data must be used appropriately by well-designed applications, search engines and interfaces. Nevertheless, the recording of clear, unambiguous, well-structured data is an essential step in the improvement of resource discovery for the user.

RDA is designed to produce data that can be stored, searched, and retrieved in traditional library catalogs. RDA data is especially designed for use in the online environment, including the Semantic Web, where the data needs to be well structured so that it can be used, reused, and aggregated in new and unexpected ways, integrated with data from other sources, and possibly used by artificial intelligence software.

During RDA development, there is a constant awareness that the standard must function as a bridge between the past and future environments, and that not all libraries will progress into new environments at the same pace. RDA in the new RDA Toolkit offers an array of options, such as different recording methods. It is these options that make it possible to use RDA in a range of different implementation scenarios.

RDA was developed with awareness of other metadata standards. It lays the groundwork for data interoperability by aligning with international models and by following the language and conventions of the online environment, especially of the linked data environment.

RDA has been broadening its scope in response to international interest in the standard. The content of the standard is designed to be flexible, to offer choices and accommodate diverse practices. It is designed for use by an international audience, but it also maintains continuity for long-standing RDA users. The governance structure has been revised to support increased international participation in RDA development. Greater international use of the standard also increases data interoperability around the globe.

RDA positions the library community to take advantage of the online environment, and to make library data widely visible and discoverable.

NOTES

1. RDA Toolkit (Chicago: American Library Association; Ottawa: Canadian Federation of Library Associations; London: Chartered Institute of Library and Information Professionals [CILIP], 2010–), https://www.rdatoolkit.org/.

2. RDA Board, "Outcomes from the 2016 Meeting" (April 2016), www.rda-rsc.org/sites/all/files/RDA%20Board%202016%20Outcomes.pdf; RDA Steering Committee, "Outcomes of the 2016 RSC Meeting" (December 4, 2016), www.rda-rsc.org/sites/all/files/RSC-Outcomes-2016.pdf.

3. "RDA Toolkit 3R Project," https://www.rdatoolkit.org/3RProject.

4. IFLA LRM is an internationally recognized bibliographic conceptual model, approved in 2017 as an official standard of the International Federation of Library Associations and Institution (IFLA): *IFLA Library Reference Model: A Conceptual Model for Bibliographic Information.* Pat Riva, Patrick Le Bœuf, and Maja Žumer (Consolidation Editorial Group of the IFLA FRBR Review Group). 2017. https://www.ifla.org/publications/node/11412.

5. These terms are defined and discussed in more detail in chapters 3 and 5.

6. "Why Isn't This Called RDA 2.0?," RDA Steering Committee, "Beta Toolkit/3R Project Frequently Asked Questions," www.rda-rsc.org/node/551#08.

7. Guidance > Introduction to RDA (RDA 84.74.84.88).

8. See chapter 3 for an explanation of IFLA's bibliographic conceptual models.

9. IFLA LRM 2.1.

10. *Bibliographic data* is used in its broadest sense, encompassing data that in some contexts is differentiated as bibliographic and authority data, such as in the MARC encoding environment.

11. *Functional Requirements for Bibliographic Records: Final Report,* IFLA Study Group on the Functional Requirements for Bibliographic Records. (Munich: K. G. Saur, 1998); also online: https://www.ifla.org/publications/functional-requirements-for-bibliographic-records.

12. Functional Requirements for Authority Data (FRAD) is an extension of the FRBR model. *Functional Requirements for Authority Data: A Conceptual Model.* IFLA Working Group on Functional Requirements and Numbering of Authority Records (FRANAR), (Munich: K. G. Saur, 2009); also online: https://www.ifla.org/publications/functional-requirements-for-authority-data.

13. Functional Requirements for Subject Authority Data (FSRAD) is also an extension of the FRBR model. *Functional Requirements for Subject Authority Data: A Conceptual Model.* IFLA Working Group on the Functional Requirements for Subject Authority Records (FRSAR). (Munich: De Gruyter Saur, 2011); also online: https://www.ifla.org/node/5849.

14. Due to disparities and contradictions between the models, it was not possible for RDA to be exactly aligned with all three models. This is discussed in more detail in chapter 3.

15. *Entity* is a word used in many different contexts. Here it refers to the entities in an entity-relationship model, the modelling technique used to develop the IFLA bibliographic conceptual models. In a computing context, a simple definition is anything about which data can be stored (see Wiktionary definition, https://en.wiktionary.org/wiki/entity).

16. Joint Steering Committee for Development of RDA, "Strategic Plan for RDA, 2005–2009" (5JSC/Strategic/1/Rev/2; November 1, 2007), www.rda-jsc.org/archivedsite/stratplan.html (last updated July 1, 2009).

17. *Well-formed data* means that "instructions are provided on how to record the values of elements, controlled vocabularies are used where appropriate, and the overall structure is governed by a formal model." Joint Steering Committee for Development of RDA, "RDA Scope and Structure." (JSC/RDA/Scope/Rev/4, 1 July 2009), cover page, www.rda-jsc.org/docs/5rda-scoperev4.pdf.

18. The International Standard Bibliographic Description is a standard developed under the auspices of IFLA to promote consistency when sharing bibliographic data. See www.ifla.org/en/about-the-isbd-review-group.

19. *Cataloger* and *metadata creator* are used interchangeably throughout the book. Metadata creator can be seen as a broader term that is less specific to libraries. Catalogers are metadata creators. Metadata creators can include those who create metadata in other domains as well.

20. For more information about MARC 21, see the MARC Standards website of the Library of Congress, Network Development and MARC Standards Office, www.loc.gov/marc/. For more information about RDF, see the W3C website, https://www.w3.org/RDF/.

21. BIBFRAME was initiated by the Library of Congress. For more information, see the Library of Congress BIBFRAME website, https://www.loc.gov/bibframe/.

22. Joint Steering Committee for Development of RDA, "Strategic Plan for RDA, 2005–2009" (5JSC/Strategic/1/Rev/2; November 1, 2007), www.rda-jsc.org/stratplan.html (last updated July 1, 2009).

23. Also called *vocabulary encoding schemes*.

24. Gordon Dunsire cites several examples in "RDA and the Semantic Web," Lectio Magistralis in Library Science, Florence, Italy, March 4, 2014 (Firenze: Casalini Libri, 2014), 36. Available online: http://digital.casalini.it/9788876560132.

25. "RDA Toolkit Glossary and RDA Reference" (RDA/Chair/17, August 7, 2016), www.rda-rsc.org/sites/all/files/RSC-Chair-17-fix.pdf.

26. The RDA Registry is the RDA namespace, http://rdaregistry.info. This is an essential part of making RDA elements and RDA vocabularies available for use as linked data.

27. For more information on the link between the Registry and the RDA Toolkit, see chapter 6, section 6.9.

28. Tim Berners-Lee, James Hendler, and Ora Lassila, "The Semantic Web," *Scientific American* 284, no. 5 (May 2001), 37, https://www.jstor.org/stable/10.2307/26059207.

29. "Linked Data," World Wide Web Consortium, 2015, https://www.w3.org/standards/semanticweb/data.

30. Barbara Tillett, "Keeping Libraries Relevant in the Semantic Web with Resource Description and Access (RDA)," *Serials*, 24, no. 3 (2011), http://doi.org/10.1629/24266.

31. Dunsire, "RDA and the Semantic Web," 19. See also "How Does RDA Support Linked Data?," RDA Steering Committee, "RDA Frequently Asked Questions," www.rda-rsc.org/content/rda_faq#10. See also early official documents, such as "RDA Scope and Structure,"

(5JSC/RDA/Scope/Rev/4, July 1, 2009), www.rda-jsc.org/archivedsite/docs/5rda-scope rev4.pdf.

32. Dunsire, "RDA and the Semantic Web," 20.

33. "Linked Data," World Wide Web Consortium, 2015.

34. See "Work Begins on RDA Vocabularies," www.rda-jsc.org/archivedsite/rdavocabularies.html. RDF = Resource Description Framework; RDFS = Resource Description Framework Schema; SKOS = Simple Knowledge Organization System. All three are compatible with Semantic Web technologies.

35. A namespace is part of preparing for the Semantic Web environment because it provides a way to ensure that the identifiers being assigned are unique and will remain unique; the namespace also reflects provenance (and hence reliability) if one uses a name that clearly identifies the source, such as "rdaregistry.info."

36. See https://www.rdaregistry.info/rgAbout/rdaref/.

37. "The RDA Registry is the source of Toolkit data for element and controlled terminology labels, definitions, scope notes, translations, and mappings, so it is integral to the operational production of the Toolkit and other RDA related publications," RDA Steering Committee, "Beta Toolkit/3R Project Frequently Asked Questions," www.rda-rsc.org/node/551#06.

38. Long term goal 1 in the Strategic Plan for RDA, 2005–2009.

39. The RDA Board's vision statement on the Board's home page (www.rda-rsc.org/rdaboard).

40. RDA. Guidance > Introduction to RDA > Principles and objectives governing RDA. Internationalization (RDA 94.23.91.09).

41. For example, see Gordon Dunsire and Ebe Kartus, "Accommodating Local Cataloguing Traditions in a Global Context" (paper presented at the Diversity of Data Conference, Kuala Lumpur, August 23, 2018), https://www.rdatoolkit.org/IFLA; Gordon Dunsire, "Cataloguing with RDA" (presentation, 1er. Coloquio sobre RDA en América Latina, National Library of Mexico, Mexico City, November 14, 2018), www.rda-rsc.org/sites/all/files/Dunsire%20Cataloguing%20With%20RDA%202018.pdf.

42. The governance structure is covered in greater detail in chapter 2.

43. RDA Board, "RDA Governance," www.rda-rsc.org/sites/all/files/RDA%20Governance%20Model%20revision%202019%20Dec.pdf. See also "RDA Governance Review Takes First Step in Implementation," www.rda-rsc.org/RDAgovernancefirststep.

44. See also chapter 2, section 2.4.

2
RDA: AN INTERNATIONAL STANDARD

Many countries around the world have implemented, are in the process of implementing, or are interested in implementing RDA. RDA evolved out of the second edition of the *Anglo-American Cataloguing Rules* (AACR2), and from the start, there was a deliberate intention to make RDA a standard that could be used in an international context more easily than its predecessor, AACR2. This intention to internationalize RDA has continued to advance and shape the standard during development work since RDA was published. A good portion of the work that happened during the 3R Project built on this intention to make RDA a fully international standard.

- 2.1 Alignment with International Principles, Models, and Standards
- 2.2 Capacity for Use in an International Context
- 2.3 Integration of Translations and the Translation Workflow
- 2.4 Shared Governance

2.1 ALIGNMENT WITH INTERNATIONAL PRINCIPLES, MODELS, AND STANDARDS

RDA uses the concepts, vocabulary, and principles that are recognized by the international cataloging community. It builds on existing cataloging traditions, while also taking into consideration how library data will be used in the future. Data produced according to RDA instructions reflects international principles and is aligned with international models for bibliographic data. This means that the data is compatible with data produced using other standards that reflect these same models and principles. RDA was developed to fit within the grid of international resource description standards.

The 1967 introduction for the first edition of the *Anglo-American Cataloguing Rules* (AACR) declares that the rules are based on the Paris Principles, the Statement of Principles adopted by the International Conference on Cataloguing Principles that was held in 1961, in Paris. Conforming to an internationally accepted set of principles lays the groundwork for enabling the exchange of bibliographic data. It is the first step in a process of standardization. Although far from the networked online environment of today, already there was a vision that standardization was an essential step in the twentieth century goal of universal bibliographic control. In the current environment, we speak of interoperability, resource sharing, and the seamless exchange and reuse of metadata. The scope has become broader, but the goal is the same: to break down the barriers that inhibit communication about bibliographic resources. Standardization remains the basic building block.

During the 1970s, with the Paris Principles as a starting point, there were fruitful efforts to develop common ground for bibliographic description at the international level. Through the work of the International Federation of Library Associations and Institutions (IFLA), a descriptive standard was developed and accepted: the International Standard Bibliographic Description (ISBD). ISBD was an internationally accepted set of descriptive elements and an agreed convention for the display of bibliographic information. Countries around the world had a common starting point.

The second edition of AACR, AACR2, began by reiterating the standard's alignment with the internationally accepted Paris Principles and also included a statement explaining its conformity with the ISBD framework.

The introduction to RDA continues this practice of situating the standard in relation to existing international standards and initiatives pertaining to bibliographic data. There are two sections that are particularly relevant:

> **Guidance > Introduction to RDA**
> Objectives and principles governing RDA
> Standards related to RDA

The information in these guidelines explicitly demonstrates that RDA is in step with the international cataloging community.[1]

2.1.1 Objectives and Principles Governing RDA

A key statement in the objectives and principles section sets out RDA's relationship to the IFLA Statement of International Cataloguing Principles:

> **The IFLA Statement of international cataloguing principles informs the cataloguing principles used throughout RDA and guides the decisions that cataloguers make.**[2]

The Paris Principles of 1961 were written at the time of the card catalog, in the context of predominantly print and paper-based resources. Forty years later, work began on producing an updated version of the international cataloging principles. Over a period of five years, from 2003 to 2007, meetings were held under the auspices of IFLA to consult with catalogers on all continents. The IFLA Meetings of Experts on an International Cataloguing Code reached consensus on a final version of the statement of principles, which was published in 2009 (and revised in 2016): *Statement of International Cataloguing Principles*.[3]

The Introduction to the Statement of International Cataloguing Principles (ICP) points to the relatedness of international initiatives in the area of cataloging and bibliographic data:

> This statement builds on the great cataloguing traditions of the world, as well as on the conceptual models in the IFLA Functional Requirements family.[4]

Even in the ICP, the importance both of connecting with past cataloging practices and aligning with other international standards is highlighted.

The International Cataloguing Principles and RDA were developed and written over the same overlapping period of years: ICP, 2003–2009; RDA, 2005–2010. The RDA development team carefully monitored the development of ICP and kept RDA in step with the substance of the principles, even though some of the names, scopes, and definitions differ. RDA also chose to divide the principles into objectives and principles. But the substance of the ICP is reflected in RDA's objectives and principles.

2.1.2 Standards Related to RDA

The section called "Standards Related to RDA" begins by declaring the relationship between RDA and IFLA's bibliographic conceptual models.[5] It is the alignment with these models that has had the greatest impact on the development and structure of RDA.

When the FRBR conceptual model was published in 1998, it was quickly recognized as a model with valid explanatory power. The FRAD and FRSAD models were developed as extensions of FRBR, and the three together provided a modelling of all the significant aspects of bibliographic data—bibliographic data, authority data and subject authority data. But the three models were developed independently, by different working groups, with different levels of granularity and different interpretations of some key points. This made it difficult to apply the models consistently in applications. Thus, from the moment that FRSAD was completed, the IFLA FRBR Review Group[6] recognized the need to consolidate the three models into one logically coherent model.

In 2017, the consolidated entity-relationship conceptual model was published: IFLA Library Reference Model (IFLA LRM).[7] IFLA LRM carries forward the essence of the three FR models, but it also introduces efficiencies in modelling and a structure that is more amenable to computer environments, as well as introducing some solutions to long-standing issues in the original FRBR model. It also introduces some new entities.

When RDA was originally published in 2010, the FRBR and FRAD models[8] provided the underlying theoretical framework that shaped RDA. In 2015, RDA enlarged its alignment to include the third entity-relationship model, FRSAD.[9]

When IFLA approved the newest entity-relationship model, IFLA Library Reference Model (IFLA LRM) in 2017, the three previous entity-relationship models became obsolete. It remains vital for RDA to be aligned with bibliographic conceptual models that are valid, current, and internationally accepted. Thus, RDA had to be aligned with IFLA LRM; the perfect opportunity was the 3R Project.

The IFLA models are not resource description standards, but they define an internationally shared understanding of bibliographic data. They are developed by working groups with international membership; they are developed under the auspices of the international library association, IFLA; and drafts are sent out for worldwide review to ensure that there is international agreement. Alignment with the conceptual models has had a major effect on the content of RDA and ensures that RDA is aligned with a global consensus about the nature of bibliographic data.

Even before IFLA LRM was published, the RDA Steering Committee was aware of the direction in which the new model was evolving. It was able to start preparing for the changes well in advance so that it could maintain alignment with the current internationally accepted model.

The text of RDA also acknowledges its relationship to other standards for resource description and access, beginning with an acknowledgment of its roots:

> RDA is built on foundations established by the *Anglo-American Cataloguing Rules*, 2nd edition (AACR2) and the cataloguing traditions on which it was based.[10]

RDA brings a new perspective to the activity of cataloging: it introduces new elements, new approaches to describing content and carrier and new ways to improve access. At the same time, it maintains continuity with the past, building on the cataloging theory embodied in earlier standards.

RDA was not developed in isolation but with an awareness of other international standards, such as IFLA's International Standard Bibliographic Description (ISBD) and the MARC 21 formats for bibliographic and authority data, as well as ONIX,[11] Dublin Core, and RDF. This awareness of other standards is essential to be able to build towards the goal of interoperability:

> The metadata standards used in archives, museums, publishers, and other communities related to libraries were taken into consideration in the design of RDA. The goal is to attain an effective level of interoperability between those standards and RDA.[12]

For a content standard to function effectively in real world situations, its data must be compatible with existing standards. To achieve interoperability with related international standards, compatibility of element sets is crucial. Compatibility does not require a perfect congruence between standards. There may be compatibility in overlapping areas, such as ISBD and RDA. RDA covers a broader spectrum of elements, but where ISBD and RDA overlap, there is compatibility. Likewise, if the elements of one standard are more granular than the other, this does not preclude compatibility. Compatibility may also exist when two standards reflect the same underlying conceptual model.

RDA encourages the formulation of data according to existing international standards when applicable. RDA does not operate in a vacuum. It fits within the grid of international bibliographic standards, ensuring that the data produced according to RDA is effective, usable, and interoperable. RDA is harmonized with the models, principles, and concepts recognized and used by international cataloging and metadata communities. This harmonization creates the opportunity for using RDA in many different contexts.

2.2 CAPACITY FOR USE IN AN INTERNATIONAL CONTEXT

When RDA was originally published, it was a standard that had been developed through a cooperative international process involving the national libraries, national library associations, and national cataloging committees of Australia, Canada, Great Britain and the United States. AACR2 was written and revised by these same institutions and organizations using the same processes. AACR2 was adopted by the four author countries and went on to be adopted by many countries around the world. AACR2 was translated into at least twenty-five languages, attesting to its widespread use beyond English-speaking countries. AACR2 was extensively used around the world, even though it was not designed for such use. Implementation was not straightforward for communities that used different languages, scripts, calendars, etc. In 1997, the International Conference on the Principles and Future Development of AACR was held in Toronto, Ontario.[13] It was hosted by the Joint Steering Committee for Revision of AACR, the body responsible for the content of AACR2. International experts were invited to identify areas for future development. One of these areas was the need to broaden the scope of the standard so that it would be easier to use in different international contexts. This recommendation went on to become one of the objectives governing RDA development.

2.2.1 Internationalization as an Objective

Since the early days of RDA's development process, there has been an effort to internationalize the standard and make it easily applicable by communities around the world.[14] This commitment has been included in the text of RDA since the beginning:

> **RDA is designed for use in an international context.**[15]

In the original RDA Toolkit, this statement was followed by a series of instructions on language and script, numerals, dates, and units of measurement.[16] The expectation was that non-English communities would make the adjustments they required in these specific areas.

In the new RDA Toolkit, wording about internationalization was moved to the "Objectives and Principles" section. Moving this piece of RDA text into the objectives section signals that internationalization is a goal that is actively pursued; it is integrated into the core guiding objectives that govern the design and future development of RDA:

> **RDA is designed for an international audience, with the expectation that cataloguing agents will make application decisions when desirable. . . . Given the flexibility of the guidance and recording methods, the metadata provided by different agents will not necessarily be identical, but as well-formed data it will be understood by any agent when shared. The emphasis is on data harmonization rather than strict compatibility.**
>
> Guidance > Introduction to RDA > Objectives and principles governing RDA

In the new RDA Toolkit, the section of RDA that addresses internationalization focuses on harmonization and interoperability. The instructions on choice of language and script, numerals, dates, and units of measurement are still in RDA, but in a section called "Adapting RDA to Local Needs" (Guidance > Introduction to RDA. Adapting RDA to local needs).

As will be seen in more detail later, RDA encourages the use of controlled vocabularies (or vocabulary encoding schemes) when recording data for many elements. RDA includes many lists of controlled vocabulary, both within RDA Toolkit, and as vocabularies for use in the Semantic Web through the RDA Registry. In the section on "Adapting RDA to Local Needs," it is understood that a single set of vocabularies cannot accommodate all communities that may want to use RDA. The most obvious example occurs when translating RDA, but there is also allowance for choice not limited to translations:

> **Some instructions specify the use of a term (e.g., *publisher not identified*, *approximately*, *unaccompanied*). An agent who creates metadata may choose to use a different but similar appropriate term. Each language version of RDA provides such terms in appropriate languages and scripts.**[17]

This underlines that RDA is intended for use by cataloging communities around the globe, and possibly also for use by communities beyond the library. The guiding principle for harmonization is "well-formed metadata" rather than rigid adherence to just one way of describing resources and creating access to them. Within particular communities, there may be decisions to adhere to one or more lists of terms; for example, the cataloging community in a bilingual country such as Canada would follow its national library's decisions for English and French cataloging and use English or French terms depending on the language of cataloging chosen for a particular description. The flexibility and presence of options built into RDA support its use by a wide range of communities.

2.2.2 Practical Support for Internationalization: Vocabulary Encoding Schemes and String Encoding Schemes

In this section, the focus is on the way RDA offers the possibility of using external schemes and not on explaining vocabulary and strong encoding schemes.[18]

A vocabulary encoding scheme (VES) can be a controlled subject vocabulary, such as the Art and Architecture Thesaurus or the RDA list of terms for content type; it can be a list of ISO codes or some other kind of standardized and structured collection of terms. A string encoding scheme (SES) can be a set of instructions about the punctuation and order of elements, such as the ISBD instructions for a publication statement, or the order and punctuation used when formulating an access point.

RDA promotes the use of recognized, identifiable schemes and offers flexibility so that a cataloging community can choose the schemes it wants to use. Using a standardized scheme facilitates automated processing for retrieval and matching and it promotes data interoperability.

RDA has its own well-developed and extensive list of vocabulary encoding schemes included as part of the standard. But RDA does not create a closed environment. RDA instructions will refer to an internal RDA vocabulary encoding scheme, such as those used for content, media, and carrier types. RDA also allows use of external schemes. See figure 2.1 for an example of the option to use an external scheme when recording *content type*.

> **OPTION**
>
> Record a term from another suitable *vocabulary encoding scheme*. For general guidance, see Guidance: Introduction to RDA. Data elements. Data values.

FIGURE 2.1
Option to use an external vocabulary encoding scheme when recording *content type*

RDA also states this flexibility as part of the general "Guidance" section:

> metadata may be recorded using any suitable vocabulary encoding scheme (e.g., ISO 3166 country codes for a place), provided the scheme is identified.
>
> Guidance > Introduction to RDA. Encoding RDA data[19]

Many RDA examples in the new RDA Toolkit demonstrate the use of external vocabulary encoding schemes (shown as VES source). See figure 2.2 for examples at *date of publication*.[20]

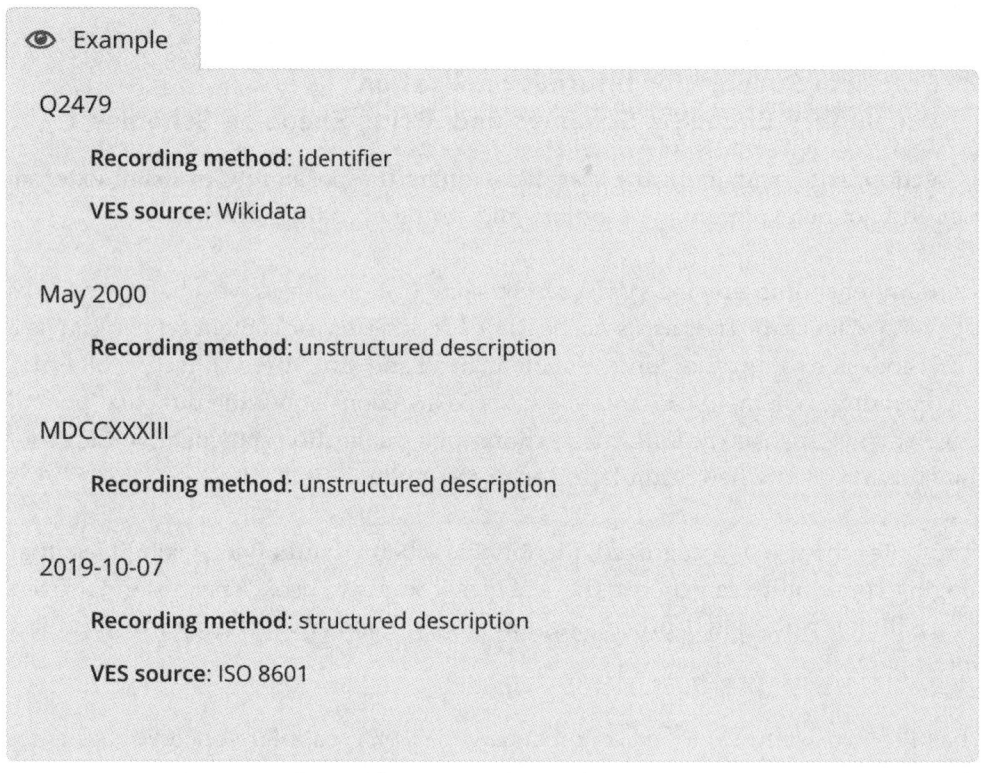

FIGURE 2.2
Examples for *date of publication*

The use of identifiers is encouraged in RDA. RDA allows for the possibility of recording a wide range of identifiers. For an identifier to have meaning and be useful, an identifier must be associated with a discernible scheme, whether it is an internal or internationally recognized scheme.

For example, the scope for *identifier for manifestation* is quite broad:

> An identifier for the manifestation includes registered identifiers from internationally recognized schemes, other identifiers assigned by publishers and others following internally devised schemes, identifiers known as fingerprints

constructed by combining groups of characters from specified pages of early printed resources, publisher's numbers for notated music, and plate numbers for notated music.[21]

The scope is broad so that a cataloging community can make its own decisions about the identifiers it wants to use.

String encoding schemes have long been interwoven in cataloging rules, such as ISBD punctuation in a publication statement. There are many practices around the globe and in different metadata communities. RDA refers to string encoding schemes but does not include them as part of the standard. String encoding schemes are used to display data in some examples. The example in figure 2.3 shows the title of the work followed by a qualifier in parentheses. The order of elements and the punctuation are part of a string encoding scheme.

View in Context Example

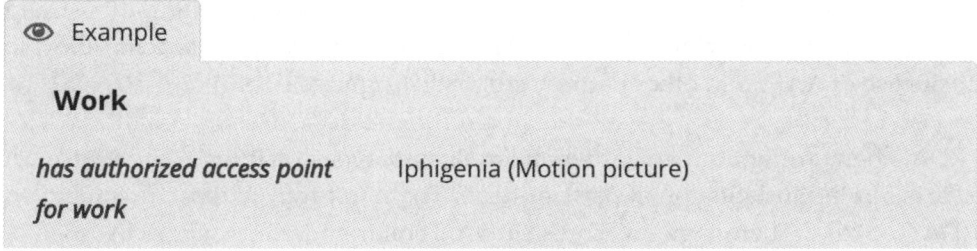

FIGURE 2.3
Excerpt from the View in Context Example for *authorized access point for work*

RDA in the new RDA Toolkit has no instructions about using parentheses when formulating an authorized access point for a work and adding the category of work. But the parentheses are useful for display in the example. Whenever a string encoding scheme is used in an example, it is not prescriptive, but simply shows how the data would look when a string encoding scheme is applied. RDA focuses on the data itself and instructs one to use recognized string encoding schemes (see figure 2.4).

OPTION

Construct an access point by applying a *string encoding scheme* to the values of one or more other elements.

FIGURE 2.4
Instruction on using string encoding schemes when constructing an access point

RDA introduces a degree of flexibility to support use in a range of different contexts. The focus of RDA is not the production of identical strings of characters. As mentioned in chapter 1, the focus is on a shared set of data elements, on the integrity of this data set, and on interoperability and harmonization. Thus, RDA can accommodate a diversity of practices.

2.3 INTEGRATION OF TRANSLATIONS AND THE TRANSLATION WORKFLOW

When RDA was published in 2010, it was delivered as an online document within a web tool, RDA Toolkit. The online version of RDA was the official version; there were print versions created, but they were produced as derivative publications, snapshots of the online standard at particular moments in time.

This switch to the online environment as the primary environment also had an impact on RDA translations. When AACR2 was translated, the translations were independent print publications, published in the countries that undertook the translations, and often invisible to the other countries using AACR2 unless there was a specific effort to investigate use of AACR2 in other parts of the world.

With RDA, there are options for different levels and types of translation. The most complete is a full translation of all parts of RDA. These full translations are integrated into RDA Toolkit.[22] There is not a Finnish RDA Toolkit and a Spanish RDA Toolkit. All full translations are integrated into the one RDA Toolkit. The translations use the same software and are closely synchronized in terms of content. The text of RDA is deconstructed into the same small granular pieces across all language versions and each translation has an identical structure. The French and German translations were the first two integrated into RDA Toolkit. It was a noteworthy innovation to be able to switch easily from one language to another and to split screens and compare any point in the text. As new full translations were added, they too were integrated and became as easily visible and accessible as any of the other language versions.

The English text is published first. However, with the focus on internationalization, there is a deliberate effort to move away from thinking that the English version has primacy. Through the process of translation, there are versions in many languages. English is one among equals (although it is the starting point for all the other translations). RDA now emphasizes that there are other language versions rather than translations.

> **RDA in the original Toolkit**: Translations of RDA will replace those terms with the same or similar appropriate terms in appropriate languages and scripts.
>
> **RDA in the new Toolkit:** Each language version of RDA provides such terms in appropriate languages and scripts.[23]

As mentioned in chapter 1, RDA has its own defined namespace, the RDA Registry. Through the RDA Registry, RDA data elements and value vocabularies are published for use in Semantic Web applications and also for use in automated workflows, such as populating parts of RDA Toolkit. The RDA Registry includes the name and scope of each RDA entity and element, as well as the name and definition of each of the terms in the RDA vocabulary encoding schemes. All language communities start their translation project by first translating the data in the Registry. They then proceed to the next workflow of translating the instructions and guidelines. But some language communities choose not to translate all of RDA; they only translate the RDA Registry terms. This is another type of RDA translation. The RDA Toolkit integrates the full translations and these full translations are always represented in the RDA Registry. But the RDA Registry also includes translations of the Registry content where there is no full equivalent translation in RDA Toolkit. So, the RDA Registry integrates an even larger number of translations (or language versions).

One important aspect of the 3R Project was the aim of improving the translations workflow. The rapid proliferation of translations within both RDA Toolkit and the Registry was straining the mechanisms for handling translations. The existing tools were considered inefficient and not scalable for the increasing amount of translation work.

The first two translations added to RDA Toolkit were the French and German language versions. It was the French and German translators who first identified a way to facilitate translation work: they noticed the presence of "recurring phrases" within the text of RDA. When they translated those phrases, they could reuse those phrases throughout the text. They carried out this reuse manually, but it still achieved some efficiency. The new RDA Toolkit exploits this simple principle of "reuse." RDA is made more efficient for all language versions by making the structure more modular, adjusting the arrangement of texts to increase the number of recurring patterns, and using templates for content. In addition, all the content that is stored in the RDA Registry is never duplicated, but automatically populates the relevant parts of RDA. This improvement in the design of the workflow benefits both new and existing translations. Translation software was also added to the workflow to provide some further support for translators.

This seamless integration of different language versions contributes to a sense of participating in a shared international cataloging community that stretches across language boundaries. As the number of language versions increased, the response of the RDA developers was to make the infrastructure changes necessary to improve the translation process and accommodate more language versions. The visibility of the language versions and the support for an efficient translation process are part of making RDA a fully international standard.

2.4 SHARED GOVERNANCE

The RDA Board is the decision-making body "responsible for setting the strategic direction for the development of RDA."[24] The RDA Steering Committee (RSC) is the body "responsible for the development and content of the standard."[25] These two bodies were formerly called the Committee of Principals (CoP) and the Joint Steering Committee for Development of RDA (JSC). The Committee of Principals changed its name to the RDA Board in November 2015, and at the same time the Joint Steering Committee became the RDA Steering Committee. These changes to the names signaled a change in governance structure.

In 2014, discussions began about changing the governance structure. The RDA Board developed a governance model and by 2016 began implementing the changes. The aim was to ensure participation from all regions of the globe. This was an important task in support of the RDA vision statement:

> **RDA: a global standard for enabling discovery of content.**[26]

To make RDA a fully international standard, it had to be attuned to a diversity of needs and be able to accommodate this diversity. It also had to become a standard developed through decisions made by representatives from every part of the globe.

The RDA Board's proposal for a new governance structure was in response to the broadening interest in RDA, both in countries that had used AACR2 and those that had not. During the development process, before RDA was published in 2010, the Steering Committee had already expanded the forum for discussion of RDA content in two ways: first, it made the drafts available to everyone around the world, by posting them on an open website; second, it formally invited comments on the drafts from the national libraries and national cataloging committees of other countries, both current AACR2 users and those that had their own national cataloging codes. Many countries responded, and their comments provided useful feedback during the development process. The first release of RDA had already begun to realize the intention of internationalizing RDA.

The German-speaking community, led by the Deutsche Nationalbibliothek (DNB), was very interested in implementing RDA as part of its plan to promote data interoperability across borders through an increased use of international standards.[27] To assess the feasibility of implementation, the DNB embarked on a complete translation of RDA. The German translation was one of the first two translations that were published in RDA Toolkit in 2013. During the process of translation, issues were identified where the former "Anglo-American" approach would cause issues for German-speaking countries. One notable example was the RDA instruction to omit initial articles from the titles of works. In 2011, DNB's Office for Library Standards submitted a formal proposal explaining that the omission of an initial article can lead to misleading results in German. The proposal requested changes to the relevant instructions. It was submitted to the Steering

Committee through the Chair of the Steering Committee (6JSC/Chair/3[28]) because the DNB had no formal relationship to the decision-making body. The amendment to RDA was made in 2012. The proposal was successful, but it highlighted the issue of having new constituencies with no representation. The Committee of Principals[29] invited DNB representatives to become involved in the decision-making committees, first inviting the DNB to send a representative as a full member of the Joint Steering Committee in 2012, and then inviting another representative to be a full member of the Committee of Principals in 2013.[30] This represented a major change in direction because the membership of these two bodies had not changed since 1986. The DNB's involvement with the RDA community marked the first step towards internationalizing RDA governance.

However, Germany and the German-speaking countries were not the only new countries interested in adopting RDA. In addition, there were many countries that had translated and used AACR2 but had not been invited to be part of the governance structure. It was not going to be practical or efficient to add representatives from all interested countries or groups of countries: it would swell the number of members on these committees, and potentially make the development process more complicated, and hence slower. There was recognition that representation needed to be broadened but also that a realistic arrangement was needed:

> As more countries implement RDA there will be additional requests and expectations of being able to join the Joint Steering Committee (JSC) and CoP or have some kind of representation on these bodies. In addition, it is important for CoP and JSC to have a greater level of international and wider community representation so that RDA can become truly relevant and internationally recognised. But providing a seat at the table for every country and/or community is not practical or financially sustainable.[31]

Work on revising governance began in 2014 and was incorporated in the 2015–2020 strategic plan of the RDA Board.[32] The new governance model revised the existing structure of both the Committee of Principals and the Joint Steering Committee. Global representation was a key element of the new plan. The globe was divided into six regions, based on the United Nations geographical regions: Africa, Asia, Europe, Latin America and the Caribbean, North America, and Oceania. The nature of the representation was geared to the needs of each body. For the RDA Board, membership would now include six National Institution representatives; the six representatives, one from each region, would be elected representatives from a national agency, such as a national library, that had implemented RDA. Terms of office were defined and the requirements were written to support rotation among institutions. For the RDA Steering Committee, membership would now include six representatives from approved regional representative bodies,[33] each body representing one of the six regions. There was an expectation that representation would also rotate among members of these representative bodies. No longer would there be fixed membership for the two main decision-making bodies.

Membership is now open to representatives from around the globe (see figures 2.5 and 2.6). The governance structure also ensures a regularly rotating membership.

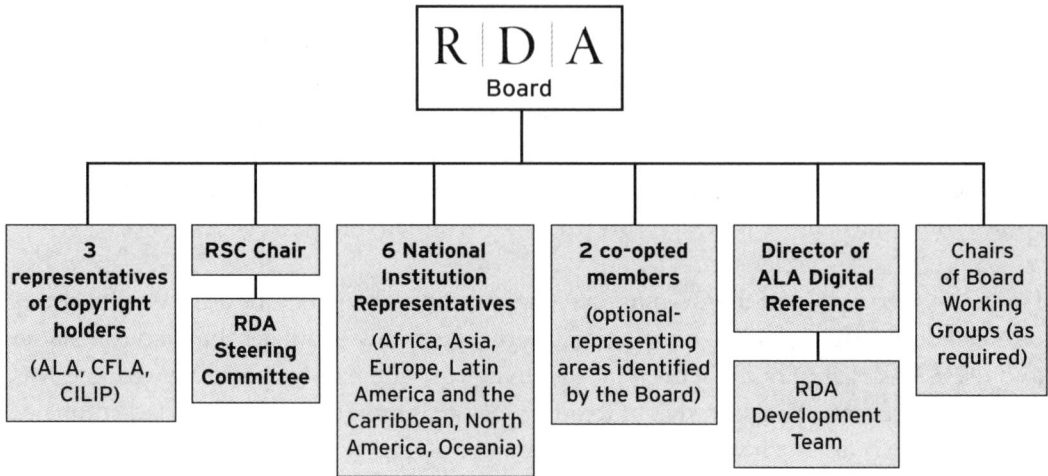

FIGURE 2.5
RDA Board organizational diagram

Source: RDA Governance Model, December 2019, appendix 1, 10. www.rda-rsc.org/sites/all/files/RDA%20 Governance%20Model%20revision%202019%20Dec.pdf.

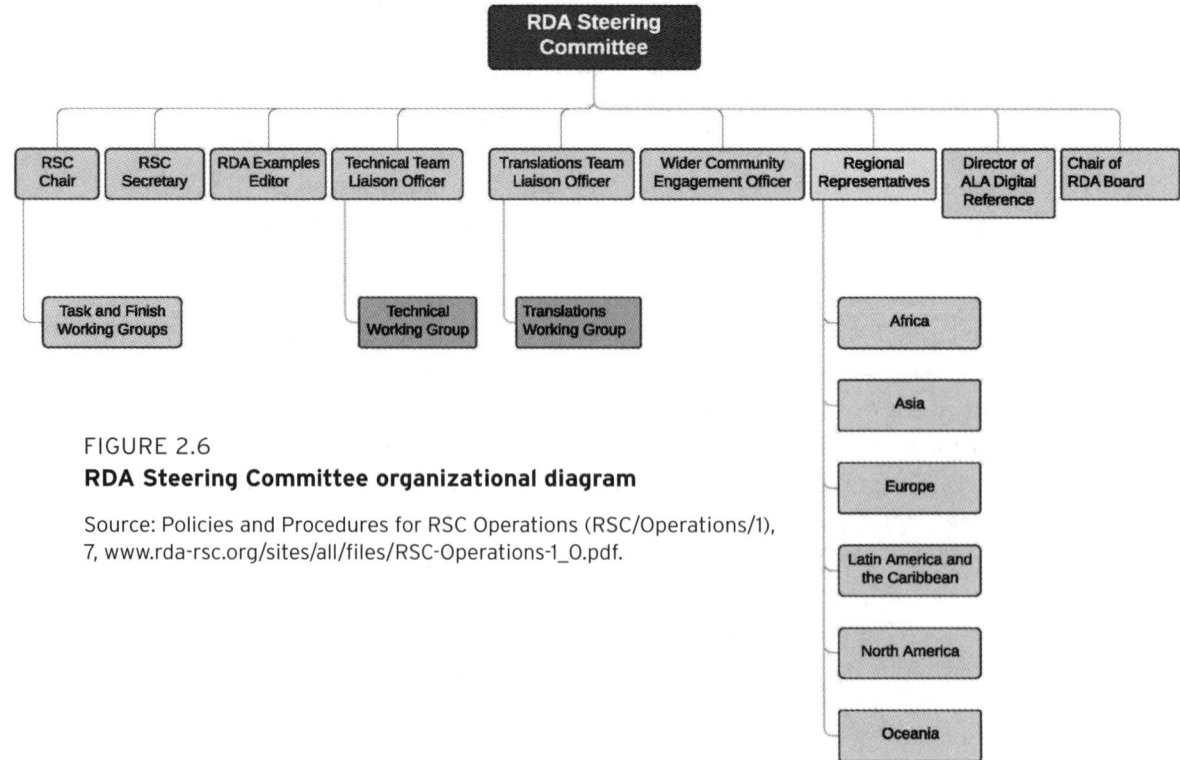

FIGURE 2.6
RDA Steering Committee organizational diagram

Source: Policies and Procedures for RSC Operations (RSC/Operations/1), 7, www.rda-rsc.org/sites/all/files/RSC-Operations-1_0.pdf.

There were also other changes to governance to support global representation. For example, the bulk of the preparatory content work would no longer be done by Steering Committee members themselves, but by "task and finish" working groups that would report to the Steering Committee for direction, decisions, and approval. When constituting a working group, the governance document states that the aim should be "to have at least one representative from each region, if possible."[34] However, there is also acknowledgment that this might not always be possible because of the requirement to find members with sufficient knowledge and expertise. But here again, there is reinforcement of the goal of global representation.

The main focus of the change in governance structure was regional representation. There were also some newly defined positions added to the RDA Steering Committee, two of which are especially geared to broadening channels of communication and participation: the Wider Community Engagement Officer, and the Translations Team Liaison Officer. The position of Wider Community Engagement Officer is an outreach position with particular responsibility for engaging with communities not represented through existing regional representative organizations. The Translations Team Liaison Officer represents the interests of the RDA translators and the Translations Working Group (a permanent working group of the Steering Committee).

The RDA Board completed its transition to the new governance structure in 2018. Due to the fact that regional representation on the RDA Steering Committee relies on the formation of regional representative bodies, the transition is slower since a regional representative body has to take shape and be approved by the RDA Board. By December 2017, three regional representative bodies had been approved by the RDA Board: EURIG (the European RDA Interest Group), NARDAC (the North American RDA Committee), and ORDAC (the Oceania RDA Committee). The transition for RSC had begun.

———

RDA is an international standard at many levels, from content to governance. It was developed with an awareness of international principles, models, and other international standards. Its content is intended for use by metadata communities around the globe. With the goal of being a global standard, infrastructure and support were developed so that all language versions are visible and have equal stature. Fundamental changes were made to governance to enable global representation on the decision-making bodies, the RDA Board, and the RDA Steering Committee. To make the goal of internationalization a reality, RDA is designed for use by communities around the globe; RDA's governance is designed to enable these communities to participate in the further development of RDA.

NOTES

1. In the original RDA Toolkit, this information was in chapter 0, "Introduction," specifically in 0.2 –0.4.

2. RDA in the original RDA Toolkit: Objectives and Principles Governing Resource Description and Access, 0.4.1. RDA in the new RDA Toolkit: Guidance > Introduction to RDA > Objectives and principles governing RDA.

3. IFLA Meetings of Experts on an International Cataloguing Code (IME-ICC), *Statement of International Cataloguing Principles,* December 2016, https://www.ifla.org/files/assets/cataloguing/icp/icp_2016-en.pdf.

4. IME-ICC, *Statement of International Cataloguing Principles,* https://www.ifla.org/files/assets/cataloguing/icp/icp_2016-en.pdf.

5. Guidelines > Introduction to RDA > Standards related to RDA. Conceptual models underlying RDA (RDA 78.56.94.00).

6. The FRBR Review Group was established by IFLA to review and maintain the bibliographic conceptual models. It is now called the Bibliographic Conceptual Models Review Group.

7. *IFLA Library Reference Model: A Conceptual Model for Bibliographic Information,* Pat Riva, Patrick Le Bœuf, and Maja Žumer (Consolidation Editorial Group of the IFLA FRBR Review Group). 2017. https://www.ifla.org/publications/node/11412.

8. *Functional Requirements for Bibliographic Records: Final Report.* IFLA Study Group on the Functional Requirements for Bibliographic Records, (Munich: K. G. Saur, 1998); also online: https://www.ifla.org/en/publications/functional-requirements-for-bibliographic-records/. *Functional Requirements for Authority Data: A Conceptual Model,* IFLA Working Group on Functional Requirements and Numbering of Authority Records (FRANAR). (München: K. G. Saur, 2009); also online: https://www.ifla.org/publications/functional-requirements-for-authority-data.

9. *Functional Requirements for Subject Authority Data: A Conceptual Model.* IFLA Working Group on the Functional Requirements for Subject Authority Records (FRSAR). (Munich: De Gruyter Saur, 2011); also online: https://www.ifla.org/node/5849.

10. Introduction to RDA > Standards related to RDA, Relationship to other standards for resource description and access (RDA 95.89.89.63).

11. ONIX = ONline Information eXchange, an international standard of the publishing industry; see www.editeur.org/74/FAQs.

12. Introduction to RDA > Standards related to RDA. Relationship to other standards for resource description and access (RDA 95.89.89.63).

13. Information about this conference can be found on the archived website of the Joint Steering Committee: www.rda-jsc.org/archivedsite/intlconf1.html.

14. Barbara B. Tillett, "The International Development of RDA: Resource Description and Access," *Alexandria* 24, no. 2 (2013), 1–10, https://doi.org/10.7227/ALX.0004; Gordon Dunsire, "Towards an Internationalization of RDA Management and Development," *Journal of Library and Information Science* 7, no. 2 (2016), 307–30, https://www.jlis.it/article/view/11708/10907.

15. RDA in the original RDA Toolkit, 0.11.1.
16. RDA in the original RDA Toolkit: 0.11.2–0.11.5.
17. RDA in the original RDA Toolkit: 0.11.2. RDA in the new RDA Toolkit: Guidance > Introduction to RDA. Adapting RDA to Local Needs (RDA 00.58.28.49).
18. See chapter 6, section 6.5, for detailed information about vocabulary encoding schemes and string encoding schemes.
19. RDA 92.57.89.91; RDA in the original RDA Toolkit: RDA 0.12.
20. Entities > Manifestation > date of publication (RDA 62.50.76.30).
21. RDA in the original RDA Toolkit: 2.15.1.1. RDA in the new RDA Toolkit: Entities > Manifestation > identifier for manifestation.
22. In the new RDA Toolkit, users select their preferred language in their user profile.
23. RDA in the original RDA Toolkit: 0.11.2. RDA in the new RDA Toolkit: Guidance > Introduction to RDA. Adapting RDA to local needs (RDA 00.58.28.49).
24. RDA Board, web page. www.rda-rsc.org/rdaboard; RDA Board, *RDA Governance Model*, section 4, www.rda-rsc.org/sites/all/files/RDA%20Governance%20Model%20revision%202019%20Dec.pdf.
25. RDA Board, "RDA Governance Model," section 5, www.rda-rsc.org/sites/all/files/RDA%20Governance%20Model%20revision%202019%20Dec.pdf.
26. See the Vision Statement at the RDA Board web page: www.rda-rsc.org/rdaboard.
27. Renate Behrens, Christine Frodl, and Renate Polak-Bennemann, "The Adoption of RDA in the German-Speaking Countries," *Cataloging and Classification Quarterly* 52, no. 6–7 (2014), 688–703, https://doi.org/10.1080/01639374.2014.882872; Ingo Caesar and Dierck Eichel, "Challenges for the Implementation of Resource Description and Access (RDA): Case Study Germany," January 1, 2009, https://www.researchgate.net/publication/28810053_Challenges_for_the_Implementation_of_Resource_Description_and_Access_RDACase_Study_Germany.
28. 6JSC/Chair/3 at the RSC website: www.rda-jsc.org/archivedsite/working2.html#chair-63.
29. The Committee of Principals did not change its name to the RDA Board until November 6th, 2015.
30. Behrens, Frodl, and Polak-Bennemann, "Adoption of RDA in German-Speaking Countries," 691–92.
31. "RDA Governance Review: A Discussion Document," 2014, 2. https://www.rdatoolkit.org/sites/default/files/rda_governance_review.pdf.
32. The 2015–2020 RDA strategic plan had four goals: (1) make RDA an internally recognized standard, (2) increase the adoption of RDA internationally, (3) develop a sustainable business model, and (4) develop a relevant governance structure.
33. For more information on RDA regional representative bodies, see RDA Governance Model, December 2019, section 5.1, www.rda-rsc.org/sites/all/files/RDA%20Governance%20Model%20revision%202019%20Dec.pdf.
34. RDA Governance Model, December 2019, section 5.7, www.rda-rsc.org/sites/all/files/RDA%20Governance%20Model%20revision%202019%20Dec.pdf.

3

THE IFLA BIBLIOGRAPHIC CONCEPTUAL MODELS

RDA is a set of data elements and practical instructions based on the IFLA bibliographic conceptual models. The concepts and vocabulary of the IFLA models played an important role in shaping RDA. It is possible to use RDA without a detailed knowledge of the models, but some knowledge of the concepts and vocabulary provides background and makes it easier to see the rationale for RDA's content and its shape and structure. This chapter looks at IFLA bibliographic conceptual models, namely the three FR models and IFLA LRM:

3.1 Overview of FRBR, FRAD, and FRSAD
3.2 IFLA LRM
3.3 Role of the Models

Bibliographic conceptual models are useful tools because they provide a shared understanding of the structure of bibliographic data. The models map out a better understanding of a real-world domain with a representation of abstract concepts and complex entities. Models can be used for analysis and as the starting point for developing data models and implementations. RDA is an example of an implementation of the IFLA bibliographic conceptual models.

When RDA was first published in 2010, it was an implementation of the FRBR and FRAD conceptual models. The FRBR and FRAD models shaped the structure of RDA and influenced the language used in the instructions. Alignment with these models defined RDA and made it fundamentally different from its predecessor, AACR2.

In 2015, RDA was aligned with FRSAD, with some changes to the text and some content added, especially at chapter 23, "General Guidelines on Recording Relationships between Works and Subjects,"[1] in the original Toolkit. These changes completed the alignment with the three inter-related IFLA models, FRBR, FRAD, and FRSAD, but the 2015 adjustments did not significantly alter the structure and language of RDA.

During the 3R Project, RDA was aligned with IFLA Library Reference Model (IFLA LRM), the model that consolidates and supersedes the three previous IFLA models,

FRBR, FRAD, and FRSAD. When RDA was aligned with IFLA LRM, this alignment has had a significant impact on both the structure and the language of RDA.

From its inception, RDA has always been defined as a standard that takes its underlying theoretical framework from the IFLA bibliographic conceptual models. Development work began from the premise of alignment with the IFLA models. These models are the key to understanding RDA, its structure, and its language. As the models evolved, so has RDA.

This chapter gives an overview of IFLA's bibliographic conceptual models, focusing on the entity-relationship models.[2] When IFLA LRM was published in 2017, it made FRBR, FRAD, and FRSAD obsolete. So, it may seem pointless to include an overview of these earlier models. But IFLA LRM is the consolidation of the three earlier models and it carries forward the essence of all three models. The chapter begins with an overview of the three FR models, FRBR, FRAD, and FRSAD, followed by a description of IFLA LRM. The overview of the three FR models is an opportunity to deepen one's understanding of IFLA LRM.

3.1 OVERVIEW OF FRBR, FRAD, AND FRSAD

3.1.1 Origins of FRBR, FRAD and FRSAD

The FRBR conceptual model has its origin in the report of a group appointed by the International Federation of Library Associations and Institutions (IFLA). In the early 1990s, the IFLA Cataloguing Section established a study group to examine the functional requirements of bibliographic records. This group had representation from many different countries. They carried out an extensive study over several years that also included a period for worldwide review. In 1997, the final report was approved by IFLA's Standing Committee on Cataloguing and the report was published the subsequent year with the title *Functional Requirements for Bibliographic Records: Final Report*.[3]

The final report contains the description of the entity-relationship model that the study group developed to analyze bibliographic records and make their recommendations.

> The study has two primary objectives. The first is to provide a clearly defined, structured framework for relating the data that are recorded in bibliographic records to the needs of the users of those records. The second objective is to recommend a basic level of functionality for records created by national bibliographic agencies.
>
> FRBR 2.1

The development of a framework or model was one of two objectives, but it is the model that had an immediate and ongoing impact. Whereas the recommendations about basic functionality were useful, it was the model itself that continued to be discussed, applied, and developed. The model led to a major change in the way bibliographic data was understood. It also introduced a common vocabulary and understanding of bibliographic data that was shared around the globe:

> FRBR's enduring strength is its neutrality as to bibliographic conventions and its theoretical approach that focuses on the user, the object and function—all of which has enabled its timelessness to application.[4]

> Since the release of FRBR in 1998, there has been a growing reflection in the bibliographic community around the ideas it represents. FRBR has provided a unifying framework and a common terminology for discussion ... Since FRBR, most theoretical studies and applications have been using FRBR terminology.[5]

Evidence of the explanatory power of the model can be seen in the volume of writing about FRBR, and the number of projects that took FRBR as their starting point. The FRBR bibliography[6] demonstrates how the FRBR model was received with great interest around the world and how it triggered a flow of commentary, new applications, new research, and new cataloging codes. In fact, the volume of additions to the bibliography was so large that the IFLA FRBR Review Group was unable to keep up and it closed the bibliography in 2008.

IFLA decided to appoint new groups to extend the FRBR model so as to include authority data (Functional Requirements for Authority Data, FRAD), and subject authority data (Functional Requirements for Subject Authority Data, FRSAD). FRAD was approved and published in 2009,[7] and FRSAD was approved in 2010 and published in 2011.[8] IFLA also decided to establish the FRBR Review Group to review and maintain the FRBR family of conceptual models and to support their application.[9]

3.1.2 Focus on the User

The FRBR, FRAD, and FRSAD models are entity-relationship models. They were developed using a similar approach and methodology. The user and their needs are the starting point for the models. The first step is to identify "key objects that are of interest to users of information in a particular domain" (FRBR 2.3, FRAD 3.1).[10] The models map out the relationship between the data that is recorded, in either bibliographic or authority records (including subject authorities), and the needs of those who use this data.

The needs of the user are defined in terms of user tasks. The user tasks are "generic tasks that are performed by users when searching and making use of national bibliographies and library catalogues" (FRBR 2.2). FRBR does not make a distinction between the end user and the library or information worker who assists the end user. FRAD and FRSAD mention that users include both the end user and intermediaries who may be working to assist end users.

The models look at data within the context of large catalogs or databases. The user tasks are tasks associated with navigating through large amounts of data in order to discover and obtain the required resource. Each model defined four tasks that are similar, overlapping, but also slightly different because each of the models had a different focus.

The four user tasks associated with bibliographic data, as defined in FRBR are:

Find to *find* entities that correspond to the user's stated search criteria (i.e., to locate either a single entity or a set of entities in a file or database as the result of a search using an attribute or relationship of the entity)

Identify to *identify* an entity (i.e., to confirm that the entity described corresponds to the entity sought, or to distinguish between two or more entities with similar characteristics)

Select to *select* an entity that is appropriate to the user's needs (i.e., to choose an entity that meets the user's requirements with respect to content, physical format, etc., or to reject an entity as being inappropriate to the user's needs)

Obtain to acquire or *obtain* access to the entity described (i.e., to acquire an entity through purchase, loan, etc., or to access an entity electronically through an online connection to a remote computer).

FRBR 6.1

These are recognizable tasks that users perform. For example, if a user needs to read Daniel Defoe's *Robinson Crusoe,* they start a search in an online catalog with a search term, such as the name of the author or the title. They start by trying to find something that matches their search term. If they have input the title, *Robinson Crusoe,* they look at the results to identify what matches their query. If there is only one result, is it what they wanted? Other resources may have the same title, but they do not want adaptations, or parodies, or criticisms; they want the original text by Defoe. If there are many results, then they identify the ones that correspond to what they want. Once they have identified one or several manifestations that contain the original text of *Robinson Crusoe,* they need to select the one that fits their needs. If they are a student completing a term paper at a time when the library building is closed, they may only be interested in electronic books. Once they have selected what they want, the last step is actually using the sought resource, either by obtaining it on a shelf, or, in the case of electronic resources, connecting to it and accessing it online.

All three models defined four user tasks. They all share the *find* and *identify* tasks, and these tasks are fundamentally the same, but the definitions have slight variations because the main focus of each model differs.

For example, *identify*

FRBR to identify an entity

FRSAD identify a subject and/or its appellation based on their attributes and relationships

The user tasks in each model match the focus of that model. Even when the tasks overlap, such as the task *identify*, the definitions are different because the task is explained within the context of the particular area of bibliographic data on which that model focuses.

The four FRBR user tasks were carried forward into IFLA LRM with some changes to the definitions to make them more general.

The four FRAD user tasks are *find, identify, contextualize,* and *justify*. The fourth task, *justify*,[11] is a task undertaken by library staff rather than by end users and so it was not carried forward into IFLA LRM. *Contextualize* was combined with one of the FRSAD tasks and was thus carried forward into IFLA LRM.

The four FRSAD tasks are *find, identify, select,* and *explore*.

The FRAD *contextualize* and FRSAD *explore* tasks have similarities:

Contextualize Place a person, corporate body, work, etc., in context; clarify the relationship between two or more persons, corporate bodies, works, etc.; or clarify the relationship between a person, corporate body, etc., and a name by which that person, corporate body, etc., is known (e.g., name used in religion versus secular name).
FRAD 6

Explore Relationships between subjects and/or their appellations (e.g., to explore relationships in order to understand the structure of a subject domain and its terminology).
FRSAD 2.2

These two tasks were consolidated into the *explore* user task in IFLA LRM.

The FRBR, FRAD, and FRSAD conceptual models set forth a framework for understanding the bibliographic universe. The models promoted a view of the bibliographic universe where the focus was on what is important to the user. The focus was not on the cataloger creating a single record, but on the user seeking a resource within the context of a large catalog or database. Both activities continue to coexist, but the defining perspective has changed.

Cataloging principles and cataloging codes have always aimed to serve the needs of the user, sometimes explicitly stating this goal, sometimes implying it. For example, in *Rules for a Printed Dictionary Catalog* (1876), Charles A. Cutter explicitly stated that the objective of the catalog was to help the user, "to enable a person to find a book … to show what the library has … and to assist in the choice of a book."[12] S. R. Ranganathan, in *The Five Laws of Library Science* (first published in 1931), also underlined the basic principle that we organize information for the benefit of the user: "books are for use; every person his or her book; every book its reader; save the time of the reader; a library is a growing organism."[13] The FRBR, FRAD, and FRSAD models continued in this tradition of focusing on the user, but went further by providing a detailed analysis of the way in which each attribute and relationship was relevant and important to the user. They each included a mapping between attributes, relationships, and user tasks.

3.1.3 Entities, Attributes, and Relationships

FRBR, FRAD, and FRSAD were developed as entity-relationship models. There are three components in an entity-relationship model: entities, attributes or characteristics of the entities, and relationships between the entities.

The key point in the models was to identify the relevant entities. Entities are the objects of interest in a specific domain. The entity is an abstract organizing category around which to cluster certain types of data. The entities identified in the IFLA bibliographic conceptual models are the objects of interest in bibliographic data (bibliographic in the broad sense of also including data known as authority data); entities are the objects of interest to users who aim to find and use a resource or explore collections of resources by using bibliographic data.

Each entity has a set of characteristics or attributes. The attributes of an entity are the data that are used to describe the entity. For example, if the entity is a work, one of its attributes might be its genre, its categorization as a poem.

An essential part of entity-relationship models is the identification and mapping of relationships between the entities. Relationships play a very important role in assisting the user to complete the tasks of finding, identifying, selecting, and exploring. Relationships are the key to navigating through the bibliographic universe. They carry information about the nature of the links that exist between entities, enable collocation, and provide pathways to improve resource discovery. By focusing attention on bibliographic relationships and relating each relationship to the user tasks, the three models emphasize the role that bibliographic relationships play when a user navigates a large catalog or database. These relationships become even more crucial when navigating the web. They are the basis for the linked data environment.

3.1.3.1 Entities in FRBR, FRAD, and FRSAD

The FRBR entities are the objects of interest to users of bibliographic data, and all the subsequent models, including IFLA LRM, reference these entities that were first defined in FRBR. There are changes and variations in FRAD and FRSAD, depending on the scope and focus of the model, but the original group of entities sets the pattern for the other models.

In FRBR, these entities were divided into three groups:

Group 1 entities:	products of intellectual or artistic endeavour
	entities: work, expression, manifestation, item
Group 2 entities:	those responsible for the intellectual or artistic content, the physical production and dissemination, or the custodianship of the entities in the first group
	entities: persons, corporate bodies
Group 3 entities:	subjects
	entities: concept, object, event, place
	+ all the entities in groups 1 and 2

The FRAD model is an extension of FRBR, and it incorporated all the FRBR entities and added more. It added *family* to the Group 2 entities. When FRAD referred to the entities that were included in the FRBR Groups 1, 2, and 3, they were collectively called the *bibliographic entities*.

FRAD also added entities related to the authority control process: *name, identifier, controlled access point, rules,* and *agency*. The FRAD model included a modelling of library processes related to authority control. Some of these entities, such as *rules* and *agency*, would not have a direct impact on the end user.

The FRAD model made a significant change from the FRBR model. In FRBR, the name of a person is categorized as an attribute of the entity *person;* the title of a work is categorized as an attribute of the entity *work*. In FRAD, they are no longer considered attributes, but are instances of the entity *name*:

Name	A character or group of words and/or characters by which an entity is known in the real world.
	Includes names by which persons, families, and corporate bodies are known. Includes titles by which works, expressions, manifestations, and items are known.

> Includes names and terms by which concepts, objects, events, and places are known.
>
> Includes real names, pseudonyms, religious names, initials, and separate letters, numerals, or symbols.
>
> [The list continues for over two pages.]
>
> FRAD 3.4

If *name* is a separate entity, then the name and the person have a relationship, the name and the work have a relationship. At first glance, it may appear a needless complication. Actually, it simplifies the conceptual model because it accommodates more complex relationships and different concepts of bibliographic identity. Different cataloging traditions treat personas and the pseudonyms used by persons in different ways.[14] With *name* as a separate entity, the FRAD model built in more flexibility to identify and define a broader range of relationships between names and entities, and also made the model applicable in a wider range of circumstances. This separation of the name from the entity to which it refers remains a key element of the IFLA bibliographic conceptual models from FRAD onwards.

FRSAD also incorporated the entities identified in the previous models, but it was a model that operated at a higher level of abstraction, and the specific FRBR and FRAD entities are not mentioned explicitly. The model had two entities that acted as "superclasses" of the other entities: *thema* and *nomen*:

> **Thema is:** any entity used as a subject of a work.
>
> FRSAD 3.4

Thema encompassed all the bibliographic entities from FRBR and FRAD: work, expression, manifestation, item, person, corporate body, family, concept, object, event, and place:

> **Nomen is:** any sign or sequence of signs (alphanumeric characters, symbols, sound, etc.) that a thema is known by, referred to, or addressed as . . . A Nomen can be human-readable or machine-readable.
>
> FRSAD 3.5

The definition goes on to specify that *nomen* is a superclass of the FRAD entities *name*, *identifier*, and *controlled access point*.

WEMI

Most of the entities in the three models are fairly self-explanatory. The four entities introduced in FRBR as Group 1, work, expression, manifestation, and item, are often referred to by the acronym "WEMI." These four entities remain at the core of all the IFLA bibliographic conceptual models.

These four entities sometimes present a challenge because the terms seem fairly straightforward but the FRBR model used these terms with precise definitions of their scope and meaning. Work, expression, manifestation, and item do not exist as separate, tangible objects. The four entities are aspects that correspond to a user's interests in the products of intellectual and artistic creation (FRBR 3.1.1). In FRBR, the definition of each entity is inextricably intertwined with the definition of the other Group 1 entities:

work: a distinct intellectual or artistic creation

expression: the intellectual or artistic realization of a *work* in the form of alpha-numeric, musical, or choreographic notation, sound, image, object, movement, etc., or any combination of such forms

manifestation: the physical embodiment of an *expression* of a *work*

item: a single exemplar of a *manifestation*

The definitions of the Group 1 entities demonstrate the primary relationships that exist between these four entities. Figure 3.1 is the diagram from section 3.1.1 of the FRBR report that illustrates these relationships:

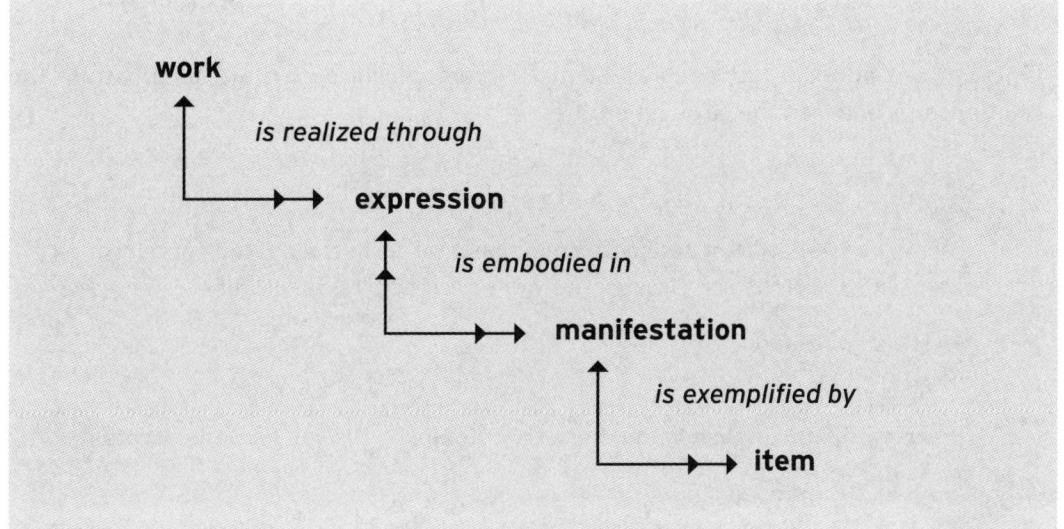

FIGURE 3.1
FRBR Figure 3.1—Group 1 entities and primary relationships

The diagram looks like a simple hierarchy, but the arrows are important because they indicate that there is a network of relationships. Some relationships are one to many (single-headed arrow), some are many to many (double-headed arrow). One work can be realized through one or more expressions. But an expression realizes only one work. An expression can be embodied in many different manifestations, and a manifestation can be the embodiment of one or more expressions. A manifestation is usually exemplified by many items, although it can also be exemplified by a single item. An item can only be the exemplar of one manifestation. These fundamental relationships between the WEMI entities exist in all the models and cannot be changed.

These four entities remain the core of the IFLA Library Reference Model. They are named in the same way, and the relationships between them remain the same. But the definitions were adjusted so that the definition is no longer simply pointing to the relationship:

> work: the intellectual or artistic content of a distinct creation
>
> expression: a distinct combination of signs conveying intellectual or artistic content
>
> manifestation: a set of all carriers that are assumed to share the same characteristics as to intellectual or artistic content and aspects of physical form. That set is defined by both the overall content and the production plan for its carrier or carriers
>
> item: an object or objects carrying signs intended to convey intellectual or artistic content
>
> IFLA LRM 4.2

One can use an example, such as Daniel Defoe's *Robinson Crusoe*, to illustrate the relationships between the Group 1 entities:

> **work**
> w = the constellation of concepts and ideas that form the shared content of all expressions of *Robinson Crusoe*, the work created by Daniel Defoe
>
> *is realized through*
>
> **expression**
> e = original English language text of *Robinson Crusoe* as Defoe wrote it
>
> *is embodied in*
>
> **manifestation**
> m = the set of physical books published in Oxford by Oxford University Press in 2007
>
> *is exemplified by*
>
> **item**
> i = a copy owned by University of Ottawa Library

Work, expression, manifestation, and item entities do not exist separately: the copy of *Robinson Crusoe* that I am reading is an item, a single physical copy that belongs to the University of Ottawa Library and carries this barcode number: 39003024567280. At the same time, it is also the exemplar of a particular manifestation, that is, the Oxford University Press manifestation published in 2007. That manifestation embodies a particular expression, the original English language text, and that alphanumeric (textual) expression was the first realization of Defoe's work, *Robinson Crusoe*. It is one book and it has all four aspects or entities: item, manifestation, expression, and work.

WORK AND ITS EXPRESSIONS

Work and expression are entities that pertain to content. They allow for more precision about similarities and differences in content and the degree of relationship that exists between resources that embody the same work.

A work is often realized in only one expression. But works that have formed an important part of our cultural and intellectual history are usually realized in many expressions. A work, such as *Robinson Crusoe,* has many expressions. Some expressions are translations of the original English text into other languages, such as French and German translations. Some expressions may be realizations into a different form of expression, for example, a spoken word version instead of text. Each expression may be published in several manifestations, and each manifestation usually has a number of identical exemplars of the manifestation.

Even if a work has only one expression, it is still important to identify both the work and expression entities. *Expression* is an important entity because it adds a degree of precision in the delineation of similarities and differences between the content of resources.

The original English text of *Robinson Crusoe* has been published many times. Each of these manifestations embodies identical content, because it embodies the same expression. The manifestations are different: for example, different dates of publication, different carrier (physical or electronic, etc.), different font size (regular or large print). But they all embody the identical content.

A work may also be realized in different expressions. For example, there may be several editions of a textbook on nanotechnology; each edition is updated with the latest developments in the field. Each edition is a slightly different expression of the work. The revised editions are realizations of the same work, but they are not the same expression. Some of the editions may have added sections or chapters; some editions may have parts where the wording has changed. The expressions are not identical.

Translations are realizations of the same work where every word is different, such as a French translation of *Robinson Crusoe*. The original English text and the French translation are different expressions. They are closely related to each other because they are expressions of the same work. But the text of these two expressions are very different from each other.

The original English words of *Robinson Crusoe* can be expressed as text or as spoken word (as in an audio reading of the original text). These are two different expressions of the same work; the content is the same, but the work is realized using two different forms of expression. However, a screenplay or a film adaptation of *Robinson Crusoe* is a related work, different from the original work, but with a relationship to the original.

In some cases, the same work in a different expression may satisfy the user's need, but in other cases, a user may need a particular expression. For example, depending on their need, a user may be equally happy with *Robinson Crusoe* as a text or as a spoken word expression. But a user with a visual impairment may only be able to access the content of *Robinson Crusoe* through a spoken word expression. A university student preparing for a final exam in nanotechnology requires the latest edition of the textbook. An earlier edition, a different expression, will be an unsatisfactory second choice. Similarly, a user doing a textual analysis of *Robinson Crusoe* will require a manifestation that embodies the original English text of the work; a French translation would not meet their need. But another user who just wants to become familiar with the story of *Robinson Crusoe* may be satisfied obtaining any expression of the work.

The identification of two content entities, work and expression, allows for more precise identification and selection. The aim is to ensure that the user will know when they have found identical content in different manifestations or when similar content may be available in different realizations or expressions. This added degree of precision supports the successful fulfillment of user tasks.

CONTENT AND CARRIER
The FRBR model also introduced a clear way to separate content and carrier data. FRBR's identification of the four WEMI entities—work, expression, manifestation, and item—allowed for a more precise definition of the boundaries between content and carrier. Work and expression are focused on the content; manifestation and item are about carriers. Taking the previous example, there may be a user with a visual impairment who needs a particular expression of *Robinson Crusoe,* the spoken word version. But carrier can be equally important to a user. The user may not be able to use any available carrier. If the user is in an area with poor internet connection, a streaming audio version would not be useful. The user may be looking for a particular expression on a physical carrier such as a CD or may need a specific encoding format, such as a DAISY audio book. The attributes of all four entities can be equally important to users and each plays a role in matching the user's selection criteria.

AGENTS

The FRBR Group 2 entities are the entities responsible for the creation of a work, the realization of an expression, the production or dissemination of a manifestation, or the ownership of an item. The FRBR model identified two Group 2 entities: *persons* and *corporate bodies*. The FRAD model expanded the Group 2 entities to include *family* as well. These entities were never collectively identified as subclasses of *agent*. This only occurred in IFLA LRM, but in putting them together as Group 2, FRBR was already setting the groundwork for this move.[15]

SUBJECT/THEMA

FRBR's Group 3 entities are the subjects of the entity *work*. There were four entities that were specific to this group: *concept, object, event,* and *place*. But Group 3 also included all the Group 1 and Group 2 entities because these too can be the subjects of works. An event, such as the Battle of Hastings, can be the subject of a work. A work, such as Defoe's *Robinson Crusoe,* can also be the subject of another work. In other words, anything can be a subject, so all entities in the FRBR model can have a subject relationship to a work.

FRBR specified particular entities. FRSAD kept the same underlying idea—that anything can be a subject. But FRSAD took a different approach by introducing a more abstract entity, *thema*:

> *Thema* any entity used as a subject of a work ... *thema* is a superclass of all FRBR entities.
>
> FRSAD 3.4

The FRBR Group 3 entities were seen as one possible categorization of *thema,* but not necessarily the only possible categorization. Different implementations would have different needs and it was not productive at the model level to decide on the granularity and type of categorization. *Thema* represented any subject system or subject vocabulary that an implementation might choose. There was an intentional decision to use the term *thema* because it had no preexisting meaning, was culturally neutral and did not require translation.[16]

3.1.3.2 Attributes

All three models identify attributes of their entities.

Lists of attributes in FRBR were very detailed. There was an explicit statement that the lists of attributes were not exhaustive, but they were fairly inclusive of all the types of data typically encountered in MARC records for library collections.

The list of attributes for a manifestation in FRBR is long, with general attributes applicable to many types of manifestations and some specific ones for certain special types of resources:

ATTRIBUTES OF A MANIFESTATION (FRBR 4.4)

- title of the manifestation
- statement of responsibility
- edition/issue designation
- place of publication/distribution
- publisher/distributor
- date of publication/distribution
- fabricator/manufacturer
- series statement
- form of carrier
- extent of the carrier
- physical medium
- capture mode
- dimensions of the carrier
- manifestation identifier
- source for acquisition/access authorization
- terms of availability
- access restrictions on the manifestation
- typeface (printed book)
- type size (printed book)
- foliation (hand-printed book)
- collation (hand-printed book)
- publication status (serial)
- numbering (serial)
- playing speed (sound recording)
- groove width (sound recording)
- kind of cutting (sound recording)
- tape configuration (sound recording)
- kind of sound (sound recording)
- special reproduction characteristic (sound recording)
- colour (image)
- reduction ratio (microform)
- polarity (microform or visual projection)
- generation (microform or visual projection)
- presentation format (visual projection)
- system requirements (electronic resource)
- file characteristics (electronic resource)
- mode of access (remote access electronic resource)
- access address (remote access electronic resource)

FRBR was the first model, and it resulted from the analysis of bibliographic records. The advantage of this specificity was that it was easy to recognize the data one regularly recorded and trace it back to the attribute and entity in the new model. FRAD continued this approach. The model was looking at data typically stored in authority records, so it looked at a narrower collection of data types than in bibliographic records, but it still included long lists of attributes, for example, for person (FRAD 4.1).

FRSAD marked a change in approach. The two FRSAD entities were both superclasses. The attributes of *thema* were succinct: *type* and *scope note*. The two attributes were intentionally general to accommodate many different types of implementations. The attribute of *type* or category allowed for a multiplicity of applications or refinements depending on the context of the implementation. The attributes of *nomen*, more numerous than those of *thema*, were still considered to be the most common and general attributes. In addition to the usual statement that the list of attributes is not exhaustive, the text encouraged the addition of implementation-specific attributes (FRSAD 4.2).

As the library community developed an increasing familiarity with conceptual models, it was no longer necessary to demonstrate in detail the link between specific types of data recorded in descriptions and how each type of data corresponded to entities, attributes, and relationships in the models. The level of specificity for attributes in the FRBR model was now reserved for implementations. A bibliographic conceptual model is intended to sketch out the big picture and identify the key entities, attributes, and relationships. Implementations are expected to refine the model for their particular use.

3.1.3.3 Relationships

Essential to all entity-relationship models is the identification and mapping of relationships between the entities:

> relationships serve as the vehicle for depicting the link between one entity and another, and thus as the means of assisting the user to "navigate" the universe that is represented in a bibliography, catalogue, or bibliographic database.
>
> FRBR 5.1

Again, the FRBR model, being the first conceptual model, mapped relationships between the entities in great detail. Before FRBR, relationships were present in bibliographic data, but they were often implied, not precisely identified, and not uniformly recorded. They were not recognized as key to navigation and exploration.

Examples of FRBR relationships between the FRBR entities:

work	*created by*	person
event	*subject of*	work
expression	*translated by*	person
manifestation	*published by*	corporate body
item	*owned by*	family
person	*subject of*	work
work A	*subject of*	work B
work C	*based on*	work D

The FRBR model started out with an identification of the relationships between work, expression, manifestation, and item. These primary relationships between Group 1 entities were already evident in the FRBR definition of the Group 1 entities: an item is the exemplar of a manifestation, which is the embodiment of an expression, which is the realization of a work.[17] The fundamental relationships between these four WEMI entities remain at the core of all the models.

FRBR also mapped out the relationships between different works. For example, going back to the *Robinson Crusoe* example, a screenplay or a film adaptation would be a different work, but would be a related work. The screenplay and the film adaptation have a relationship of "being based on" on the original work, or, more precisely, of transforming the original work. FRBR mapped out a large number of relationships between different works, relationships such as imitation, adaptation, transformation, supplement, successor, whole-part, etc. These bibliographic relationships were not new. However, the level of information recorded about bibliographic relationships and about the exact nature of the relationship had varied over time and in different cataloging contexts. The FRBR model focused attention on the importance of recording the existence of a relationship, and also on the importance of identifying the exact nature of the relationship. Clarifying bibliographic relationships is essential for the successful completion of user tasks, especially in the current context of large agglomerations of bibliographic data, such as shared catalogs, databases, and the web.

The FRAD model also put a strong emphasis on the role of relationships between entities. One of the basic relationships was the relationship between a name or identifier and one of the bibliographic entities. There were also the relationships easily recognized as the basis for authority control work:

Entity	Relationship	Entity
person	*has appellation*	name
work	*has appellation*	name
corporate body	*is assigned*	identifier
manifestation	*is assigned*	identifier
person	*is member of*	corporate body
name	*alternate linguistic form*	name

There was some overlap between FRBR and FRAD relationships. For example, FRBR and FRAD both mapped out the relationships between different works—relationships such as imitation, adaptation, transformation, supplement, and successor. FRBR's aim was to identify the nature of bibliographic relationships. FRAD looked at how these relationships were expressed in authority data.

With FRAD's introduction of the *name* entity, there was now a relationship between the name and the entity to which it referred. FRAD introduced the *appellation relationship* and this relationship is carried forward into the subsequent models.

The FRSAD model maintains the subject relationship first defined in FRBR—all entities in all three FRBR groups can be the subject of a work. The FRBR Group 3 entities were replaced by the broader entity *thema*. *Thema* encompasses all the entities.

Entity	Relationship	Entity
thema	*is subject of*	work

FRSAD defines additional relationships. FRSAD only had two entities, so there were only a limited number of categories of relationships: *relationships between thema and nomen*; *relationships between thema*; and *relationships between nomens*. Relationships involving *nomens* generalized some of the FRAD relationships:

nomen	*is appellation of*	thema
thema	*is associated with*	thema
nomen	*is equivalent to*	nomen

The appellation relationship was a generalization, in the sense that it applied to the broader entity *nomen* that encompassed three of FRAD's entities: *name, identifier*, and *controlled access point*. It was also adapted for the model's focus on subject authority data, and thus was a relationship between *nomen* and *thema*. The relationship between *nomens* generalized the FRAD relationships between names, between access points, and between identifiers. For the *thema-thema* and *nomen-nomen* relationships, there was also a detailed identification of subcategories for each of these general relationships.[18]

FRSAD, like FRBR and FRAD, focused attention on a detailed analysis and identification of relationships, looking specifically at relationships in the area of subject authority data. Although the model appeared highly abstract at the entity level, when one moves to the relationships section, the model is categorizing relationships that are easily recognizable for anyone who has used a classification system, a subject thesaurus, a subject heading system, or other knowledge management system.[19]

3.2 IFLA LIBRARY REFERENCE MODEL

Preceding the publication of FRAD and FRSAD, there was recognition of the need to consolidate the three FR models into one coherent model:

> Inevitably the three FR models, although all created in an entity-relationship modelling framework, adopted different points of view and differing solutions for common issues. Even though all three models are needed in a complete bibliographic system, attempting to adopt the three models in a single system required solving complex issues in an ad hoc manner with little guidance from

> the models. Even as FRAD and FRSAD were being finalized in 2009 and 2010, it became clear that it would be necessary to combine or consolidate the FR family into a single coherent model to clarify the understanding of the overall model and remove barriers to its adoption.
>
> IFLA LRM 1.1

Putting the three FR models together required a new modelling exercise. FRBR, FRAD, and FRSAD had very different levels of granularity. For example, FRSAD had one superclass entity, *thema,* to cover all the entities that could be the subjects of works. In contrast, FRBR had ten entities that could be the subjects of a work. The models also took different approaches. In FRBR, *name* was an attribute of the entity to which it referred. FRAD and FRSAD modelled *name* or *nomen* as a separate entity. In places, the models were actually contradictory: the definition of *person* in FRBR is significantly different from the definition in FRAD.

The consolidation process yielded one consistent model that had a uniform level of granularity, resolved contradictions, and solved some outstanding issues. While still using entity-relationship modelling, the methodology was adjusted to be in tune with modelling for the current technological environment. The model also incorporated research into user experience and insights from implementing the previous FR models.[20] It accommodated the global diversity of descriptive practices with the manifestation statement, proposed a solution to the aggregates debate,[21] and encompassed the modelling of serials. But, despite all the changes, the model remains true to the essence of FRBR, FRAD, and FRSAD. In the words of Pat Riva, "The process of consolidation has been evolutionary, not disruptive."[22]

3.2.1 LRM User Tasks

In the user tasks, one immediately sees the continuity with the three FR models:

LRM User tasks

Find	To bring together information about one or more resources of interest by searching on any relevant criteria
Identify	To clearly understand the nature of the resources found and to distinguish between similar resources
Select	To determine the suitability of the resources found, and to be enabled to either accept or reject specific resources
Obtain	To access the content of the resource
Explore	To discover resources using the relationships between them and thus place the resources in a context

LRM has five user tasks. The definitions are slightly different from those in the FR models, because LRM models bibliographic data in its broadest meaning, so it encompasses the perspectives of the three previous models. All the definitions had to be adjusted.

For example, the essential meaning of "find" remains the same, but in each model, it was defined differently because each model focused on different types of data (bibliographic, authority, and subject authority data):

> **FRBR:** To find entities that correspond to the user's stated search criteria . . .
>
> **FRAD:** Find an entity or set of entities corresponding to stated criteria . . . or to explore the universe of bibliographic entities using those attributes and relationships.
>
> **FRSAD:** Find one or more subjects and/or their appellations, that correspond(s) to the user's stated criteria, using attributes and relationships.

During the development of LRM, it became obvious that it would not be possible to simply choose one of the three definitions. While all three definitions mean the same thing, each reflects the particular perspective of its model. Choosing one of the three was not a good option. Instead, each definition had to be examined, and a new definition developed that took the essential meaning of the three definitions and worked it into one generalized definition. This process had to be repeated for every entity, attribute, relationship, and their definitions.

LRM set aside the *justify* user task from FRAD because it was too specific to the library process of authority control rather than focusing on the end user. Then LRM combined the remaining user tasks into these five tasks and redefined them to make them appropriate for the consolidated model. Most are obvious because they keep the same names. FRAD's "contextualize" was mapped to "explore,"[23] a task that first appeared in FRSAD.

As in the previous models, the user tasks provide the lens through which to examine bibliographic data and map out the relevant entities, attributes, and relationships that support successful completion of these tasks.

3.2.2 LRM Entities

In the process of consolidating the three FR models, all the FR entities were examined. Some of the FR entities were brought forward into IFLA LRM unchanged, some were generalized, some removed in favor of broader entities, and some were simply removed. The model also introduced some new entities. In IFLA LRM, there are eleven entities.

Some of the FR entities remain unchanged, such as work, expression, manifestation, and item. FRSAD's "thema" was generalized to become *res*, the superclass that encompasses all other entities. The model also introduced new entities: *agent, collective agent,* and *time-span*. IFLA LRM focuses on the entities of interest to the end user so some entities were removed as being out of scope: FRAD's "rules" and "agency" because they relate to a library process rather than directly relating to the data. FRSAD's "nomen" was also generalized so it no longer applies only to subject data, and FRAD's "name" was merged into *nomen*. For FRBR's "place," the name of the entity was retained, but the entity was completely redefined, so in effect, a new entity. Some entities were removed in favor of a broader entity, such as FRAD's "identifier" and "controlled access point" being subsumed into *nomen*, and "family" and "corporate body" being subsumed into *collective agent*.[24]

The LRM entities are presented in a different way because LRM uses hierarchies in its modelling, with superclasses and subclasses. FRSAD had already introduced the idea of superclasses, in the definitions of its two entities, "thema" and "nomen." LRM takes this further and integrates this notion into the structure of the model. This is the first major difference between LRM and the previous FR models.

ENTITY HIERARCHY		
Top Level	**Second Level**	**Third Level**
LRM-E1 Res		
--	LRM-E2 Work	
--	LRM-E3 Expression	
--	LRM-E4 Manifestation	
--	LRM-E5 Item	
--	LRM-E6 Agent	
--	--	LRM-E7 Person
--	--	LRM-E8 Collective Agent
--	LRM-E9 Nomen	
--	LRM-E10 Place	
--	LRM-E11 Time-span	

FIGURE 3.2
IFLA LRM Table 4.1—Entity Hierarchy

A hierarchical structure is efficient and reduces repetition in the model itself. It is also an efficient structure for programming and makes the model more easily adaptable for current technological environments. Anything that is valid for a superclass is automatically valid for all the subclasses. So, if an attribute or relationship is defined at the superclass level, it is a valid attribute or relationship for all the subclasses. Instead of reiterating an attribute for a person, family, or corporate body, one can simply state the attribute at the *agent* level and it then applies to all the subclasses of *agent*. The subclasses inherit all the properties of the superclass.

Res is the superclass of all entities in the model.[25] It is the starting point at the top of the entity hierarchy in LRM. It encompasses any entity in the universe of discourse, namely, the bibliographic universe, and it includes both physical and conceptual entities. *Res* appears to be a new entity but in fact, it is not: Maja Žumer, who worked on the development of both FRSAD and IFLA LRM, has pointed out that *res* has its roots in FRSAD's "thema," with its name and definition generalized beyond the scope of subject.[26]

Res includes all the other entities in LRM, as well as other ones that may be specified in the future. Thus, *res* includes an author such as Louise Penny, who is a *person*, and *person* is a specified subclass of *res*; *res* includes Hamlet, a *work*, and *work* is a specified subclass of *res*. *Res* can include a *place*, such as Paris, France, or a *timespan*, such as the Ming Dynasty. *Res* can also include things and concepts that are not members of one of the specified subclasses of *res*: it can include an animal performer, a legendary place such as Atlantis, the field of mathematics, or a group of people that is not a collective agent, such as Italians living in Canada. These are simply modelled as instances of *res*. By having *res*, implementations or applications of LRM can respect the fundamental structure of LRM data and refine the model for specific uses by defining further subclasses of *res*.

The WEMI entities continue to be the central part of the model. As mentioned earlier, the definitions of *work, expression, manifestation,* and *item* were reworded so that the definitions did not simply summarize the relationships between the entities, but the entities themselves remain the same.

A further level of hierarchy was introduced with the entity *agent*. *Agent* is a subclass of *res* and it is also a superclass. It is the superclass that encompasses any "entity capable of deliberate actions, of being granted rights, and of being held accountable for its actions" (Definition, LRM E-6). These are the entities that have "intentional relationships" with the "entities of bibliographic interest (*works, expressions, manifestations, items*)" (Scope Notes, LRM E-6). *Agent* encompasses the three entities defined in the FR models: persons, family, and corporate bodies. IFLA LRM does not define "family" and "corporate body." Instead, LRM introduces another new entity, *collective agent,* that acts as a broader entity than "family" or "corporate body" (see figure 3.3). In LRM, there are two subclasses of *agent*: *person* and *collective agent*.

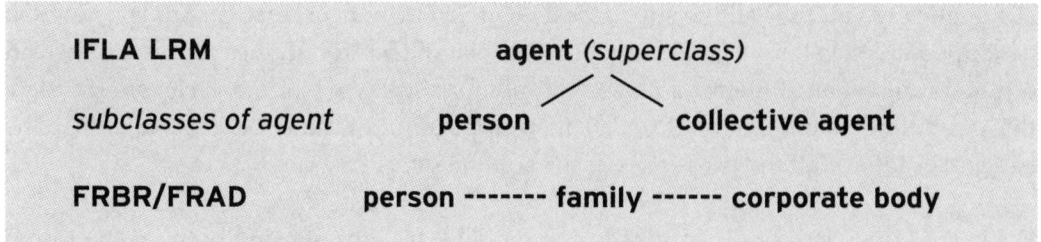

FIGURE 3.3
Hierarchy in IFLA LRM, versus FRBR/FRAD with multiple entities all at the same level

IFLA LRM does not define subclasses of *collective agent*. If an implementation requires greater granularity, developers can further refine *collective agent* (as is the case with RDA, where "family" and "corporate body" are retained by modelling them as subclasses of *collective agent*).[27]

IFLA LRM continues the approach introduced in FRAD of modelling "name" as an entity, separate from the entity to which it refers (instead of the FRBR approach, which makes the name an attribute of the entity). LRM uses the broader entity *nomen*, as FRSAD did. LRM *nomen* has a generalized definition so it no longer applies only to subject entities:

> Nomen   an association between an entity and a designation that refers to it.
> IFLA LRM, LRM-E9

The use of the Latin term "nomen" is a reminder not to limit this entity to the conventional understanding of "name." All entities have *nomens*: the name of a person, the title of a work, the name of a place, a date (name for a timespan), the term used for a subject.[28]

> In a library context, the *nomens* for *persons*, *collective agents* (such as families and corporate bodies), or *places* have been traditionally referred to as names, the *nomens* for *works*, *expressions*, and *manifestations* as titles, while the *nomens* for *res* used in a subject context are variously referred to as terms, descriptors, subject headings, and classification notation.
> IFLA LRM 5.4

There are also different types of *nomens*, such as a string of characters in common usage, an authorized access point, or an identifier.

IFLA LRM has two entities, *place* and *time-span*, that make the model more efficient and flexible:

> Place   a given extent of space
>
> IFLA LRM, LRM-E10
>
> Time-span   a temporal extent having a beginning, an end, and a duration.
>
> IFLA LRM, LRM-E11

IFLA LRM defines a top-level, general relationship that exists between all entities: *is associated with*. By using the association relationship and these two entities, many data elements can be modelled as relationships instead of attributes.

Place in LRM is not the same as "place" in FRBR. "Place" in FRBR was also a location but was limited to place as a subject of the work. LRM's *place* is broader. It is an extent of space, a geographic area;[29] it can be used as the subject of a work; it can also be associated with other entities. For example, FRAD defined three attributes of person related to place: place of birth, place of death, place of residence. IFLA LRM simply has the relationship *res has association with place*. In an implementation, such as RDA, the association relationship can be further refined to *person has association with place*, and even further refined to *person has place of birth*. *Place* can similarly be associated with *manifestation*. The IFLA LRM relationship *res has association with place* can be refined in an implementation, such as *manifestation has association with place*, and even further refined to *manifestation has place of publication*.

Like *place*, the *time-span* entity also streamlines the modelling by shifting attributes to relationships. The relationship *res has association with time-span* means that *time-span* can have a relationship with any other entity. Taking the same two examples as above, *person* and *manifestation*, the relationship of *association* can be further refined in an implementation. The *person* to *time-span* relationship could be of the types: *has date of birth, has date of death, has period of activity*, etc. The *manifestation* to *time-span* relationship could be of the types: *has date of publication, has date of distribution, has copyright date*.

Person is an entity defined in FRBR and FRAD but is not mentioned specifically in FRSAD. The entity *person* is retained in IFLA LRM, but its definition required some analysis. In consolidating the three models, IFLA LRM had to determine which of the two definitions of person would be used in LRM:

Person

> FRBR: An individual.
>
> Encompasses individuals that are deceased as well as those that are living.
>
> FRBR 3.2.5

> FRAD: An individual or a persona or identity established or adopted by an individual or group.
>
> Includes real individuals; personas or identities established or adopted by an individual through the use of more than one name; personas or identities established or adopted jointly by two or more individuals; literary figures, legendary figures, divinities, and named animals as literary figures, actors, and performers; personas or identities established or adopted by a group, etc.
>
> FRAD 3.4

FRBR and FRAD had significantly different definitions. In FRBR, person was "an individual," living or deceased. In FRAD, the scope was broadened: a person is "an individual or a persona established or adopted by an individual or group." One individual may have many personas; several people may together adopt a single persona. Person also included legendary and literary figures, divinities, etc.

The definitions of the entity *person* in FRBR and FRAD were in conflict with each other, thus making it challenging for anyone attempting to implement the models together in one implementation.[30] As stated in IFLA LRM's introduction, when the models cannot provide guidance, people will make ad hoc decisions, which undermine the point of referencing a bibliographic conceptual model. Ad hoc decisions jeopardize the goal of consistency and a common, shared understanding.

The decision for IFLA LRM was to use the definition of person from FRBR and to underline that the individual is understood to be a real human being:

Person

> IFLA LRM: an individual human being

The scope note further reinforces the definition: the entity *person* is restricted to real persons who live or are assumed to have lived. The narrower definition of *person* does not cause a loss of modelling for personas and bibliographic identities. In IFLA LRM, these are handled through the *nomen* entity.

As mentioned before in the description of FRAD entities, it was FRAD that moved *name* from attribute to an entity in its own right. By making this modelling change, FRAD introduced flexibility to accommodate many different ways of dealing with bibliographic identities in different cataloging communities around the globe.[31] IFLA LRM carries forward this modelling and this flexibility but uses the more generalized entity *nomen*. By having the *appellation* relationship between *nomens* and an agent such as a p*erson*, one can have:

> two *nomens* associated with one *person*
>> *for example,* one person—two names used in different contexts: Lewis Carroll, Charles Lutwidge Dodgson
>
> many *nomens* associated with one *person*
>> *for example,* one person—many names used in different contexts: Agatha Christie, Mary Westmacott, Lady Mallowan, Agatha Mary Clarissa Miller
>
> two *persons* associated with one n*omen*
>> *for example,* Manfred B. Lee and Frederic Dannay using the name Ellery Queen
>
> many *persons* associated with one *nomen*
>> *for example,* Victoria Holmes, Kate Cary, Cherith Baldry, Gillian Philip, Inbali Iserles, Tui Sutherland, Dan Jolley and Rosie Best, using the name Erin Hunter

Modelling *nomen* as an entity allows the model to cover many different scenarios in the bibliographic universe, including different approaches to handling bibliographic identities:

> In the model, a bibliographic identity is a cluster of *nomens* used by a *person* in the same bibliographically significant context or contexts. Which kinds of differences in *context of use* trigger the recognition, and consequent specific handling, of distinct bibliographic identities, depend on the cataloguing rules or knowledge organization system. For example, multiple pseudonyms for the same *person* may require multiple preferred access points in the cataloguing rules, but only a single classification number.
>
> IFLA LRM 5.5

If an implementation needs to include another entity, for example, an entity for performing animals, the implementation can model an extension starting from the *res* entity. IFLA LRM did not include this modelling because performing animals are a specialized use case. LRM is intended to be a high-level model covering the most generally used types of data:

> data elements that are viewed as specialized or are specific to certain types of resources, are generally not represented in the model.
>
> IFLA LRM 2.1

The *Transition Mappings* document[32] that accompanied the publication of IFLA LRM provides a detailed mapping of the transition from the entities that were defined in FRBR, FRAD, and FRSAD to the eleven entities in IFLA LRM.

3.2.3 IFLA LRM Attributes and Relationships

Attributes and relationships are an important part of IFLA LRM, but they appear a bit differently than they did in the earlier models. IFLA LRM has fewer attributes and fewer relationships. There are thirty-seven attributes and thirty-six relationships. Attributes and relationships have been streamlined.

IFLA LRM is intended to be high-level and cover "the most essential, commonly found attributes."[33] Similarly, relationships are declared at a general level. FRBR and FRAD had detailed lists of attributes and relationships that were long but still never considered to be exhaustive. IFLA LRM, like FRSAD, intentionally remains at a more general level:

> The model considers bibliographic information pertinent to all types of resources generally of interest to libraries; however, the model seeks to reveal the commonalities and underlying structure of bibliographic resources. . . . [D]ata elements that are viewed as specialized or are specific to certain types of resources, are generally not represented in the model. . . . The model is comprehensive at the conceptual level, but only indicative in terms of the attributes and relationships that are defined.
>
> IFLA LRM 2.1

IFLA LRM is a high-level model and its structure is more streamlined than FRBR and FRAD. It has a hierarchical superclass/subclass structure, and it transforms many attributes into relationships.

3.2.3.1 From Attributes to Relationships

As mentioned above in the discussion of LRM's entities, *place* and *time-span*, a major design consideration was the preference for relationships over attributes as a way of recording the data. By using the entities *place* and *time-span*, all the date and place attributes from FRBR and FRAD were moved to relationships. In IFLA LRM, these relationships were established at a very high level of "association," through the *res has association with place*, or *res has association with time-span* relationships. In a hierarchical model, if the relationship is valid for res, it is valid for all subclasses of res. An implementation can further refine the relationship, resulting in *manifestation has association with time-span*. Where FRBR had identified *date of publication* as an attribute of the manifestation, IFLA LRM uses the relationship *res has association with time-span* as the means to model that data.

Attributes provide descriptive information, but, especially in a linked data environment, they do not provide as much support for exploration as relationships do. Attributes are often recorded as *literals,* as strings of text, or strings of characters. But relationships between entities are a more fruitful way to record data in the linked data environment because each entity can also be the launching point for other relationships, and the links created by relationships support increased capacity to explore. This is one of the ways in which IFLA LRM becomes better optimized for use in linked data environments:

> When an entity-relationship model is translated into the semantic web, both relationships and attributes are rendered as properties in RDF triples. The difference is that a property derived from an attribute can only have either a literal (a text string) or a value from a controlled vocabulary as its object, while a property derived from a relationship will always have an instance of an entity as both its subject and its object. In a sense, attributes (although still important) are a "dead-end" in the semantic web, while relationships play a part in growing the network.[34]

3.2.3.2 Superclass/Subclass

In IFLA LRM, the hierarchical structure for entities also extends to attributes and relationships. IFLA LRM defines some of the key subtypes, to give a sense of how the model works, but there is the expectation that implementations will further subtype entities, attributes, or relationships as required for the particular context.

Attributes are defined for the entity highest in the hierarchy to which they apply. Attributes are valid for a particular entity, and for all subclasses of that entity. Any entity inherits all the attributes applicable to the superclass to which it belongs. So, if one is looking at the attributes attached to manifestation, one must also look at the attributes attached to its superclass, res, namely the attributes of *category* and *note*.

For relationships, all relationships are subtypes of the one high-level relationship: *res is associated with res* (LRM-R1):

> The first relationship in Table 4.7 in section 4.3.3 (*res* 'is associated with' *res*) is the top-level, general relationship. All other relationships declared in the model are specific refinements of this relationship which add to the semantic content of the specific association between particular domain and range entities . . . Any additional relationships needed by a particular implementation can be defined as refinements of the additional relationships defined in the model, or of the top relationship.
>
> IFLA LRM 4.3.1

Most of the relationships continue the earlier relationships declared in the FR models, although they may be renamed, merged, or generalized. For example, in FRBR, there was a list of relationships between works, such as summarizations, adaptations, imitations, and transformations. IFLA LRM continues the practice of categorizing types of relationships between works, but the categorization is a bit different. For example, summarizations are merged with the subject relationship; adaptations and imitations are merged with transformations. IFLA LRM also adds a new relationship between works: the *inspiration relationship,* "where the content of the first served as the source of ideas for the second" (LRM-R21). This relationship is considered to be different from transformation because in the inspiration relationship "the new work may not use any actual part of the original work."[35]

3.2.3.3 New Attributes

There are two new attributes that were not in any way present among the FR lists of attributes: the *representative expression* attribute and the *manifestation statement* attribute.

REPRESENTATIVE EXPRESSION

In the succinct definition in the IFLA LRM model, a *representative expression* attribute is:

> an attribute which is deemed essential in characterizing the *work* and whose values are taken from a representative or canonical expression of the *work*.
>
> IFLA LRM, LRM-E2-A2

At first glance, this seems contradictory—a *work* attribute that takes *expression* values? This is an attribute that can record several *expression* values, and the type of data recorded will vary according to the category of *work*, such as whether it is a textual or a cartographic work. But these values are recorded for the purpose of identifying the *expression* that most closely represents the *work*. The values remain values of *expression* attributes in the model, but the values can be "parked" in this *work* attribute to provide a means for sorting *expressions*:

> In a strict formal sense, within the [IFLA LRM] model all the *expressions* of a *work* are equal as realizations of the *work*. However, research with end-users indicates that they consider certain characteristics as inherent in *works* and that *expressions* that reflect those characteristics can be felt to best represent the intention of the creators of that *work*.
>
> . . .
>
> End-users intuitively understand that William Shakespeare's *Hamlet* is linked to the English language and that its literary form is a play. Users will consider that derived *expressions*, such as abridgements or translations, are distinct *expressions* of the *work* that are more distant from the "original" *expression* than full-length English language editions.
>
> IFLA LRM 5.6

Especially in cases where a work has a large number of expressions, such as *Hamlet*, the *representative expression* attribute records data that can be used to guide a user through multiple expressions to the ones that are most representative of the work, such as a full-length English language edition of *Hamlet*.

MANIFESTATION STATEMENT
IFLA LRM introduces a useful attribute that enables the model to accommodate a range of different descriptive practices:

> Manifestation statement: a statement appearing in exemplars of the *manifestation* and deemed to be significant for users to understand how the resource represents itself.
>
> IFLA LRM, LRM-E4-A4, Definition

It is the sum of information that appears on exemplars of a *manifestation* and that are used to identify and distinguish the *manifestation*. In an RDA context, it is the information that is usually transcribed. This attribute could be used as defined in IFLA LRM, but in cataloging contexts will usually be refined into more granular attributes. There is a clear example in the scope notes:

> In most implementations, these statements would likely be typed at a level of granularity considered appropriate for user needs. For example, the *manifestation statement* attribute may include transcribed elements such as: publication statement (as a whole), or alternatively, place of publication statement + publisher name statement + date of publication statement (as three individual statements).
>
> IFLA LRM, LRM-E4-A4, Scope Notes

The *manifestation statement* attribute indicates the place within the structure of the model for this type of information. But it is totally non-prescriptive about how an implementation decides to record this information and how an implementation decides to subtype this attribute. As an internationally endorsed model, IFLA LRM is designed to be open to different descriptive practices. It maintains a robust model structure for the high-level entities, attributes, and relationships to support interoperability. The *manifestation statement* attribute is a practical solution that accommodates different ways of recording this information, whether by a type of transcription or by digital capture, whether at a general level or at a more granular level.

The *manifestation statement* attribute ends up as an umbrella for many of the very specific FRBR manifestation attributes.[36] However, it is not simply a question of merging previous attributes into a more general attribute. The *manifestation statement* attribute also makes explicit that there is a difference between manifestation information taken from an exemplar, for example, a transcribed name of a publisher, and the recording of an actual relationship of association between the *manifestation* and an *agent*. The assumption is that a *manifestation* would carry information from which one could infer that there is an actual association between the *manifestation* and the *agent*. But the information recorded in the publication statement is simply a statement taken from the exemplar. So, the inference could be true or false (as with title pages that carry deliberately false imprints). One can record identifying statements that appear on the exemplars of a *manifestation* to support identification. And, when considered important, one can also explicitly record an association relationship between the *manifestation* and an *agent*. In the model, it is clear that these two processes are different: one is an attribute and the other is a relationship between two entities. The Transition Mappings table clearly states that the FRBR attribute "publisher/distributor" could either map to a *manifestation statement* attribute, as a subtype of that statement, or could map to a relationship between *manifestation* and *agent*.[37]

3.2.3.4 Modelling of Aggregates

An important new relationship that cannot be traced back to any relationships in the earlier models is the aggregation relationship. FRBR had not provided satisfactory modelling for any type of aggregate, and this had been seen as an impediment to implementing FRBR.[38] In 2005, IFLA's FRBR Review Group had created a Working Group on Aggregates to address the modelling of collections, anthologies, series, journals, and other types of aggregates. This was a difficult area to model and it took six years for the Working Group to produce its report. Its recommendations were accepted by the FRBR Review Group and the decision was made to integrate these recommendations during the development of the new consolidated model, IFLA LRM.

An aggregate by its very definition contains more than one *expression*.

> An **aggregate** is defined as a *manifestation embodying multiple expressions.*
> IFLA LRM 5.7

IFLA LRM identifies three types of aggregates:

- Aggregate collections of expressions
    - A collection of *expressions* of different *works*, such as a collection of children's stories written by different authors, a collection of novels by the same author, an anthology of poems, a compilation of songs on a CD.
- Aggregates resulting from augmentation
    - A main *work* with augmentations, for example, a novel such as Trollope's *Barchester Towers* with a preface by John Kenneth Galbraith, *La grande Bible de Tours* with illustrations by Gustave Doré.

- Aggregates of parallel *expressions*
  - more than one *expression* of the same *work*, such as the Greek text of the *Iliad* and a parallel English translation of the *Iliad*, a government document in the three official languages of that government, or a motion picture in a DVD with a choice of spoken languages.

What is the entity where the *expressions* are brought together? The conclusion was that it was the *manifestation*. The relationship is the same relationship that exists between all *expressions* and *manifestations:* an expression is embodied in a manifestation. When the *manifestation* embodies more than one *expression,* the *manifestation* is an aggregate *manifestation*. This is not a new *manifestation* entity, simply a particular case of the *manifestation* entity.

But how did those multiple expressions end up embodied in the same manifestation? Here, IFLA LRM introduces the notion of an *aggregating work* and *aggregating expression*:

> **The essence of the *aggregating work* is the selection and arrangement criteria. It does not contain the aggregated *works* themselves and the whole-part relationship is not applicable.**
>
> IFLA LRM 5.7

The *aggregating work* and *aggregating expression* are basically the plan for a particular *manifestation* to embody several *expressions*.

> **Modelling an aggregate simply as an embodiment of discrete *expressions* may fail to recognize the creative effort of the aggregator or editor. The process of aggregating the *expressions* is itself an intellectual or artistic effort and therefore meets the criteria for a *work* . . . This effort may be relatively minor—two existing novels published together—or it may represent a major effort resulting in an aggregate that is significantly more than a sum of its parts (for example an anthology).[39]**

The diagram in IFLA LRM (see figure 3.4) shows clearly that there are two separate processes taking place—the embodying and the aggregating (planning):

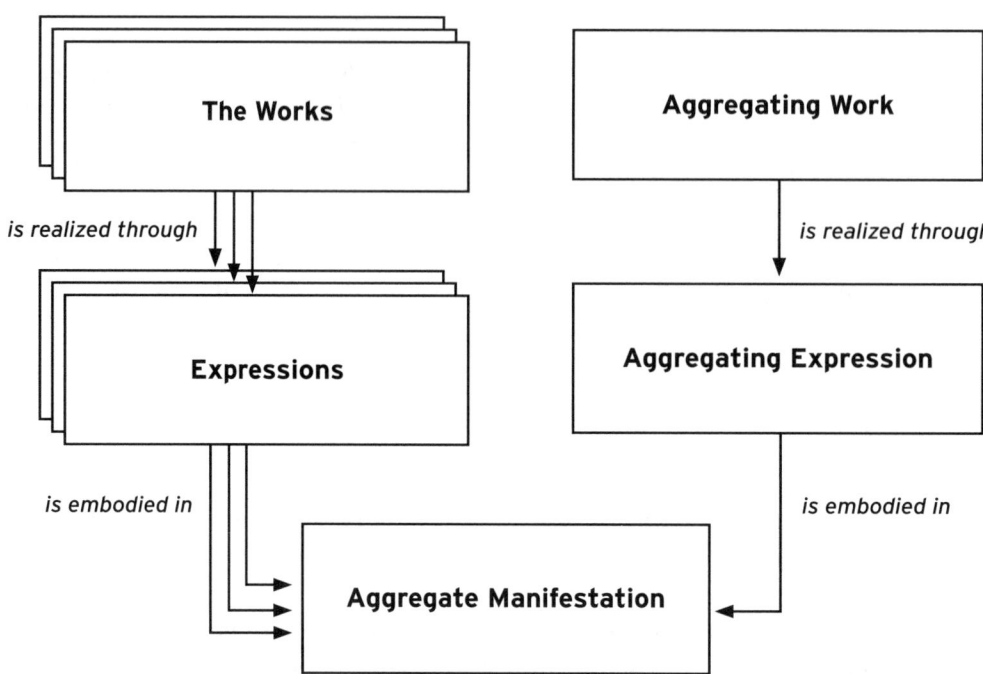

FIGURE 3.4
IFLA LRM figure 5.7 General model for aggregates

Together they result in the aggregate *manifestation*. In many cases, there may be no need for a cataloger to record the plan (the *aggregating work* and *aggregating expression*). Data about the plan can also be recorded afterwards. But the plan exists, and it is a key part of the model. The introduction of the *aggregating work* and *aggregating expression* provides the bridge between WEMI and the challenge of modelling any type of collection or aggregate in a way that is consistent and useful.

Aggregation is not a type of whole-part relationship. The *has part/is part of* relationship is a completely different relationship. For works and expressions, the whole-part relationship is inherent and always applies. In a collection of children's stories, a single story does not have an inherent relationship to the collection. It happens to have been selected to be part of an anthology of favorite children's stories from around the world. But Dante's *Inferno is* always part of *La divina commedia*, regardless of the manifestation in which it appears: it could be published alone or with the other parts, *Purgatorio* and *Paradiso*. But *Inferno* always remains the first part of *La divina commedia*. The single children's story may be published in an anthology of favorite children's stories from around the world, then republished in a collection of bedtime stories by famous British writers, and then republished in an illustrated treasury of animal stories for children. There is no inherent whole-part relationship between the story and these collections. But there definitely is a relationship.

IFLA LRM identifies the *aggregated by/aggregated* relationship that produces the aggregate *manifestation*. The aggregate *manifestation* embodies two types of *expressions*: a) the individual *expressions* of *works* and b) the *aggregating expression* that realizes the *aggregating work,* the plan to bring together these *expressions* and produce the aggregate *manifestation*:

> was aggregated by/aggregated
>
> An *aggregating expression* will select multiple specific *expressions* of other *works* so that they can be embodied together in an aggregate *manifestation*. An *expression* may be chosen by multiple *aggregating expressions.*
>
> . . .
>
> Unlike the whole-part relationship between *expressions*, the *expressions* selected to appear together in the aggregate *manifestation* do not become components of the *aggregating expression.*
>
> IFLA LRM, LRM-R25, Scope Notes

At first glance, the modelling seems complex. But the modelling maintains the integrity of the original *work-expression-manifestation* relationships while also accommodating real-life situations, such as the reality that an e*xpression* may be chosen by many different *aggregating expressions*: the same short story appearing in many different anthologies, an introductory essay by a famous philosopher appearing first in one aggregate manifestation simply as an introduction and later in another aggregate manifestation that collects the philosopher's works.

THE IMPACT OF AGGREGATION ON SERIALS

The modelling of aggregation has a significant impact on serials. Again, the original FRBR model was criticized because it did not provide satisfactory guidance in the area of serials. The experience of any cataloger who has wrestled with serials is that serials are complex, and IFLA LRM confirms this complexity. When dealing with serials, there are three different levels—the article, the issue, and the whole serial.

- Each **article** in a serial is the *expression* of an individual *work*. The articles are embodied in serial issues.
- Each **issue** of a serial is an aggregate *manifestation* that embodies a collection of articles, that is, a collection of *expressions* of *works* created by different persons. The modelling for each serial issue is the same as the diagram in IFLA LRM figure 5.7 (see figure 3.4 above): an issue is an aggregate *manifestation* that embodies multiple *expressions* of different *works*. It also includes the plan for that issue: the *aggregating work* and *aggregating expression* that resulted in that issue.

- The **sequence of serial issues** is a sequence of *manifestations* where the individual issues/manifestations share certain characteristics. The individual serial issue has a whole-part relationship to the sequence. But this whole-part relationship is only at the *manifestation* level. In common library usage, the term "serial" refers to a sequence of issues. In the model, this sequence of issues is a sequence of aggregate *manifestations*. But this sequence is not the serial *work*.
- The **serial** *work* is the overall plan, the purpose and scope of the journal, the editorial criteria used when selecting articles. It is not a new entity, but a particular case of the *work* entity.

A single serial issue is an aggregate *manifestation*. For an aggregate *manifestation* to exist, there must be an *aggregating work* and *aggregating expression*: the plan, the criteria, etc., that resulted in the selection of the articles for that particular issue. There is also the overall plan, the editorial policy of the serial as a whole. This overall *aggregating work*, the editorial policy, is the serial *work*:

> the "commonality of content" that defines a serial *work* resides in both the publisher's and the editor's intention to convey the feeling to end-users that all individual issues do belong to an identifiable whole, and in the collection of editorial concepts (a title, an overall topic, a recognizable layout, a regular frequency, etc.) that will help to convey that feeling.
>
> IFLA LRM 5.8

> The serial *work* gives rise to the sequence of *aggregating works* resulting in the individual issues through the work-inspiration relationship (LRM-R21). Despite their differences, these *aggregating works* are each inspired by the overall editorial policy, scope and style of the serial *work*.
>
> IFLA LRM 5.8

A serial has a whole-part relationship only at the *manifestation* level. The complete set of serial issues, for example, the set of print volumes, has a whole-part relationship to the individual issues. But this whole-part relationship does not exist at the *work* or *expression* level.[40]

IFLA LRM uses a complex set of relationships to model serials. The complexity of the model underlines the reality that the description of serials has been challenging cataloging communities for decades. It brings out that the distinctive feature of a serial is its overall plan or editorial policy. It confirms that each article is an *expression* of a *work* that may be aggregated by more than one *aggregating expression*, such as the original serial issue, a later collection of articles on a particular topic, a course pack for reserves, etc. From a user perspective, it matches more closely how users interact with the content of serials, not as large monolithic *works* but as collections of articles with reliability linked to the editorial plan and the selection criteria used by the editors.

3.3 ROLE OF THE MODELS

Bibliographic data has not changed. The IFLA bibliographic conceptual models introduced a systematic theoretical framework for understanding the nature of this data. The models focus on the aspects of that data that are most important for the successful completion of resource discovery tasks carried out by users.

The models promote a change in perspective because the data is analyzed in terms of its utility for those who will use the data. The models also take the perspective of looking at data in the context of navigating through very large collections of data. The focus is not a single record but the sum of bibliographic data in large catalogs, databases, or the web.

The models are understood to be the starting point for developing applications, for creating data models for those applications, and for designing standards such as cataloging codes. The models clarify the underlying structure of bibliographic data and act as a basic road map in the process of developing and revising cataloging standards. They can be used as the reference point against which to measure and test that cataloging instructions are comprehensive and consistent, and to evaluate if the instructions produce effective metadata that correspond to user needs.

Models are not intended to cover every detail but to provide an overall structure. Thus, IFLA LRM clearly states in 2.2 that an application may need to expand or omit parts. It is possible to refine or expand depending on the degree of detail that an implementation requires. Also, everything that is modelled does not necessarily have to be used. For example, it is important to model the *aggregating work* and *aggregating expression* for every aggregate *manifestation*, but it may not necessarily be important to record the *aggregating work* and *aggregating expression* for every aggregate *manifestation*. The model aims to provide the overall structure of data and to explain that structure so that someone who refines the model for an implementation maintains logical consistency with the overall model.

The models also promote data interoperability between communities with different descriptive traditions and practices. If two cataloging standards both reference the same bibliographic conceptual model, bibliographic data produced using the different cataloging standards would use the same entities and share the same structure of data. By aligning with IFLA bibliographic conceptual models, standards and applications take the same starting point. The data should then be interoperable even if not identical.

The models also make library bibliographic data easier for communities outside the library to understand. In the early 1990s, the FRBR Study Group chose the methodology of entity-relationship modelling, a technique used for developing conceptual models for relational database systems (FRBR 2.3). They adopted a modelling methodology used in other communities and began the process of building bridges to communities outside the library.

By referencing an explicit conceptual model, communities outside the library, such as museums and other cultural heritage communities, or those designing web applications, can see the structure of the data and identify points of contact and paths for interoperability.

One notable example is the cooperation between the museum and library communities. During the time when FRBR was being developed by IFLA, the International Council of Museums (ICOM) was also developing its own conceptual model called CIDOC CRM (CIDOC Conceptual Reference Model).[41] The two communities explored the possibility of mapping to each other's models as a way of supporting data interoperability in a broader cultural heritage context. This exploration became an ongoing partnership to harmonize the models.

CIDOC CRM was modelled taking an object-oriented approach instead of a relational (entity-relationship) approach as was used with FRBR. So harmonization would be required. A joint working group with representatives from both IFLA and ICOM was created to develop this harmonization. The harmonization group decided to take the FRBR model and map it as an extension of the CIDOC CRM model, which resulted in an object-oriented formulation of FRBR, called $FRBR_{OO}$ ("oo" stands for object-oriented).[42] As the IFLA models evolved, $FRBR_{OO}$ also continued to evolve. With the publication of IFLA LRM, the name of the next version of $FRBR_{OO}$ was changed to LRM_{OO}.

The collaboration between the library and museum community is an important step towards realizing the vision of data interoperability beyond the library. This collaboration with ICOM has benefits beyond linking with the museum community. $FRBR_{OO}$ was the first extension of the CIDOC CRM. But there are a growing number of extensions to CIDOC CRM. There are extensions for scientific observation, archeological buildings, and social phenomena, to name a few. When the library's conceptual model links to CIDOC CRM, it means it also links to every other extension. With an ever-expanding proliferation of compatible models, the possibilities for data interoperability are also expanding.

At the time that FRBR was published, the Semantic Web was a nebulous concept, a promise for the future. But the decision to choose a modelling technique from the computing domain positioned all the IFLA bibliographic conceptual models to be models that could be adapted for use in the web. By the time IFLA LRM was published in 2017, development of Semantic Web technology had advanced to make linked data a viable environment. LRM was explicitly optimized for use in the linked data environment:

> IFLA LRM is presented as a concise model definition document, principally consisting of formatted tables and diagrams. Previous experience in creating IFLA vocabularies for the FR family of conceptual models indicated that a highly structured document will, for example, make the task of specifying namespaces for use with linked open data applications easier and reduce the potential for ambiguity. The context has changed since the FRBR model was originally developed, and new needs have emerged, particularly in terms of reuse of data in semantic web applications, making this consideration an integral part of the initial planning of presentation of the model definition.
>
> IFLA LRM 2.3

> this model is developed very much with semantic web technologies in mind.
>
> IFLA LRM 4.2.4

The context has indeed changed since the FRBR model was originally developed. IFLA LRM continues the role of FRBR/FRAD/FRSAD in making the structure of bibliographic data explicit and understandable for those within and outside the library, whether to develop metadata standards or design applications and discovery tools. The earlier model descriptions were written as discursive texts for human interpretation. The format of IFLA LRM underlines that the context has changed. It combines explanatory guidance with a format that is also ready for publication in an IFLA namespace, a necessary requirement for the linked data environment.

NOTES

1. "Subject Relationship Element in RDA Chapter 23" (6JSC/ALA/31/rev/Sec final) March 12 2015, www.rda-jsc.org/archivedsite/docs/6JSC-ALA-31-rev-Sec-final-rev.pdf.

2. The IFLA conceptual models are maintained using two different types of modelling: entity-relationship and object-oriented. RDA aligns explicitly with the IFLA entity-relationship models: FRBR, FRAD, FRSAD, and IFLA LRM. The object-oriented models, $FRBR_{OO}$ and LRM_{OO}, mirror the same fundamental conceptual structure but are better suited for working with object-oriented tools and methodologies and provide common ground for interoperability with the models of other cultural heritage institutions. The ERM models are the focus of this chapter. $FRBR_{OO}$ and LRM_{OO} are outside the scope of this chapter except for a brief mention in section 3.3.

3. *Functional Requirements for Bibliographic Records: Final Report.* IFLA Study Group on the Functional Requirements for Bibliographic Records. (Munich: K. G. Saur, 1998); also online: https://www.ifla.org/publications/functional-requirements-for-bibliographic-records.

4. Olivia Madison, "Utilizing the FRBR Framework in Designing User-Focused Digital Content and Access Systems," *Library Resources and Technical Services* 50, no. 1 (2006): 15. www.ala.org/alcts/sites/ala.org.alcts/files/content/resources/lrts/archive/50n1.pdf.

5. Pat Riva, "Introducing the Functional Requirements for Bibliographic Records and Related IFLA Developments," *Bulletin of the American Society for Information Science and Technology* 33, no. 6 (2007): 9-10, https://asistdl.onlinelibrary.wiley.com/doi/10.1002/bult.2007.1720330604.

6. FRBR Review Group, *FRBR Bibliography*, https://www.ifla.org/node/881.

7. *Functional Requirements for Authority Data: A Conceptual Model*. IFLA Working Group on Functional Requirements and Numbering of Authority Records (FRANAR). (Munich: Saur, 2009); also online: https://www.ifla.org/publications/functional-requirements-for-authority-data.

8. *Functional Requirements for Subject Authority Data (FRSAD): A Conceptual Model*. IFLA Working Group on the Functional Requirements for Subject Authority Records (FRSAR). (Munich: De Gruyter Saur, 2011); also online: https://www.ifla.org/node/5849.

9. The FRBR Review Group changed its name to the Bibliographic Conceptual Models Review Group in 2018: https://www.ifla.org/about-the-bcm-review-group.

10. Different words are used in FRSAD (2.4, point 2) but the entities identified are still "the objects of interest."

11. FRAD *Justify:* Document the authority data creator's reason for choosing the name or form of name on which a controlled access point is based. (FRAD 6).

12. Charles A. Cutter. *Rules for a Printed Dictionary Catalog,* 4th ed. (Washington: Government Printing Office, 1904): 12. Available online in the University of North Texas Digital Collections, digital.library.unt.edu/permalink/meta-dc-1048.

13. S. R. Ranganathan, *The Five Laws of Library Science* (Madras: Madras Library Association, 1931).

14. The note in FRAD gives a brief outline of two different approaches to pseudonyms. *Functional Requirements for Authority Data,* 8, https://www.ifla.org/publications/functional-requirements-for-authority-data.

15. There is more detailed discussion of the entity *person* in the section on the LRM entities, including a comparison of the FRBR/FRAD definitions, in section 3.2.2 of this chapter.

16. FRSAD 3.3.

17. The relationships between the Group 1 entities are sometimes called "inherent" because the nature of the relationship is essentially the definition of the entity.

18. See FRSAD 5.3 and 5.4.

19. For example, *nomen to nomen* relationships: equivalence; whole-part (FRSAD 5.4).

20. Maya Žumer, "IFLA Library Reference Model (LRM): Harmonisation of the FRBR Family," in *ISKO Encyclopedia of Knowledge Organization*, 2017, www.isko.org/cyclo/lrm.

21. In 2005, the FRBR Review Group created the Working Group on Aggregates. The WG produced a final report in 2011. The report presents the majority view of the WG but also includes an appendix with the description of an alternative approach; see https://www.ifla.org/files/assets/cataloguing/frbrrg/AggregatesFinalReport.pdf.

22. Pat Riva, "The IFLA Library Reference Model," Lectio Magistralis in Library Science, Florence, Italy, March 6, 2018 (Firenze: Casalini Libri, 2014), 8. Available online: http://digital.casalini.it/9788876560255.

23. A full mapping of the three FR models to IFLA LRM was published at the time that IFLA LRM was published. Pat Riva, Patrick Le Bœuf, and Maja Žumer, *Transitions Mapping: User Tasks, Entities, Attributes, and Relationships in FRBR, FRAD, and FRSAD Mapped to Their Equivalents in the IFLA Library Reference Model,* 2017, https://www.ifla.org/files/assets/cataloguing/frbr-lrm/transitionmappings201708.pdf.

24. For complete details, see Riva, Le Bœuf, and Žumer, *Transitions Mapping*.

25. Žumer, "IFLA LRM: Harmonisation of the FRBR Family," in ISKO Encyclopedia of Knowledge Organization. 2017, www.isko.org/cyclo/lrm.

26. Žumer, "IFLA LRM: Harmonisation of the FRBR Family."

27. Discussed in more detail in chapter 5, section 5.2.2.

28. The only entity that does not have an appellation relationship with *nomen* is the entity *nomen*.

29. IFLA LRM specifies that one should not confuse *place* with the government that has jurisdiction over a territory. The government body is a *collective agent*. *Place* is an extent of space, a geographic area. (Scope Notes, LRM-E10).

30. For example, the RDA treatment of names in Pat Riva and Chris Oliver, "Evaluation of RDA as an Implementation of FRBR and FRAD," *Cataloging and Classification Quarterly* 50 (2012) 5-7; 579-80, https://doi.org/10.1080/01639374.2012.680848.

31. See section 3.1.3.1 of this chapter, above. See also the note in FRAD 3.4 outlining two different approaches to pseudonyms, *Functional Requirements for Authority Data*, 8, https://www.ifla.org/publications/functional-requirements-for-authority-data.

32. Riva, Le Bœuf, and Žumer, *Transitions Mapping*.

33. Riva, Le Bœuf, and Žumer, *Transition Mappings*, 3.

34. Riva, "IFLA Library Reference Model: Lectio Magistralis," 13.

35. Riva, Le Bœuf, and Žumer, *Transition Mappings*, 64.

36. See the detailed information for manifestation attributes in Riva, Le Bœuf, and Žumer, *Transitions Mapping*, 24-30.

37. Riva, Le Bœuf, and Žumer, *Transition Mappings*, 25.

38. Working Group on Aggregates. Final Report, 2011, 1, https://www.ifla.org/files/assets/cataloguing/frbrrg/AggregatesFinalReport.pdf.

39. IFLA LRM 5.7, 93-94.

40. For a more detailed discussion and diagrams, see Riva, "IFLA Library Reference Model: Lectio Magistralis," section IV B, "Serials, a Special Kind of Aggregate."

41. For more information about CIDOC Conceptual Reference Model, see www.cidoc-crm.org/.

42. For more information about $FRBR_{oo}$, see https://www.ifla.org/publications/node/11240 or www.cidoc-crm.org/collaborations; for more information on the working group, see https://www.ifla.org/node/928.

4

RDA'S BACKGROUND: EVOLUTION FROM AACR2 INTO RDA

RDA was born out of an initial attempt to do a radical revision of AACR2, the second edition of the *Anglo-American Cataloguing Rules*. RDA introduced significant changes that made it a standard that was very different from AACR2. But AACR2 was RDA's predecessor and the text of RDA acknowledges this link:

> RDA is built on foundations established by the *Anglo-American Cataloguing Rules* (AACR) and the cataloguing traditions on which it was based.

This statement is found in RDA in both the old and the new RDA Toolkits.[1] It is an important acknowledgment of the tie between a former standard and the new standard that evolved out of it. Since RDA was first published, it has continued to develop in ways that make it increasingly different from its predecessor. But work on RDA started by building on the foundations of AACR2. RDA now presents a multiplicity of ways to apply the standard and to accommodate different cataloging traditions, but there is still a clear place for accommodating the cataloging traditions and practices on which AACR2 was based.

This chapter takes a brief look at the evolution of RDA.

- 4.1 Building on the Foundations of AACR
- 4.2 Deconstruction of AACR2
- 4.3 Continuity with AACR2
- 4.4 Moving away from AACR2

4.1 BUILDING ON THE FOUNDATIONS OF AACR

An initial question might be: why not begin with a totally blank slate and create something that is entirely new? The answer lies in the evidence that AACR was successful in fulfilling an important role and that it had become a widely adopted standard. Thus, in developing a new standard, it made sense to build on the foundations of AACR.

During the twentieth century, library communities around the world made significant steps towards coordination of their activities and international standardization. The Paris Principles (1961) remains a landmark document in the history of cataloging because it represents the transformation from well-intentioned expressions of the desire to cooperate into a tangible road map for future harmonization. The Paris Principles provided a shaping structure for many cataloging codes around the world, including AACR. The American, British, and Canadian cataloging communities, and later also the Australian cataloging community, developed the set of cataloging rules known as AACR. AACR was their shared standard, but it also went on to be adopted more broadly. One can almost hear the element of surprise in the preface to the second edition of AACR:

> The starting point for this new edition is, indeed, the very clear success of the 1967 texts ... not only in the three "Anglo-American" countries for which AACR was established, but throughout the world. AACR has been adopted ... in most English-speaking countries, and has had a considerable influence on the formation or revision of local and national cataloguing rules in a number of others.[2]

AACR2 was translated into twenty-five different languages, demonstrating widespread adoption beyond the original author countries and beyond English-speaking cataloging communities.

With its widespread use around the world, AACR2 encouraged consistency in the recording of bibliographic data. This consistency supported an efficient sharing of records between libraries and greater cooperation between cataloging agencies and institutions. A widely shared standard made it possible to share and reuse bibliographic data.

When the Joint Steering Committee judged that it was not possible to achieve the required changes within the shell of AACR2, it also recognized that there were valuable aspects in the old standard. Thus, the aim was to build on "foundations established by the *Anglo-American Cataloguing Rules* (AACR)." This aim first appeared in the *Strategic Plan for RDA 2005–2009*[3] and became part of the introductory text of RDA. RDA was intentionally built on the foundations of AACR.

4.2 DECONSTRUCTION OF AACR2

The history of RDA goes back to the need to address deep-seated problems in AACR2. RDA is now very different from AACR2. But RDA was born out of an initial attempt to do a radical revision of AACR2.

Instructions and wording have changed, but the key to RDA is its alignment with IFLA's bibliographic conceptual models. RDA instructions are applied within the context of this new theoretical framework and this transforms RDA far beyond a revision of AACR2.

Using the analogy of a major renovation project shows how the content of RDA and AACR2 are related and yet fundamentally different. One way to think about the development of RDA is to see it as the product of a process of deconstruction and then reconstruction around a new framework.

Up to the 1990s, the amendment process had proved to be sufficient for dealing with change. By the mid-1990s, with the proliferation of new publication practices, new electronic resources and new methods of scholarly and creative communication, it became increasingly clear that there were substantive issues beyond the scope of a simple amendment process. The committee responsible for AACR2's content was the Joint Steering Committee for Revision of AACR (JSC). JSC hosted a conference of experts in 1997 to discuss the future direction of AACR. The International Conference on the Principles and Future Deve lopment of AACR was held in Toronto, Ontario, on October 23–25, 1997. As a result of the conference, the JSC compiled a list of action items[4] and embarked on a process of revision that began within the AACR2 structure and then pushed beyond.

Two action items, in particular, began a process of revision that resulted in a complete deconstruction of AACR2:

> *Action:* Pursue the recommendation that a data modeling technique be used to provide a logical analysis of the principles and structures that underlie AACR.
>
> *Action:* Solicit a proposal to revise rule 0.24 to advance the discussion on the primacy of intellectual content over physical format.

The two action items overlap to a certain extent because they are both related to the "class of materials" concept. In AACR2, how a resource is described is determined by the class of material to which it belongs. Both action items led to the conclusion that the class of material concept was a major stumbling block for the flexibility and extensibility of AACR2.

The first action item, the logical analysis, was carried out by Tom Delsey, and reported in the document *The Logical Structure of the Anglo-American Cataloguing Rules.*[5] One of the fundamental problems in the logical structure of AACR was the categorization used in the class of materials concepts and for the general material designations. The assumption was that the categories were defined by physical carrier. However, on closer examination, it became clear that the categories were a mixture of content and carrier. For example, taking classes of material, only five classes were actually defined by physical carrier: sound recordings, motion pictures, videorecordings, computer files, and microforms. Cartographic material, graphic materials, and three-dimensional artifacts and realia are actually types of content, and these types of content are delivered on a variety of physical carriers, few of which are exclusive to one content type. For example, a sheet can carry cartographic content, still image content, or musical notation content. Music was also a problem. The AACR2 chapter on music focused only on music expressed through musical notation, that is, scores, and there was little explicit accommodation for performed music as a content type except through the chapter that focused on sound recordings. But this was a chapter that actually focused on a type of physical carrier not on content.

The FRBR model had just been approved and published at the same time as Delsey's logical analysis of AACR2. The FRBR model provided clarity because the FRBR entities and attributes clearly demonstrated which AACR2 types of material were associated with content and which ones with carrier. The model illuminated the contradictions and inconsistencies in the AACR2 classes of material.

For example, the class of material *microform* aligns with the FRBR manifestation attribute, form of carrier; the class *music* was really only notated music or scores and aligns with the expression attribute, *form of expression*; some classes, such as *cartographic material*, were defined according to a work attribute, *form of work*.

With this patchwork of categorizations, it was difficult to extend AACR2 to describe new types of resources and difficult to describe resources consisting of different types of content. The instructions in AACR2 were organized according to class of material chapters. It was often unclear how a cataloger should proceed when they needed to consult multiple chapters, which chapters had precedence, and how to resolve conflicts if the chapters gave different instructions.

The *Logical Structure* report included recommendations. The recommendation for the class of material issue was to consider the possibility of "deconstructing" class of materials and developing a more flexible approach, so that AACR2 could easily extend to the description of new types of resources. Given that part I of AACR2 was organized according to the class of materials, the way forward must also include deconstructing part I. The recommendation was worded as "use the model developed for this study to assess the options for restructuring part I of the code."[6] Delsey also went on to suggest the possibility of reorganizing part I according to the ISBD areas.

As early as 1999, work had begun on an experimental "alpha" prototype of a reorganized part I of AACR2, created by Bruce Johnson and Bob Ewald. The prototype simply rearranged the rules, but it was the first step in the deconstruction process. The prototype took the part I rules out of the chapter structure based on class of material and organized them according to the ISBD areas. The rearrangement highlighted some problems and discrepancies. Then the ALA Task Force on Consistency across Part I of AACR2 took the process of deconstruction a step further. Taking the prototype of rearranged text, the Task Force was asked to analyze the consistency of AACR2 rules by looking at the degree of overlap between similar rules originating from different chapters, and to identify inconsistencies, discrepancies, or conflicts between these similar rules. The task force proposed revisions to increase consistency and prepared another prototype for a reorganized part I.[7] The action of taking the rules out of their chapters and rearranging them began a process of visualizing a new organization for the structure of the cataloging code.

Another action item from the Toronto conference was focused on bringing out the primacy of content over carrier.[8] This action item also pointed to the need to deconstruct part I of AACR2. The rule 0.24 instructed catalogers to give primacy to the physical carrier, and to follow the rules for one class of materials:

> It is a cardinal principle of the use of part I that the description of a physical item should be based in the first instance on the chapter dealing with the class of materials to which that item belongs. In short, the starting point for description is the physical form of the item in hand, not the original or any previous form in which the work has been published.[9]

The American Library Association's Committee on Cataloging: Description and Access (CC:DA) was asked to examine 0.24 and prepare a rule revision proposal. The CC:DA task force, Task Force on Rule 0.24, identified two aspects of the problem: (1) how to describe a bibliographic resource that has multiple characteristics and (2) how to deal with identical intellectual content existing on a variety of carriers, also called the "format variation problem" in their report.[10] It prepared a revision proposal that partially dealt with the first aspect and led to the amendment of rule 0.24 in 2001. The amendment instructed the cataloger to "bring out all aspects of the item being described, including its content, its carrier, its type of publication, its bibliographic relationships, and whether it is published or unpublished." It replaced the previous instruction that focused on the "physical form."

The revision did not indicate any precedence among the classes of materials, nor did it address the inconsistency in categorization of the classes of materials. The task force recognized that any changes to the class of materials concept would necessarily entail changes to the structure of part I of AACR2. The task force clearly indicated that its proposed revision was an interim step because a full resolution of the problem would require an extensive reorganization of AACR2.[11] They supported and encouraged the reorganization of part I.

In April 2004, the Committee of Principals (CoP) and JSC decided that the degree of reorganization and changes required had surpassed the level of "amendments" and warranted a comprehensive revision of the rules. They named the new revision AACR3. JSC endorsed the process of deconstruction. They also explicitly provided the new organizing framework with the intention to align the rules with the concepts and terminology used in the FRBR model.[12] A new draft of part I was prepared. The proposed changes for AACR3 increased the integration of FRBR into the cataloging rules. The division into parts I and II continued to mirror AACR2's structure, with the addition of a third part for authority control. But there was a new structure for the chapters within part I. The draft also demonstrated a new approach to class of materials and GMDs, where there was a conscious differentiation between the type of content and the type of medium. The class of materials concept was in the process of being removed and replaced with a new, more logically rigorous and extensible framework for the technical and content description of resources.

As the new changes were proposed, tested, and discussed, it became evident that the standard was moving in the right direction, but it had not yet gone far enough.[13] In April 2005, the Committee of Principles and the Joint Steering Committee announced a further change in approach. Rather than trying to work within the AACR2 structure, the decision was made to abandon totally AACR2's structure and move to a more complete alignment with the FRBR model. The name of the standard was also changed to Resource Description and Access to indicate the degree of change.

The origin of RDA was in the thorough deconstruction of AACR2 and the rebuilding into a new standard around the framework of the FRBR and FRAD conceptual models. During the collective deconstruction of part I of AACR2, the individual rules were taken out of their chapters. They were removed from the "class of material" structure that had defined part I of AACR2. A few rules or instructions were eliminated, some were changed, some were generalized, and new ones were added. A large number of the AACR2 rules were reworded to fit with the vocabulary from the IFLA models and were placed in a new location within RDA's structure but were essentially kept the same. RDA used many of the old building blocks and rearranged them in a new structure built on the theoretical framework expressed in the FRBR and FRAD conceptual models. Thus, there were recognizable links to AACR2, especially in the text of RDA as published in the original RDA Toolkit. There were many RDA instructions that were simply reworked AACR2 rules, but the orientation of the standard as a whole had changed. In its alignment with the FRBR and FRAD conceptual models, RDA was built around an explicit and logically sound theoretical framework and incorporated a new understanding of the structure of bibliographic data.

RDA in the new RDA Toolkit continues in this same direction: a standard built on the theoretical framework rooted in the IFLA bibliographic conceptual models. It aligns with the most current IFLA bibliographic conceptual model, IFLA LRM, so its structure has some differences, but the principle of building a standard on a sound and explicit theoretical framework continues. The design of RDA has also evolved to accommodate greater international use, more automated data description contexts, and a spectrum of implementation scenarios, such as creating structured data for the linked data environment. It still has visible links to AACR2 instructions, but these are found among an array of options. Instructions that have links to those that originate from AACR2 are found among the instructions for recording unstructured and structured descriptions.[14]

As RDA develops, the wording of the instructions continues to be refined to eliminate conceptual stumbling blocks where instructions were carried over from AACR2 but are out of alignment with the principles and concepts of the IFLA bibliographic conceptual models. For example, old instructions that included the word *place* may be referring to place in the context of different entities, such as *nomen, corporate body,* or the geographic entity, *place*. RDA in the new RDA Toolkit addresses this long-standing issue.

4.3 CONTINUITY WITH AACR2

4.3.1 Fundamentals of Governance

AACR was a cooperative venture that began with three author countries, Canada, Great Britain, and the United States, and then expanded to four when Australia joined during the 1980s. There was a formal governance structure to manage both content development and publication:

> The Committee of Principals (CoP) oversaw the management and finances related to the development and publication of the standard.
>
> The Joint Steering Committee (JSC) was responsible for the content of the standard and for the ongoing review and amendment of the standard.[15]
>
> The Co-Publishers published the work created by the Joint Steering Committee and were members of the Committee of Principals.
>
> The Trustees or Fund Committee managed the financial aspects and reported to the Committee of Principals.

This governance structure remained essentially the same until late 2016, when the transition to a new governance structure began, starting with the change of names for the bodies that make up the organizational structure. The new governance structure (see chapter 2 of this book for more details) retained a similar configuration. The names of all the bodies were updated, and the membership of the bodies were also changed to broaden representation from all areas of the globe.

- The RDA Board oversees the strategic planning, management, and finances related to the development and publication of the standard. *Formerly the Committee of Principals.*
- The RDA Steering Committee (RSC) is responsible for the content of the standard and for the ongoing review and development of the standard. *Formerly the Joint Steering Committee.*
- The Copyright Holders share the copyright for RDA and RDA Toolkit and are part of the RDA Board. *Formerly the Co-Publishers.*
- The Trustees manage the financial aspects and report to the Board

The traditional method of operation has continued in the new governance structure: consensus-building remains the preferred way to operate. All ideas are brought to the table and discussed, and decisions are reached after deliberate consideration and a careful weighing of impacts.

One of AACR's strengths was the active and robust amendment process that was managed by the Joint Steering Committee. The first edition of AACR was originally developed in a print-based, card catalog environment. It was able to remain the cataloging standard that was in active use for decades because of the revision process, including the major revision that produced the second edition, AACR2. When there were changes in publication practices or catalogers confronted new situations, AACR's amendment process kept the cataloging code up-to-date. With the advent of online catalogs and electronic resources, AACR2 went through many significant changes in order to respond to the challenges of the changing environment until the point when it became evident that a total rewrite was required. Until that point, many problems had at least partially been addressed through the amendment process.

The RDA Steering Committee maintains the same commitment to ongoing development and amendment but also operates in a new context. The mechanics of the process have slightly changed; for example, the path for a revision proposal now goes through a regional representative body first.[16] With a web tool, it is possible to publish updates more frequently than before and move away from the amendment cycle that took at least a year from proposal to implementation. In early 2019, Kathy Glennan, RSC Chair, signaled that the revision process would be more efficient and prompt, with an aim of making amendments four times a year, instead of only annually.[17] RSC updated their operations documents to reflect this plan for an efficient process within a shorter timeline.[18] The change processes and timelines are updated to meet current needs. RSC manages an active and robust development process that encourages a wide range of input and careful deliberations about changes.

4.3.2 Some RDA Instructions Visibly Derived from AACR2 Rules

There are new instructions in RDA that have no equivalent in AACR2, and there are instructions that are changed and different in intent compared to their equivalent rule in AACR2. However, there are also some instructions where the wording is totally different, but the intent of the instruction remains fundamentally the same. These instructions are "reworked" versions of traditional cataloging practices that were also part of AACR2. The RDA instruction is given within the context of the FRBR/FRAD/FRSAD or the LRM conceptual framework, using new vocabulary and concepts, in an updated technological context, and in a new place within the structure of the standard. But one is still being guided to record the same bibliographic data:

AACR2 1.1B Title Proper
1.1B4

Abridge a long title proper only if this can be done without loss of essential information. Never omit any of the first five words of the title proper (excluding the alternative title). Indicate omissions by the mark of omission.

RDA in the original Toolkit

2.3.1.4 Recording Titles

Optional Omission

Abridge a long title only if it can be abridged without loss of essential information. Use a mark of omission (...) to indicate such an omission. Never omit any of the first five words.

RDA in the new Toolkit

Entities > Manifestation > title of manifestation

Abridging long titles of manifestation

CONDITION

A value of Manifestation: **manifestation title and responsibility statement** includes a long title.

> **OPTION**
> Record a value of the first five or more words followed by a mark of omission (...) if there is no loss of essential information.

The instruction remains the same from AACR2 to the new RDA Toolkit. The same data is being recorded. In this case, the wording in AACR2 and RDA in the original RDA Toolkit are quite similar. The wording in the new RDA Toolkit follows the patterns used throughout the new RDA Toolkit but relays the same intention.

In some cases, the intention and the net result of the instruction clearly remain the same, even though there is a difference in wording that reflects the new context for the instructions:

AACR2 1.1F Statements of Responsibility
1.1F4

Transcribe a single statement of responsibility as such whether the two or more persons or corporate bodies named in it perform the same function or different functions.

> **RDA 2.4.1.5 in the original Toolkit (until April 2016)**
> **Statement Naming More Than One Person, Etc.**
>
> Record a statement of responsibility naming more than one person, family, or corporate body as a single statement whether those persons, etc., perform the same function or different functions.
>
> **RDA 2.4.1.5 in the original Toolkit (2016 onwards)**
> **Statement Naming More Than One Agent**
>
> Record a statement of responsibility naming more than one agent as a single statement whether those agents perform the same function or different functions.
>
> **RDA in the new Toolkit**
> **Entities > Manifestation > statement of responsibility**
> **Statements that name two or more agents**
>
> > **OPTION**
> > Record a statement of responsibility that names two or more agents as a single statement whether those agents perform the same function or different functions.[19]

There are two differences in wording since the original AACR2 instruction: the use of agent instead of person and corporate body; and the use of "record" instead of "transcribe."

In the first case, the difference in wording between AACR2 and RDA is significant, not because it changes the intent of the instruction, but because the change demonstrates the alignment with the IFLA bibliographic conceptual models. The FRAD conceptual model had identified three entities that can have a relationship of responsibility for a resource: *persons, families,* and *corporate bodies*. Originally the RDA instruction listed these three entities. IFLA LRM introduced the superclass *agent* to encompass all three. RDA, in this instruction and elsewhere, uses the most encompassing entity, *agent,* instead of using *person* and *corporate body* as AACR2 did. This change was made before the 3R Project, in 2016, but with the knowledge that IFLA LRM would be using the superclass *agent*.

In the second instance, the instruction in RDA uses the verb "record." When RDA was first published, the transcription part of the instruction was not repeated at every sub-instruction. One was expected to reference the general instruction and apply that to all the sub-instructions. For example, when applying 2.4.2.3, Recording Statement of Responsibility Relating to Title Proper, the cataloger would refer to the general instruction at 2.4.1.4 Recording Statement of Responsibility, where the instruction was to transcribe, and then also apply the specific instructions. In the new RDA Toolkit, the instructions are presented slightly differently, with the introduction of choices for recording methods.[20] If there is more than one way to record the data, a cataloger may choose from recording methods according to the context in which they work, the policy statements they follow, etc. For this instruction, the only applicable option is *recording an unstructured description,* and transcription is the predominant method. As in the original RDA Toolkit, information about transcription is not found at the specific instruction, but at the more general one. The intent of the original AACR2 rule is still evident, even though the wording and context are changed. The same bibliographic data can be recorded in the same way as it was originally recorded using AACR2.

In some cases, the original instruction remains but the instruction has been generalized.

AACR2   7.7.B10
Note on physical description of motion pictures and videorecordings

e) Film base

Give the film base (i.e., *nitrate, acetate,* or *polyester*). . . .

RDA in the original Toolkit
3.6 Base Material

3.6.1.3 Record a base material of the manifestation if considered important for identification or selection. Use one or more appropriate terms from the following list.

>   acetate
>   acrylic paint
>   aluminium
>   Bristol board
>   canvas
>   . . . [list of terms is not limited to films and videorecordings; list includes *nitrate* and *polyester*]

RDA in the new Toolkit
Entities > Manifestation > base material

Recording an unstructured description

Recording a structured description

Recording an identifier

Recording an IRI

In this case, the AACR2 instruction has been moved from the nonspecific note to its own specific element—*base material.* Base material is an attribute element that describes a manifestation. The instruction has been generalized to apply to all carriers, not simply for photographic film used to record motion pictures. RDA in the new RDA Toolkit then expands the ways in which this information can be recorded, giving instructions for all four recording methods, not simply as an unstructured description (as a note). The controlled vocabulary is still there, but it is now associated with the broader element *material*. One can still record that the film base is "polyester" but RDA provides instructions so that the data support resource discovery in a range of technological contexts.

There are legacies from AACR2 that are not helpful, such as Western and Christian perspectives. These perspectives were never deliberately written into AACR2 but evolved unconsciously because of who the main contributors were. Right from the beginning of RDA, the Steering Committee was well aware that these "Anglo-American" viewpoints existed and aimed to reduce them while developing RDA. There were small steps such as the preferred titles for books of the Bible (more detail in 4.3.3, below) or adding explicit options for recording data in an agency's preferred languages and scripts. The Steering Committee continues to keep this work in scope. For example, it was a topic for discussion at the 2019 RDA Steering Committee meeting.[21]

4.3.3 Compatibility of RDA and AACR2 MARC Records

In the *Strategic Plan for RDA, 2005–2009,* there was recognition of the need for change, and also the need to maintain a certain level of continuity. The plan demonstrated the aim of building on the foundation of AACR. The plan also acknowledged the practical reality that when RDA was implemented, RDA MARC records would need to coexist in databases full of legacy MARC records that were created using AACR2 and other standards.

In terms of description, there was general agreement among libraries that there was no necessity to change AACR2 records. In addition, it would be impractical to make changes to transcribed fields because one would need the item in hand or on the screen so as to re-describe.

MARC records created according to the RDA contained more data elements, such as new elements that were not included in AACR2 and the precise description of relationships. RDA also dropped the use of many cataloger-supplied abbreviations and Latin abbreviations. These kinds of changes enriched the records without impairing compatibility.

In a MARC environment, the issue of compatibility is particularly critical when considering access points. The Joint Steering Committee did make some changes, but these cases were carefully scrutinized to ensure that modifications could be carried out with global updating procedures. For example, preferred titles for individual books of the Bible were simplified. This was partly to simplify the formulation of the access points, and partly to begin a more "balanced, neutral, and culturally-sensitive approach to formulating certain headings."[22] The division of the Bible into the Old and New Testaments is a Christian way of aggregating the content. It does not make sense from a Jewish perspective. Thus, when referring to the Book of Genesis, the RDA access point eliminated the mention of the Old Testament:

       Bible. Genesis   *instead of*   Bible. O.T. Genesis

For consistency, this was also applied for books considered part of the New Testament:

       Bible. Acts   *instead of*   Bible. N.T. Acts

The original 2006 proposal recognized that use of the term "Bible" was also problematic, but there was no simple solution; more extensive changes were shelved until a later date.

This modification was also made because it was considered possible to achieve with global change functionality. JSC went ahead because it expected that changing these access points would not require case-by-case scrutinization.

Even though there were no radical changes to the way that access points were formulated, there were enough other modifications in RDA practices that a number of existing access points were not well-aligned with RDA.

There was an ambitious and successful multiphase project to update the LC/NACO authority file and bring a large number of authority records in conformity with RDA practices, under the direction of the Program for Cooperative Cataloging (PCC).[23] The original PCC Task Group on AACR2 and RDA Acceptable Headings Categories issued a report in 2011; the group analyzed where changes were required and took into consideration the potential for large-scale machine manipulations, while also recognizing that many existing access points would not need to be changed. This was then translated into a series of programming changes by the PCC Acceptable Headings Implementation Task Group and these changes were carried out on the entire file of authority records.[24] Some were simple changes such as spelling out abbreviations. Some were replacing data, such as changing from Koran to Qur'an. Some were changing the placement and coding of elements in access points, such as the changes when the term "Selections" was part of a preferred title. There was also recognition that some changes could not be handled with machine manipulations but had to wait for human decisions on a case-by-case basis. The changes that were carried out for these authority records then impacted bibliographic records containing the affected access points. By updating the access points of all the records, the impact of this project was to increase the compatibility of MARC 21 bibliographic records within databases and catalogues, whether created by following AACR2 or RDA. It also illustrated the merit of JSC's assumption that necessary updates to access points could largely be achieved through global changes.

This compatibility of access points is essential in a MARC environment. But in a linked data environment, it is less urgent to have precise conformity in the formulation of access points. Linked data relies heavily on the use of identifiers, especially IRIs (Internationalized Resource Identifiers). The advantage of using an identifier, especially a machine-actionable identifier, is that one no longer relies on the precise order of a character string. An identifier may have several clusters of data associated with it or bring together several different iterations of the data coming from different metadata communities. An early form of this linked data environment can be seen in the Virtual International Authority File (VIAF).[25] VIAF brings together multiple name authority files from national libraries and cataloging agencies from around the world. For example, a VIAF identifier for a person clusters together multiple forms of names for the same person (see figure 4.1). There is no single "correct" form. All are valid and related.

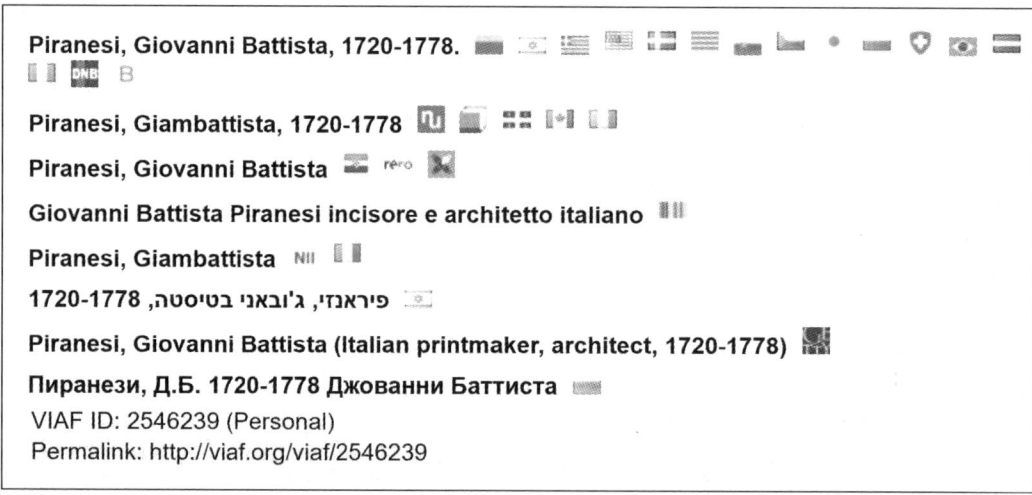

FIGURE 4.1
VIAF ID for the artist Piranesi and a few different forms of name associated with this VIAF ID

When RDA was first published in 2010, it had been developed as a standard that was in no way tied to the MARC record, as stated in "RDA Scope and Structure" (last updated in 2009):

> RDA does not specify a record syntax for the encoding or presentation of descriptive data or access point control data. Property/value statements formulated according to the guidelines and instructions in RDA are treated as discrete statements that can be stored or presented in a variety of record syntaxes.

5JSC/RDA/Scope/Rev/4[26]

The practical reality of access points in a MARC environment is important for a significant number of current RDA implementations. But RDA was written for many implementation contexts and this is clearly evident in the new RDA Toolkit. Access points continue to be crucial, but there are different ways to record them: a structured description or an IRI. RDA opens up the option to use IRIs in preparation for the linked data environment, but at the same time continues to deliver the instructions necessary to create an authorized access point as would be used in a MARC record. RDA instructions together with a community's accepted policy statements will ensure continued conformance of access points in MARC record catalogs.

As RDA evolves, its links to the past become increasingly less visible. Issues such as the compatibility of MARC records will also lessen in importance, while the issue of data interoperability in the web environment will increase. Therefore, the compatibility of data elements and of controlled vocabularies will be more important in the future rather than the precise conformity of access points.

4.4 MOVING AWAY FROM AACR2

It is hard to see the breadth of change when one looks at RDA data encoded in a MARC record. However, even in a MARC record, there are noticeable differences between AACR2 records and records created using RDA. Chapter 5 looks at the concepts that define RDA and that are key to understanding RDA. This section looks at some small changes in descriptive practices that were particularly noticeable to AACR2 catalogers. These changes are now such an accepted part of RDA that they no longer need commenting, but when RDA was first published, they were noteworthy.

4.4.1 Abbreviations and Inaccuracies

Abbreviations were important in the era of card catalogs, when the information had to be recorded on a small rectangle of cardboard. AACR2 frequently instructed catalogers to abbreviate, even in data elements when the cataloger was transcribing. For example, when transcribing an edition statement, the AACR2 rule at 1.2B1 instructed one to replace full words such as "edition" with the abbreviation "ed." and numerals for spelled out numbers, such as "2nd" instead of "Second." In the current era of online catalogs, there is no longer a pressing need to limit the number of characters used to describe a resource. For transcribed data, RDA does not have any instructions that introduce abbreviations when they do not appear on the manifestation. RDA follows the principle of representation more closely than AACR2.

RDA also moves away from the use of abbreviations in elements that are not transcribed. This change also responds to the objective of being responsive to user needs by reducing ambiguity and improving precision. For example, when recording extent, common abbreviations such as p. and v. are no longer used. The full words, pages, volumes, are used instead. Likewise, Latin abbreviations are no longer used. Latin abbreviations, such as "S.l.," "s.n.," and "et al." were used to supply information succinctly to the user and were prevalent in the era of the card catalog. These abbreviations are no longer universally understood, nor are they needed. RDA instructs one to supply a short descriptive phrase, such as "place of publication not identified," and "publisher not identified." These phrases are given in English, but the understanding is that the agencies that operate in other languages and scripts will find equivalent terms in the languages and scripts that they prefer.

The RDA instructions on recording inaccuracies or spelling mistakes in a title were also different from those in AACR2. In AACR2 rule 1.0F, the instruction was to transcribe the inaccuracy or misspelled word and supply the correction in the same place: transcribe the inaccuracy and then add "[sic]"; or transcribe the inaccuracy and add "i.e." and the correction in square brackets. In RDA, there is no equivalent to this rule. In RDA as originally published, there was an instruction on inaccuracies (RDA 1.7.9). The cataloger was instructed to transcribe the inaccuracy, and, if considered important for identification or access, to make a note correcting the inaccuracy in a *note on manifestation*. If the inaccuracy was in the title, there was an explicit instruction to consider recording the corrected title as a *variant title*. In the new RDA Toolkit, RDA still provides the option to record a corrected form of the title in a *note on title* (a subtype of n*ote on manifestation*). The transcription guidelines do not explicitly state that one should transcribe an inaccuracy because it is understood by the very nature of transcription. When RDA was first published, it was necessary to state this explicitly because it was a significant change from AACR2. After ten years of using RDA, this is no longer something that has to be said. But it can certainly be inferred from the instruction for *note on title*:

> **RDA in the new Toolkit**
> Entity > Manifestation > note on title
>
> **CONDITION**
> An inaccuracy in a title has been transcribed as it appears on the source of information.
>
> > **OPTION**
> > Record a note giving the corrected form of the title.

RDA follows the principle of representation and provides the means to ensure identification without disturbing the transcribed element.

4.4.2 More Relationships

One of the ways in which RDA promotes the recording of relationships is that it places no limits on the number of relationships than can be recorded. In contrast to its predecessor,

AACR2, RDA eliminates the "rule of three" when describing the resource and when giving access to the resource. For example, chapter 21 of AACR2 had numerous rules that restricted the number of access points for collaborative works.

> **From AACR2 21.7B1:**
>
> Make added entries under the headings for the compilers/editors if there are not more than three and if they are named prominently in the item being catalogued. If there are more than three compilers/editors named prominently, make an added entry under the heading for the principal compiler/editor and/or for the one named first.

Equivalent instructions are absent in RDA. RDA allows one to record all significant relationships. RDA itself does not prescribe a maximum number of relationships. Policy statements and application profiles may prescribe minimums and maximums, but RDA does not.

4.4.3 Elements for a Computing Environment

The term "element" is not new. It was used in AACR2. Although AACR2 and RDA both use the word "element," RDA's use of the term is different. An RDA element is intended to be precise and unambiguous, used for only one kind of data. Each element can stand alone and does not need to be clustered into areas or paragraphs of bibliographic information.

When RDA was first published, it signaled an important shift away from past practices where bibliographic information was recorded in long strings of characters, decipherable by humans, but not necessarily by computers. With RDA, bibliographic information is parsed into independent elements so that the information can be used as reliable data in computing and web environments. RDA data elements are labelled and precise so that one can predict the information that will be contained in that element.

If one thinks of past cataloging standards such as AACR2, the data was not structured and parsed in a way that was conducive for use in automated environments. For example, many different types of information were recorded in the same place. The AACR2 element "other physical details" could include a range of information, from information about illustrative content when describing a book, to details about base material, applied material, projection speed, track configuration, etc. It is difficult to use AACR2's "other physical details" as a fruitful way to improve searching, filter a search, or map to web ontologies because there are too many different types of information recorded in the same place.

AACR2	RDA
all recorded as "other physical details"	*separately defined data elements*
(book) illustrative matter	illustrative content
(sound recording)	
type of recording	type of recording
playing speed	playing speed
groove characteristic (analog discs)	groove characteristic
track configuration (sound track films)	track configuration
number of tracks (tapes)	tape configuration
number of sound channels	configuration of playback channels
recording and reproduction characteristics	special playback characteristic
(motion picture/videorecording)	
aspect ratio	aspect ratio
and special projection characteristics	presentation format
sound characteristics	sound characteristic
colour	colour content
projection speed	projection speed

FIGURE 4.2

Granularity of RDA data elements in comparison to AACR2

RDA segments the data into separate data elements. Different kinds of data are recorded in appropriate elements and these elements are unambiguously identified and defined. This results in RDA having a large set of data elements, but they are well-identified, unambiguous elements. RDA started with over 300 elements. As RDA has evolved, there has been increasing precision in the definition of elements to make them better suited for machine manipulation. This increasing precision has resulted in a larger number of elements, now numbering over 3,000.

AACR2 and RDA are very different standards. But there are visible and acknowledged links between RDA and its predecessor, AACR2. RDA evolved out of the deconstruction of AACR2 and some of the building blocks—the instructions—were carried forward into RDA. The visible links in the instructions become less obvious as RDA evolves. The historical link between the two standards will never change. It is part of RDA's development history.

When RDA was first published, it signaled a new way of understanding and handling bibliographic data. RDA acknowledges the cataloging traditions and practices on which AACR2 was based. With its multiplicity of options, it can also accommodate some traditional descriptive practices carried over from AACR2.

NOTES

1. RDA in the original RDA Toolkit at 0.31. AACR refers collectively to the first and second editions of the *Anglo-American Cataloguing Rules*. RDA in the new RDA Toolkit has a slight variation because it specifies being built on the foundations of AACR2; Guidance > Introduction to RDA > Standards related to RDA (95.89.89.63).

2. *Anglo-American Cataloguing Rules*, 2nd edition (Chicago: American Library Association; Ottawa: Canadian Library Association, 1978).

3. Joint Steering Committee for Development of RDA, *Strategic Plan for RDA, 2005-2009* (5JSC/Strategic/1/Rev/2; November 1, 2007), www.rda-jsc.org/archivedsite/stratplan.html (last updated July 1, 2009).

4. The list of action items is a list of issues that urgently needed action. See Joint Steering Committee for Revision of AACR, *Action Items, Progress Report, July 2005*, www.rda-jsc.org/archivedsite/intlconf2.html.

5. Tom Delsey, *The Logical Structure of the Anglo-American Cataloguing Rules*, 1998, www.rda-jsc.org/archivedsite/docs.html#logical.

6. Delsey, *Logical Structure of AACR*, Part 1, Recommendation no. 1. (The report and recommendations are divided into two parts).

7. ALCTS Committee on Cataloging: Description and Access. Task Force on Consistency across Part 1 of AACR, "Prototype of revised Part 1 of AACR," https://www.libraries.psu.edu/tas/jca/ccda/tf-con1.html#list.

8. One of the invited papers for the Toronto conference was explicitly devoted to this topic; see Lynne C. Howarth, " Content versus Carrier" (paper presented at The Principles and Future of AACR, Toronto, Ontario, October 23-25, 1997). Available online: www.rda-jsc.org/archivedsite/intlconf1.html.

9. AACR2, 8.

10. ALCTS Committee on Cataloging: Description and Access, Task Force on Rule 0.24, "Overview and Recommendations Concerning Revision of Rule 0.24" (4JSC/ALA/30, August 16, 1999), 3. Available online: https://www.libraries.psu.edu/tas/jca/ccda/docs/tf-024h.pdf.

11. "Overview and Recommendations Concerning Revision of Rule 0.24," 5.

12. Joint Steering Committee for Revision of AACR. "AACR3. Part I. Constituency Review of December 2004 Draft" (5JSC/AACR3/I, December 17, 2004), 3, www.rda-jsc.org/archivedsite/docs/5aacr3-part1.pdf.

13. For example, see the responses of the Library of Congress and the British Library. Library of Congress, "AACR3. Part I. Constituency Review of December 2004 Draft: Library of Congress Response" (5JSC/AACR3/I/LC response, March 25, 2005): 1, www.rda-jsc.org/archivedsite/docs/5aacr3-part1-lcresp.pdf; British Library, "AACR3. Part I. Constituency

Review of December 2004 Draft: British Library Response" (5JSC/AACR3/BL response, March 31, 2005), 1, www.rda-jsc.org/archivedsite/docs/5aacr3-part1-blresp.pdf.

14. For examples of RDA instructions that have links to AACR2, see chapter 4, section 4.3.2.

15. The full name of JSC was the Joint Steering Committee for Revision of AACR until 2007 when the name changed to Joint Steering Committee for Development of RDA.

16. Or through the Wider Community Engagement Officer when a regional representative body has not yet been created and approved.

17. Kathy Glennan, "New Ways of Working: The RSC in the Post 3R Era" (presentation, ALA Midwinter Meeting, January 28, 2019), Slide 14, www.rda-rsc.org/sites/all/files/Glennan%20New%20Ways%20of%20Working%2028%20Jan.pdf.

18. RDA Steering Committee, *RSC Operations Documents,* www.rda-rsc.org/node/608.

19. RDA in the original RDA Toolkit, 2.4.1.5; RDA in the new RDA Toolkit: RDA Entity > Manifestation > statement of responsibility (87.62.68.89).

20. For more detail about recording methods, see chapter 6, section 6.2.

21. RDA Steering Committee. *Public Agenda*, 21–25 October 2019, 2, agenda item 166 = discussion of the report "Western and Christian Bias in the 3R RDA Toolkit," www.rda-rsc.org/sites/all/files/RSC-Public%20Agenda-159-203.pdf.

22. "Bible Uniform Titles." (5JSC/LC/8, June 1, 2006). Report prepared by the Library of Congress representative on JSC, www.rda-jsc.org/archivedsite/docs/5lc8.pdf.

23. *Summary of Programmatic Changes to the LC/NACO Authority File: What LC-PCC RDA Catalogers Need to Know,* July 30, 2012, https://www.loc.gov/aba/rda/pdf/lcnaf_rdaphase.pdf.

24. Reports prepared by the PCC Task Group on AACR2 and RDA Acceptable Heading Categories and the PCC Acceptable Headings Implementation Task Group, http://files.library.northwestern.edu/public/pccahitg/.

25. VIAF: The Virtual International Authority File https://viaf.org/.

26. Joint Steering Committee for Development of RDA, "RDA Scope and Structure" (5JSC/RDA/Scope/Rev/4, July 1, 2009), 7, http://rda-jsc.org/sites/all/files/5rda-scoperev4_0.pdf.

5
RDA: SOME KEY ASPECTS

The aim of this chapter is to give an overview of RDA, by looking at key concepts and focusing particularly on areas where there are new ideas or changes in approach. Policy statements and application profiles will provide comprehensive, step-by-step coverage of the ways in which to apply RDA, geared to the needs of different cataloging and metadata communities. This chapter walks through key features to increase familiarity with RDA and provide background when using RDA:

5.1 Focus on the User

5.2 Structure of RDA

5.3 Content and Carrier

5.4 RDA Elements

5.5 Aggregates

5.6 Shortcuts

5.7 Nomen

5.8 New Ways of Thinking about Resource Description

    5.8.1 Fictitious and Non-Human Entities

    5.8.2 Diachronic Works

    5.8.3 Representative Expression

    5.8.4 Manifestation Statement

5.9 Summary

5.1 FOCUS ON THE USER

The very first objective for RDA is responsiveness to user needs.[1] This objective is given priority of place in the list of objectives. It relates back to the user tasks identified in the IFLA bibliographic conceptual models. From FRBR to IFLA LRM, the user tasks are the starting point for each of the models. The user tasks underline the "outward orientation" of the models.[2] When RDA aligns with the IFLA bibliographic conceptual models, it inherits this outward orientation to user needs. The user tasks are the lens through which to analyze and evaluate the importance of bibliographic data elements for successful resource discovery. Focus on the user is translated into elements and instructions that concretely serve the user, by recording data with the user's needs in mind.

When RDA was first published, the focus on the user tasks appeared throughout the text. The different sections of RDA each started with a general guidelines chapter. These chapters always included the functional objectives specific to that section of RDA; the objectives pointed out how the instructions of that section related back to the user tasks.

For example, from section 2, "Recording Attributes of Work and Expression:"

> **Chapter 5.** General Guidelines on Recording Attributes of Works and Expressions
>
> **5.2** Functional Objectives and Principles
>
> The data recorded to reflect the attributes of a work or expression should enable the user to:
>
> a. *find* works and expressions that correspond to the user's stated search criteria
> b. *identify* the work or expression represented by the data (i.e., confirm that the work or expression represented is the one sought, or distinguish between two or more works or expressions with the same or similar titles)
> c. *understand* the relationship between the title used to represent the work and another title by which that work is known (e.g., a different language form of the title)
> d. *understand* why a particular title has been recorded as a preferred or variant title
> e. *select* a work or expression that is appropriate to the user's requirements with respect to form, intended audience, language, etc.

In the new RDA Toolkit, the structure of RDA is radically different. It is no longer subdivided into sections and chapters. Text from all the general guidelines chapters was merged and summarized in the "Guidance" section of the new RDA Toolkit. Instead of reiterating the links to objectives and principles and to user tasks throughout the text, this content is centralized in "Guidance." Objectives and principles are presented front and center as part of the Introduction to RDA (Guidance > Introduction to RDA > Objectives and principles governing RDA). Information about the relationship between user tasks and successful resource discovery are condensed into the "User Tasks" section (Guidance > User tasks). Centralizing the information into the "Guidance" section simply reflects the new structure of RDA. It does not lessen the importance of this information. The objectives and principles and the user tasks continue to provide the context and priorities when creating metadata.

The scope for cataloger judgment is an important aspect of RDA. When RDA was first published, the scope for cataloger judgment was explicitly stated and had many instructions referencing the user tasks. In these cases, a decision on whether to record a data element would depend on the cataloger's judgment of how important this information may be for the user; the criterion was the successful completion of one or several user tasks. These instructions include phrases such as "if considered important for identification," or "if considered important for access," or "if considered important for identification or selection." This phrasing continues to be used.

RDA in the new RDA Toolkit is structured differently. It presents an array of options. In a sense, almost everything is left open to cataloger judgment. On the other hand, metadata communities will likely provide policy statements or application profiles that define the limits within which a cataloger may make judgments.

Focusing on the relationship between bibliographic data and a user task was a new approach when RDA was first published. It remains an essential and defining aspect of RDA. The first objective remains the same: responsiveness to user needs. The user tasks are an integral part of the standard. One difference in the new RDA Toolkit is a broader scope for assessing the relationship between an element and a user task. There is recognition that a data element is not necessarily tied to only one or two user tasks, and that the utility of an element to complete a user task may vary, depending on the recording method chosen.

> **User tasks and RDA recording method**
>
> A single RDA metadata statement may support one or more user tasks.
>
> The utility of a statement in supporting a specific task is dependent on the RDA element and recording method that is used for the statement.[3]

RDA in the new RDA Toolkit maintains the focus on the user. RDA instructions provide practical guidance to record and create data that will support user tasks.

5.2 STRUCTURE OF RDA

5.2.1 Organized According to the Entities

When RDA was first published, the standard was organized into a sequence of sections and chapters. The sections and chapters were organized according to the entities of IFLA's first bibliographic conceptual model, FRBR.

RDA instructions and guidance continue to be organized according to entities, but there are two big areas of change in the new RDA Toolkit that affect the structure of the standard:

    a) RDA chapters were deconstructed into individual data elements.

    b) RDA's structure was realigned to fit with the IFLA LRM entities.

RDA's defining feature has always been its alignment with the IFLA bibliographic conceptual models. The original table of contents of RDA reflected the FRBR entities and followed an order loosely based on a probable order in which a cataloger might go about describing a resource and its relationships to other entities.

Looking at the section titles of RDA in the original RDA Toolkit, especially looking at original titles, one can see the alignment with the FRBR entities (plus *family* from FRAD):

Section 1   Recording Attributes of *Manifestation & Item*

Section 2   Recording Attributes of *Work & Expression*

Section 3   Recording Attributes of *Agent*
(previously Recording Attributes of *Person, Family & Corporate Body*)

Section 4   Recording Attributes of *Concept, Object, Event, & Place*

Section 5   Recording Primary Relationships between *Work, Expression, Manifestation, & Item*

Section 6   Recording Relationships to Agents
(previously Recording Relationships to *Person, Family & Corporate Body* Associated with a Resource)

Section 7   Recording Relationships to *Concepts, Objects, Events, & Places*
(previously Recording the *Subject of a Work*)

Section 8   Recording Relationships between *Works, Expressions, Manifestations, & Items*

Section 9   Recording Relationships between Agents
(previously Recording Relationships between *Persons, Families, & Corporate Bodies*)

Section 10   Recording Relationships between *Concepts, Objects, Events, & Places*

When RDA was first published, it was set up to align with all the FRBR entities. The chapters and sections relating to the FRBR Group 3 entities were empty placeholder chapters.[4] Their presence in the table of contents demonstrated full alignment with the FRBR entities. These chapters were included even if there was no content because, at the time, there was the idea that content would be developed after RDA's initial release. After FRSAD was published, it became evident that RDA should not include specific instructions for the attributes and relationships of entities that would most probably be deprecated when the three FR models were consolidated. When RDA was revised in 2015 to include the general subject relationship, content was added to section 7, chapter 23, "General Guidelines on Recording Relationships between Works and Subjects" (thus aligning with FRSAD). The other chapters were left as empty placeholders until after the alignment with IFLA LRM during the 3R Project.

IFLA LRM introduced new entities and shifted many attributes to relationships. To maintain alignment, the content of RDA had to be reorganized. In the new RDA Toolkit, one can see that RDA has a different structure. The standard is now organized according to the IFLA LRM entities (see figure 5.1).

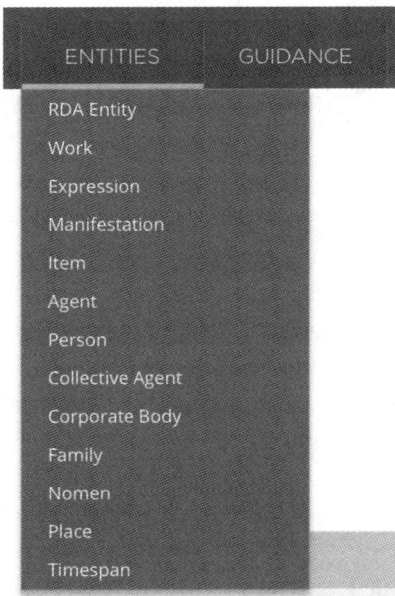

FIGURE 5.1
Entities drop-down menu in RDA Toolkit

The list of entities in RDA matches closely to the list of entities in IFLA LRM. There are two differences: RDA uses *RDA entity* instead of *res*; RDA extends *collective agent* into two narrower entities: *corporate body* and *family*.

RDA entity is narrower than *res*. *Res* is "everything considered relevant to the bibliographic universe."[5] *RDA entity* is also a high level and encompassing entity but it is limited to those conceptual objects that are "a focus of interest to users of RDA metadata in a system for resource discovery."[6] In hierarchical models such as IFLA LRM, one needs a high-level entity—a superclass—that includes all the other entities whether specifically defined in the model or not. It also allows for future extensions of the model where there may be a need to define a new entity that cannot be a subclass of any entities already defined. *RDA entity* has the same role in the model as *res* does in IFLA LRM, but it is narrower than *res*. It is "limited to the set of entities defined in RDA, rather than all things or entities in the universe of human discourse."[7]

All the other IFLA LRM entities are in the list of RDA entities, plus there are the two RDA extensions or refinements, *corporate body* and *family*. RDA extends the model by making the *collective agent* entity more granular. This also maintains continuity with RDA's original instructions and guidance related to *corporate body* and *family*.

5.2.2 Hierarchy of Entities

IFLA LRM introduces a hierarchical structure with superclasses and subclasses, which allows for more efficient modelling. RDA adopts IFLA LRM's hierarchical structure. All attributes and relationships associated with a superclass entity are immediately inherited by all the subclasses.

In the FR models, there was no superclass/subclass structure. Entities had relationships to each other, but they were all in the same plane. IFLA LRM introduces hierarchy, and RDA implements it.

IFLA LRM introduces the entity *agent,* which is a superclass of all entities that have intentional relationships to works, expressions, manifestations, and items. Even before alignment with IFLA LRM, RDA had already adopted the use of the term "agent" instead of repeating the phrase that listed the three entities: *person, family,* and *corporate body.* Many instructions and elements applied to all three entities and the phrase *person, family, and corporate body* had been repeated innumerable times throughout the original text of the standard. Using the term "agent" was an efficient shortcut, but it was not yet a full introduction of the entity *agent.*

RDA in the new RDA Toolkit continues the use of the term "agent," but more importantly adopts the structure of IFLA LRM. First, there is the RDA entity that is the RDA superclass entity. Then RDA also introduces the hierarchical structure used in IFLA LRM for *agent* by formally adding *agent* and *collective agent* to its defined entities (see figure 5.2). RDA maintained continuity with its previous entities by defining *corporate body* and *family* as extensions or subclasses of the *collective agent* entity.

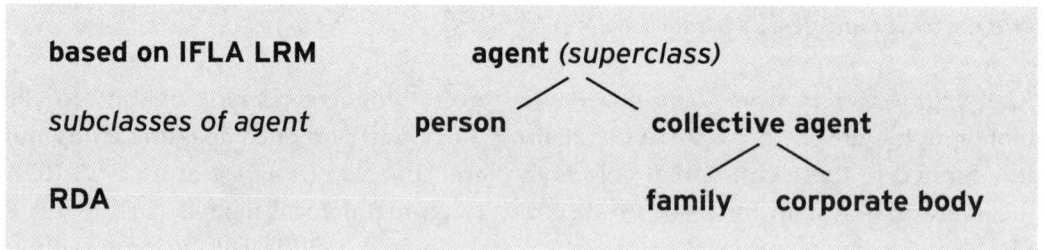

FIGURE 5.2
Implementation of IFLA LRM in RDA with RDA extension for collective agent

Subclasses are defined when there are attributes or relationships that only hold for that subclass and not for all members of the superclass. For RDA, there was sufficient reason to maintain the more granular entities, *family* and *corporate body,* because there were some differences in elements and instructions that justified this differentiation.

For example, *agents* have relationships to *timespans* and IFLA LRM simply declares a general association relationship at this superclass level. RDA has a general relationship:

period of activity of agent. This *agent* to *timespan* relationship is inherited by the subclasses of *agent*, *person*, and *collective agent*, and in turn, by the subclasses of *collective agent*, *corporate body* and *family*. On the other hand, a specific relationship such as *date of birth* is valid only for a person but not for a collective agent. In RDA, the *date of birth* relationship is only valid between *person* and *timespan*. Similarly, *date of establishment* is specific to a corporate body but not to a person nor to a family. So, it cannot be a relationship between *agent* and *timespan*, and it cannot be a relationship between *collective agent* and *timespan*. The relationship only exists between *corporate body* and *timespan*. RDA needed the *corporate body* entity because there were attributes and relationships that only hold for a corporate body and not for a *collective agent* nor for an *agent* in general. It also maintains continuity with instructions specifically related to *corporate body*.

The use of a hierarchy means that all subclasses will inherit the attribute and relationship elements that apply for the superclass. For example, the relationship LRM-R5 in IFLA LRM is *work was created by agent* and its inverse is *agent created work* (LRM-R5i). IFLA LRM did not add a relationship for each subclass of agent because it is understood that this relationship applies for all the subclasses of *agent*. IFLA LRM simply defined one general creator relationship between *agent* and *work*. RDA as an implementation of IFLA LRM provides much more detail to facilitate implementation. The creator relationship is broken down into specific types, such as author, cartographer, composer, etc. These types of relationships are defined at a general level—between *agent* and *work*.

RDA has the general relationships:

> *creator agent of work*
> *author agent*
> *filmmaker agent*

But RDA also defines these relationships for all the subclasses. The specific relationships could be inferred from the general relationship because all the subclasses inherit the same relationship. But for ease of implementation and accuracy, all the specific relationship elements are also individually defined:

> For example,
>> *author agent*
>> *author collective agent*
>> *author corporate body*
>> *author family*
>> *author person*

5.2.3 Not a Linear Text

When RDA was first being developed, there was a conscious decision to make the structure of RDA align with FRBR. The total set of instructions and guidelines not only had content that was aligned with the models, but the way that the instructions and guidelines were organized was in a shape that aligned with the models (see the original RDA table of contents in section 5.2.1, above). When RDA was first published, the way that RDA was structured caused some concerns about navigating the new standard because it was so different from its predecessor, AACR2. But the structure of RDA also helped to reinforce an understanding of bibliographic data as expressed in the FRBR and FRAD conceptual models.

When RDA was aligned with IFLA LRM, there was some work to be done at the conceptual level, but it was not insurmountable because IFLA LRM consolidated and carried forward the essence of the three previous models. What was insurmountable was grafting the changes into the existing infrastructure of the standard within the original RDA Toolkit. For example, it was unclear where to add new entities such as *timespan* or *nomen*; in addition, introducing *nomen* would also affect every existing chapter with instructions on recording names or titles. It was going to be a major challenge.

RDA in the original RDA Toolkit was a web tool, with many internal links and links to outside resources. It was an integrating resource, with updates seamlessly added over the years. But its fundamental structure was linear, with sections and chapters, and every instruction was sequentially numbered within each chapter. Previous experience during the amendment process between 2011 and 2016 had already illustrated that changes, even on a small scale, were difficult. For example, in 2014, the simple split of *note* into *note on manifestation* and *note on item* necessitated a series of changes: to insert *note on manifestation* in its logical place in the linear sequence of instructions, all the subsequent instructions had to be renumbered.

The chapter structure also presented problems because the chapters were very different in size. Chapters 2, 6, and 11 in the original RDA Toolkit were notably huge chapters. The chapters had to be broken down into subsections to improve the speed of navigation. Figure 5.3 is a screenshot from original RDA Toolkit.

The original structure of RDA consisting of sections and chapters with sequential numbering of instructions was well-suited to a book-like resource, where only minor changes might be made. It was too rigid a structure to allow for a significant change in shape, such as aligning with a new conceptual model. In addition, there were concerns about the age of the software and RDA Toolkit's conformance with accessibility standards.

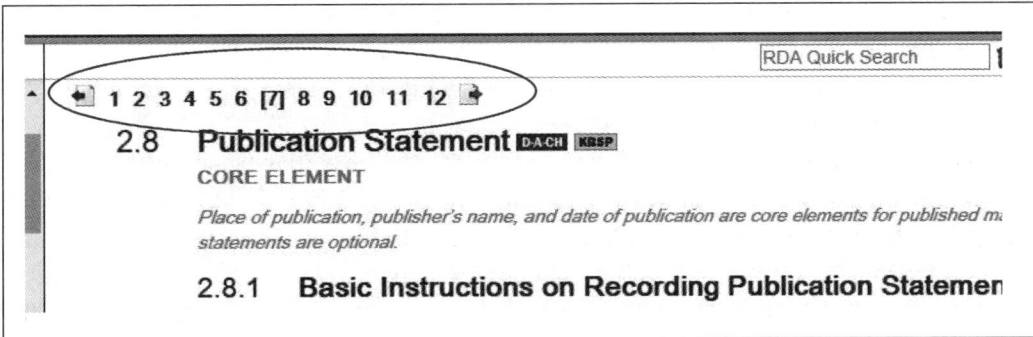

FIGURE 5.3
Chapter 2 in the original RDA Toolkit broken down into twelve subsections to speed up navigation

It became evident that RDA Toolkit needed a new way of storing and organizing the instructions that would be flexible and efficient, not only for the alignment with IFLA LRM, but also for future developments.

RDA in the new RDA Toolkit looks radically different because of the deconstruction of chapters into separate units for each data element. The basic organizational unit is no longer the book chapter but the element. This makes the units smaller and easier to handle. If, in the future, there were a new conceptual model that introduced additional entities, it would be easy to make the changes needed to align with a new model. It would no longer be difficult to add new entities and their attributes and relationships. The whole structure becomes more streamlined and agile for future maintenance and development of the standard.

Each element has its own page. All the pages for elements have a similar structure, beginning with the definition and scope, a section called "Element Reference" that has technical data, then instructions and guidance, as well as examples and links to related elements. The instructions include as many recording methods as are applicable for that element, up to four. All the information pertaining to one data element is collected together in one cluster, and these clusters are the basic building block of RDA Toolkit. RDA is a large collection of data elements, each with its own applicable instructions, supported with additional guidance and supplementary documents. With this modular redesign, the underlying structure is a collection of elements. This is not a random collection because the elements are carefully structured around the thirteen entities. But it is a structure that no longer resembles a book.

In the new RDA Toolkit, the elements are no longer embedded in chapters so, at first glance, it is not obvious how a metadata creator will recognize where they are in the standard. But there are several ways to start seeing the underlying structure of the standard. Some are described in chapter 6 of this book, such as the breadcrumb trails at the top of the page (see 6.1.1.3) and the element reference area (see 6.3). There is also a style of citing an RDA element by preceding the element name with the name of the entity to which it belongs. This is the pattern used throughout the new RDA Toolkit when referring (and linking) to other elements. The part in bold is the element (and is also an active link to that element's page), and the part preceding it is the name of the entity to which it belongs:

> Manifestation: **title proper**
>
> Work: **preferred title of work**
>
> Person: **date of birth**

For example, in figure 5.4, the instruction makes a reference to *carrier type*. *Carrier type* is clearly labelled as an element that describes a manifestation.

Entities > Manifestation > title proper

> **OPTION**
>
> Record a Manifestation: note on title ⤵ to indicate the source of a title proper.

FIGURE 5.4
Element name preceded by the entity to which it belongs

The organization of the sections and chapters in the original RDA Toolkit implied a workflow moving from manifestation and item to work and expression, moving from attributes to relationships. Some procedure documents may mirror this flow, but many catalogers entered and searched the original RDA Toolkit going directly to the information they needed to complete a MARC template or to follow another type of procedure document. Even if the original RDA Toolkit had a linear design, few people read it as a book.

RDA in the original RDA Toolkit had already moved away from looking like a cataloging manual. RDA in the new RDA Toolkit moves even further away.[8] A user enters the standard where they choose. There is no beginning, middle, or end. There is no implied order or workflow. Individuals and communities are free to develop workflows that organize the steps in the order they prefer.

There are navigational structures in the new RDA Toolkit. The most obvious one is the division into four tabs. There are four major sections, each with its own drop-down menu. The four tabs appear on every page at the top of the screen:

| ENTITIES | GUIDANCE | POLICIES | RESOURCES |

From the "Entities" drop-down menu, the metadata creator can navigate to the entity they are describing and from there to the data element they need. Or, the metadata creator can go to the "Search" box if they already know the name of the data element they want.[9] The individual data element pages are efficient and streamlined; they bring together all the information required to record that element. The "Guidance" section provides context, background, and in-depth information for concepts that apply to several elements. The new RDA Toolkit continues to accommodate the policy statements from different cataloging communities (Policies) and provides supplementary documentation in the "Resources" tab, such as access to the glossary and revision history. The new RDA Toolkit also includes improved space and functionality for sharing documentation between RDA Toolkit users.[10]

RDA in the new RDA Toolkit has a different look and feel due to the major restructuring of the original RDA Toolkit. This restructuring was driven by the need to reorganize both at the conceptual level and at the practical level.

5.3 CONTENT AND CARRIER

One of the key goals for the development of RDA was to:

> Provide a consistent, flexible, and extensible framework for both the technical and content description of all types of resources and all types of content.[11]

A major weakness of AACR2 had been its inability to extend to the description of new kinds of publications. There were fundamental logical flaws that prevented flexibility and extensibility.[12] RDA introduced a new approach. RDA's framework is not based on a predefined set of "classes of material." RDA's framework is a set of entities, with attribute and relationship elements that can be used in any combination, as required. The entities, attributes, and relationships are aligned with the IFLA bibliographic conceptual models and are designed to support the successful completion of user tasks. Data elements can be used in familiar combinations for known resources, and also in new combinations as new types of resources are created. The underlying conceptual framework permits flexibility and extensibility and maintains consistency by acting as the point of reference against which to test any future expansion of the element set. New elements can be introduced, but they must fit with the underlying conceptual model.[13]

RDA also introduces a new approach to the categorization of technical and content aspects of a resource. RDA replaced the old AACR2 practice of predefined general material designations (GMDs) and classes of material because these categorizations were logically inconsistent and thus difficult to extend. Information about the type of content, media, and carrier is important for the user, whether as a means to discover resources, or to filter searches. RDA affirms the importance of this information for the user but takes a different approach from AACR2. RDA uses a grid or framework that consists of three basic elements: *content type, media type,* and *carrier type*. This framework can provide a large number of combinations of data to cover both current and future types of resources.

This categorization of content and carrier with the three types is based on work done in collaboration with the ONIX community. ONIX is a metadata format of the publishing community used for the exchange of information. Representatives from the RDA and ONIX communities worked on the development of the *RDA/ONIX Framework for Resource Categorization (ROF)*.[14]

The collaboration with the ONIX community began during the early development of RDA. This link with ONIX for developing the content and carrier categorizations has been mentioned in RDA since it was first published. In the new RDA Toolkit, RDA has incorporated more information about the *RDA/ONIX Framework for Resource Categorization*. There is even a link to the original 2006 framework document (Guidance > Content and carrier). Content and carrier has several subsections: two subsections provide additional context and background on the relationship with ROF: RDA resource categorization; RDA carrier and content categories. There is also another subsection that sets out the means for making future additions or refinements to RDA categorizations: RDA resource category extension.[15] The potential for extensibility is an important aspect of RDA's design.

The ROF is larger than what is seen in the content, media, and carrier types. For example, content type is based on the ROF categories of character, sensory mode, image dimensionality, and image movement. But there are also additional categories that have not yet been used, such as capture method or form/genre. The framework offers the possibility of extending current categorizations while still maintaining harmonization with the ONIX community.[16]

Each of the three elements, *content, media,* and *carrier types*, has its own vocabulary encoding scheme or set of controlled vocabulary. The vocabulary for all three elements was jointly developed by the Joint Steering Committee for Development of RDA, the RDA Editor, and developers of the ONIX schema. The terms chosen were considered appropriate for the element and sufficiently differentiated one from another; the total set of terms for each type had to cover all possible, known types without leaving gaps; the terms for each type were intended to be at a consistent level of abstraction and granularity.

CONTENT TYPE

Content type is an element that describes an expression. Content type is:

> A categorization reflecting the fundamental form of communication in which the content is expressed and the human sense through which it is intended to be perceived.
>
> Content type also reflects the number of spatial dimensions and the presence or absence of movement in which content expressed in the form of an image or images is intended to be perceived.
>
> Entities > Expression > content type

RDA's definition of *content type* may seem a little philosophical, but it sets the scope for this element at a particular level of abstraction. For content type, the significant aspect is how the content is expressed and through which human sense the content is perceived. A difference in content type signals a different expression.

The terms used for content type capture the essence of the communication process:

- cartographic dataset
- cartographic image
- cartographic moving image
- cartographic tactile image
- cartographic tactile three-dimensional form
- cartographic three-dimensional form
- computer dataset
- computer program
- notated movement
- notated music
- performed movement
- performed music
- sounds
- spoken word
- still image
- tactile image
- tactile notated movement
- tactile notated music
- tactile text
- tactile three-dimensional form
- text
- three-dimensional form
- three-dimensional moving image
- two-dimensional form
- two-dimensional moving image

When recording a structured description, RDA instructs the metadata creator to use a term from the above vocabulary. There are instructions when none of the terms apply or when one cannot ascertain which content type it may be. There is the possibility of using *other* and *unspecified*, but these two terms are not considered part of the formal vocabulary encoding scheme, nor do they appear as part of the vocabulary set at the RDA Registry. The instructions allow the option of using *other* and *unspecified* when needed, but they are considered uncontrolled terms. This applies to content type and also to media and carrier types.

RDA gives prominence to its own vocabulary encoding scheme, the *RDA content type* vocabulary encoding scheme. But RDA also offers the option of recording a term from another suitable vocabulary encoding scheme.[17] This option is one of the ways in which the standard includes flexibility to support the use of RDA by many different communities. This option applies throughout the standard whenever an RDA vocabulary encoding scheme is mentioned, not just at content type. There is also the option to record a suitable uncontrolled term as an unstructured description.[18]

MEDIA TYPE

Media type is an element that describes a manifestation. It is an attribute of the carrier, an attribute that distinguishes manifestations.

The definition of *media type* is very succinct. *Media type* is:

> A categorization reflecting the general type of intermediation device required to view, play, run, etc., the content of a manifestation.
>
> Entities > Manifestation > media type

When recording a structured description, the vocabulary used for media type is:

audio	projected
computer	stereographic
microform	unmediated
microscopic	video

Media type is closely related to carrier type. In theory, it can be inferred from the carrier type, because carrier types are explicitly associated with a particular media type. In some implementation scenarios, it may be possible to avoid recording media type explicitly, and programming would populate the data element based on the carrier type.

Media type is a valuable clustering element that allows a user to narrow a search to several carrier types that all use the same type of intermediation. For example, a user with a visual impairment may only want resources whose media type is audio; the user may be able to use a range of different carriers. Using media type would permit the user to find all audio resources, regardless of the particular carrier.

CARRIER TYPE

Carrier type is also an attribute that describes a manifestation. The definition of *carrier type* is closely intertwined with media type, but it is more concrete and specific than media type.

Carrier type is:

> A categorization reflecting the format of the storage medium and housing of a carrier in combination with the type of intermediation device required to view, play, run, etc., the content of a manifestation.
>
> Entities > Manifestation > carrier type

Examples of terms in the vocabulary encoding scheme: computer disc, film reel, online resource, sheet, volume. Carrier types are closely correlated with media types: computer disc and online resource with media type "computer," film reel with "projected," sheet and volume with "unmediated." Each carrier type is associated with a single media type. Each media type encompasses several carrier types.

When recording a structured description, the metadata creator is instructed to record a term as the carrier type, and the term is recorded using the precise vocabulary in the vocabulary encoding scheme. The term is used in the singular, with no further extensions, additions, or qualifiers. It is the use of precise terms (or the use of the matching identifiers/codes or IRIs) that will enable precision and reliability when searching.

Carrier type is not the same as *extent of manifestation*. RDA encourages the use of carrier type vocabulary when recording extent, but there are many more options when recording the extent of a manifestation. For example, one can choose to record an unstructured description—a free text description, such as using a term in common usage, including a trade name. Or one can also choose to record a structured description that has stricter parameters, such as using the *carrier type* terms..

CONTENT, MEDIA, AND CARRIER TYPES

RDA has instructions on recording content, media, and carrier types. In the event that there is more than one content, media, or carrier type, one can record all the applicable types, the type that applies to the predominant part, or the types that apply to the most substantial parts.

The metadata creator is instructed to record this data, but RDA does not indicate how to use or display this data. As long as the data is recorded, then an implementation can make decisions about how to map this data for display or how to use it as a filter, etc. An implementation may choose not to map the values, and to display them as recorded.

But terms in a vocabulary encoding scheme, whether RDA or not, can be mapped to user-friendly labels that are appropriate for one's particular audience. For example, if the data recorded were content type=moving image, media type=computer, carrier type=online resource, it could map to show the type of resource as "online video." Some communities may prefer to use icons. The terminology used to display the information can also vary between different communities, so one community may want to take those three types and map it to display as "online video," and another to display it as "e-video" or "video (digital)." A community could also decide that only certain types or combination of types would display to the user. A highly specialized community might take the three categorization types in combination with another element to develop more precise terms for its user group, such as "streaming video" or "video game." Likewise, if the data is recorded as content type=text, media type=unmediated, carrier type=volume, this could map to show the type of resource as a printed text or combine with other data to show "book" or "journal."

The underlying principle is consistency in recording the data and then flexibility in displaying it or using it in discovery tools. Another aspect of flexibility is the ease of making changes over time. We can map the elements to a set of terminology. There may be decisions later on to change this terminology. The original data in the elements remains the same. It is just a matter of changing the mapping to another version of the display terminology. Tom Delsey made this point in the 2006 document *Categorization of Content and Carrier* (5JSC/RDA/Part A/Categorization):

> Although the terms are designed to reflect common usage, it is recognized that usage varies from one community to another and changes over time. The terms used in the drafts should be treated simply as "labels" to designate the categories. . . . The instructions do not prescribe how the categories are to be displayed. The intent is to provide agencies using RDA flexibility to adapt displays to the needs and preferences of their user communities. Agencies may choose to be selective in which elements they display, and may display them either as separate elements or in combination. They may also choose to display the categories using different terms than those that are listed . . . The only requirement is that the elements be recorded so that they map directly to the categories as they are defined.[19]

The three elements *content, media,* and *carrier type* bring a logically consistent approach to the description of content and carrier. There is a clear distinction between content (content type) and carrier (media/carrier types). When encountering a new type of expression or manifestation, data can be recorded by using a combination of the types. At a later point, decisions can be made about labels or icons to display to the user. By having a framework, we can record data about a new type of resource even before the community has agreed upon a term to call it.

5.4 RDA ELEMENTS

The RDA elements correspond to the attributes and relationships that are defined in the IFLA bibliographic conceptual models. They are often refined or extended beyond what is presented in the IFLA models because the models present a high-level overview that establishes the basic structure of the data. IFLA LRM explicitly states:

> Any practical application will need to determine an appropriate level of precision, requiring either expansion within the context of the model, or possibly some omissions. However, for an implementation to be viewed as a faithful implementation of the model, the basic structure of the entities and the relationships among them (including the cardinality constraints), and the attachment of those attributes implemented, needs to be respected.
>
> IFLA LRM 2.2

The elements carry information about the RDA entities:

> The elements in RDA reflect the attributes and relationships associated with the RDA entities. They often provide a greater level of granularity than LRM itself.[20]
>
> Guidance > Introduction to RDA > Data elements. RDA elements

The elements are organized according to the entity being described, for example all the elements associated with a person, all the elements associated with a work, all the elements associated with a place, etc.

As mentioned in chapter 4, the use of the term "element" is not new. AACR2 and RDA both use the word "element," but RDA's use of the term is different and is closer to the meaning of element as part of a predefined element set used in a metadata schema. In 2007, the RDA editor, Tom Delsey, prepared a document showing the similarities between RDA's elements and metadata element sets:

RDA as a metadata element set

RDA can be viewed as a metadata element set (similar to the Dublin Core Metadata Element Set) insofar as it:

  a) specifies a set of elements, element sub-types, and sub-elements that reflect the properties of a resource

  b) defines each element, element sub-type, and sub-element

  c) establishes parameters for the value representations recorded for each element, element sub-type, and sub-element.[21]

From the beginning, RDA was moving towards becoming an element set. In the original RDA Toolkit, RDA still retained the appearance of a traditional cataloging code, with the emphasis on the instructions and the guidelines:

> **RDA in the original Toolkit**
>
> RDA provides a set of guidelines and instructions on recording data to support resource discovery.
>
> RDA 0.0

The purpose and scope of RDA in the new RDA Toolkit emphasizes the fact that RDA is a data element set:

> **RDA in the new Toolkit**
>
> *RDA: Resource Description and Access* is a package of data elements, guidelines, and instructions for creating library and cultural heritage metadata that are well-formed according to international models.
>
> Guidance > Introduction to RDA

Note that "package of data elements" appears first.

Recording data in defined, unambiguous elements has been a key feature of RDA since it was first introduced. These elements are precisely defined, they do not overlap, each element contains only a single type of data, and the instructions for many of these elements recommend the use of a controlled vocabulary, now called a vocabulary encoding scheme. Each element is defined at a fairly granular or fine-grained level, so that it is clear what kind of data is recorded in that element. The granularity of the elements and their precise scope and definition reduces ambiguity and increases reliability when navigating through large collections of bibliographic data.

5.4.1 Many New Elements

The careful parsing of bibliographic information into distinct data elements has led to the creation of many new types of elements:

a) Some new elements record bibliographic information that had been recorded in the past, but not in ways that could be deciphered and used by computers, such as the example in figure 4.2, in the discussion of AACR2's treatment of "other physical details." Another example is RDA's careful distinction between different types of dates associated with a manifestation—production, publication, distribution, manufacturing, and copyright.

b) Some elements add greater precision and better serve specific user populations. Taking the example of resources for those with a visual impairment, RDA includes data elements that record the description more precisely and that have the potential to improve searching. RDA considers the "tactile" dimension of a resource as an aspect of its content. A tactile resource is a different form of expression from an audiobook or a printed book. There are provisions for recording a full range of tactile content types, from *cartographic tactile image* to *tactile notated music*. Tactile content is delivered on media and carrier types that are also used to deliver other content types. A braille book will have the content type "tactile text," but shares the same media type and carrier type as a regular print book, "unmediated" and "volume." Additional details specific to a tactile resource are recorded in other data elements. There is a data element to record the *form of tactile notation* and controlled vocabulary or a vocabulary encoding scheme for this element includes terms such as "braille code," "mathematics braille code," or "tactile musical notation." RDA also includes separate data elements for recording *production method* and *layout*. Since 2016, these two data elements were generalized so that they can be used for many types of resources. The vocabulary encoding scheme recommended for these data elements include the terms required for describing the manifestation of a tactile expression, such as "solid dot" for *production method* or "short form scoring" for *layout.*

c) In the process of aligning RDA with the IFLA conceptual models, many data elements were introduced to match the entities, attributes, and relationships defined in the conceptual models. For example, the *person* entity was not directly addressed in AACR2. In AACR2, there was a chapter on "Headings for Persons." The focus was on distinguishing between two persons with the same name. RDA was structured to align with the IFLA conceptual models. Thus, data can be recorded about the entity *person* as well as about the *nomens* associated with the person. Data about the person is not just the data required to formulate a unique authorized access point. It moves towards data about the entity, a cluster of data associated with the person, data that can be used not only for identification but also for exploration.

d) In the process of aligning RDA with IFLA LRM, some new entities were introduced into RDA, such as *agent* and *timespan*. All the elements associated with new entities also had to be added to RDA.

The structuring of data into independent, well-defined data elements permits flexibility that is not particularly evident when working with RDA data in a MARC environment. For example, access points can be very different according to the environment in which one is working. In a linked data environment that relies on IRIs, the access point is an IRI. It is no longer essential to have detailed instructions about the choice and order of data elements. In a MARC environment, access points have a preset structure; they follow a predetermined pattern. Collocation is dependent on this conformity for the order of data elements.

However, once data is recorded in separate RDA elements, it can potentially be stored, searched, and displayed in different ways, which opens up new possibilities. An access point could be presented differently for different user communities or assembled on demand in response to an actual query, with the presentation of data adjusted to respond to the user's needs. For example, if a user were searching using the name of the creator of a work and was presented with a list of identical or similar names, the interface might present options. Instead of presenting a list of names disambiguated according to an authority file, a user might be able to choose or add elements to assist with their tasks of identification and selection. Dates of birth and death may not always be a useful way for a user to select the author they seek; the option to use profession, or a corporate body with which the person is associated, might be more useful to them. The capacity to develop new and responsive interfaces for navigating through bibliographic data is predicated on the recording of data in well-defined and unambiguous data elements.

5.4.2 Domain and Range

As mentioned earlier in the chapter, each RDA element has its own page. All the pages begin with the definition and scope, followed by a section called "Element Reference," which in turn is followed by the relevant instructions, examples, and links to related elements (see figure 5.5).

Entities > Person > date of birth

date of birth

Definition and Scope

A timespan during which a person was born.

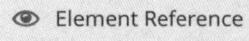 Element Reference

FIGURE 5.5
Top of the element page for *date of birth*

Element Reference is where one finds information in terms of how the element maps to other standards, such as MARC 21. The IRI of the element is always given. Domain and range information is also found here.[22] One also finds alternate labels for the element. See figure 5.6 for an example of the information included in Element Reference.

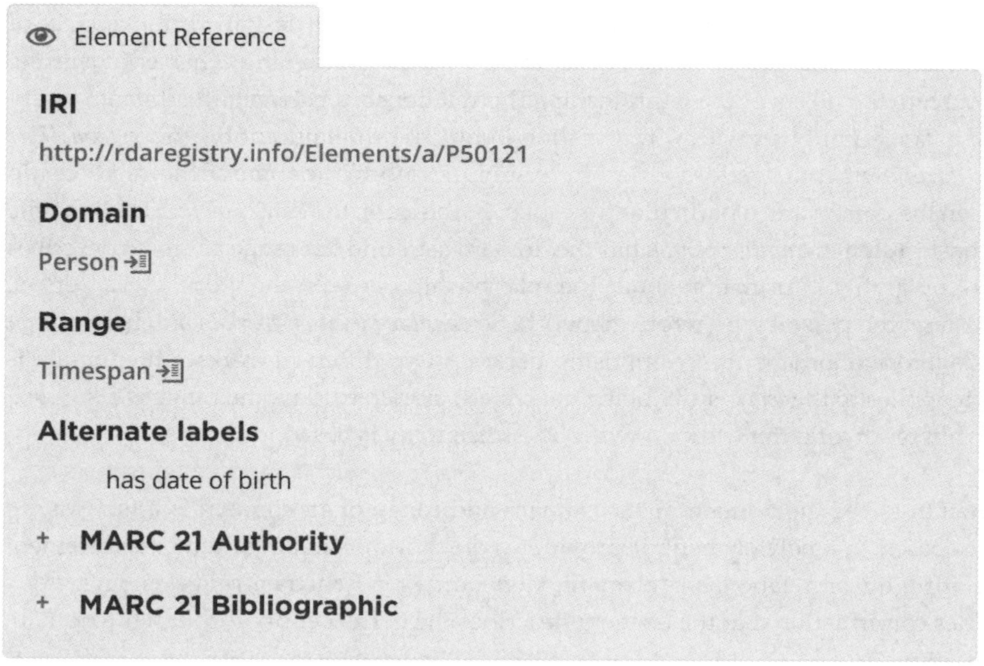

> **Element Reference**
>
> **IRI**
> http://rdaregistry.info/Elements/a/P50121
>
> **Domain**
> Person
>
> **Range**
> Timespan
>
> **Alternate labels**
> has date of birth
>
> + **MARC 21 Authority**
>
> + **MARC 21 Bibliographic**

FIGURE 5.6
Element Reference for *date of birth* (opened)

Domain and range are terms commonly used in schema optimized for the Semantic Web, such as RDFS (Resource Description Framework Schema).[23] The terms are a way of referring to the entities that are associated with a particular element and provide a precise and concise way to check what the element is about, which entity it describes and whether it is the valid element to use.

From the RDA Glossary:

> **domain** the RDA entity that is described by an element
>
> **range**   the RDA entity that is the value of a relationship element

If an element is an attribute element, such as *profession or occupation*, there is only a domain; there is no range. For the *profession or occupation* element, the domain is *person*. When one uses the *profession or occupation* element, one is recording information that applies to the *person* entity; one is recording information that describes a person: "composer" describes Ludwig van Beethoven; "physicist" and "chemist" describe Marie Curie; "actor" describes Morgan Freeman. It is a valid element to use when describing a person.

If an element is a relationship element, there is both a domain and a range. *Date of birth* has the domain *person* and the range *timespan*. When one uses the *date of birth* element, one is recording information that applies to the *person* entity. It is a relationship element that relates two entities. *Domain* is the entity being described, the subject of the relationship. The entity that is designated as the range is the other entity in the relationship, the object of the relationship. The relationship between the domain entity and the range entity provides information about the domain entity, the *person*. The *date of birth* element describes a person by giving information about the relationship between the person and a particular timespan, in this case, the *date of birth*. Similarly, the relationship element *author person* has the domain *work* and the range *person*; it describes a work by giving information about the relationship between the work and a person, in this case, the person who wrote the work. *Screenplay based on work* is an element that records information about a relationship between two different works. The domain is *work*: it applies to the *work* entity being described, the screenplay; the range is also *work*, but a different work, the work on which the screenplay is based.

The ability to see the domain or the domain and range of an element is a fast way to orient oneself to a new element: it provides a quick indication of whether the element is an attribute or relationship element, depending on whether range is present; it provides confirmation that the element describes the correct entity through the domain information.

5.4.3 Relationships

As an implementation of the IFLA bibliographic conceptual models, RDA places great importance on relationships. RDA is a package of data elements, with guidelines and instructions on how to use those data elements to produce well-formed metadata. Many of the data elements record relationships. The instructions encourage the explicit identification of relationships. This emphasis is an intentional part of the design of RDA.

One of the RDA principles is *Relationships:*

> **The metadata describing an entity should indicate significant relationships between entities.**
>
> Guidance > Introduction to RDA > Objectives and principles governing RDA

This principle is fundamental and unchanged from the beginning of RDA. The wording in the original text is a bit more elaborate but the essence remains the same.

When RDA was first published, it was divided into sections, then chapters. Of the ten sections, six were devoted to recording relationships. The focus on relationships was one of the new and distinctive features of RDA. It was useful to have this feature reinforced in the table of contents. RDA in the new RDA Toolkit continues to emphasize the recording of relationships. But it has a different structure and a different approach. There is no simplistic glance at a table of contents to see the preponderance of attention devoted to relationships. Attributes and relationships are not split apart into separate areas. All elements are simply organized by entity. All elements associated with one entity appear together in the one list of elements for that entity. There is only one list, but RDA Toolkit does provide a filter so that one can narrow the list to attribute or relationship elements (see figure 5.7).[24]

Elements

○ All   ○ Attribute Elements   ○ Relationship Elements ⌄

[Find Element]

    abbreviated title →

    access point for manifestation →

    accessibility content →

FIGURE 5.7
Elements filter on Manifestation page

RDA provides ways to record the nature of the relationship. Records created using earlier standards, such as AACR2, did include some information about relationships, but the nature of the relationship usually had to be ascertained by reading the record. Precise information about relationships can potentially create useful pathways through large amounts of data, enabling a user to navigate successfully through large catalogs or databases; this information can also be used to improve the sorting, collocating, and display of search results. However, to use this information in an online environment, it is important to add consistent data about the nature of the relationship.

When RDA was first published, this precise description of the relationship was called a *relationship designator.* The Glossary in the original RDA Toolkit defines it as:

> A designator that indicates the nature of a relationship between entities represented by authorized access points, descriptions, and/or identifiers.

The relationship designators were a set of controlled vocabulary terms to indicate the nature of the relationship. The relationship designators gave clear information about relationships that might otherwise be embedded in other elements such as transcribed data elements or notes. Promoting the use of a controlled vocabulary meant that this information was present, and it was present in a recognizable form, so that it could be picked up by automated processes and used for navigation and data display.

RDA as published in 2010:

Section 6: Recording Relationships to Persons, Families, and Corporate Bodies Associated with a Resource (later changed to *Recording Relationships to Agents*)

> 18.5.1.3 Recording Relationship Designators
>
> Record one or more appropriate terms from the list in appendix I with an identifier and/or authorized access point representing the person, family, or corporate body to indicate the nature of the relationship more specifically than is indicated by the defined scope of the relationship element itself.

There were expected terms for the creator of a work, such as *author, composer, cartographer*. There were also terms for other types of relationships to the work, such as *production company, issuing body*. There were designators at the expression level: agents who had contributed to the creation of an expression, such as *abridger, editor, recording engineer, translator, transcriber, performer*. There were agents whose contribution might be at the manifestation level, by having a role in manufacturing or publishing the manifestation: *braille embosser, lithographer, broadcaster*. In addition, there were the item-level relationship designators, such as *former owner, illuminator, inscriber*.

There were also relationship designators to describe relationships between works and subjects, relationships between works, expressions, manifestations, and items, and relationships between agents. There were four appendixes that contained lists of approved relationship designators. The designators made the relationship visible and identified the relationship precisely; use of the designators meant that the data was found in a consistent and identifiable location and could be used in automated processes for data navigation and data display. The designators could also be used simply to present information for a user to read.

RDA in the new RDA Toolkit continues the principle of precise identification of relationships with controlled terminology to ensure consistency. But in the original RDA Toolkit, *relationship designator* was a part of recording the relationship element. It was a term added to a relationship element to provide a more precise refinement of the relationship. It was applicable for use with an authorized access point or an identifier. The relationship designator terms were listed in appendixes rather than being integrated into the standard.

In the new RDA Toolkit, the *relationship designators* become *relationship elements*.[25] They are treated as any other *relationship element*:

> **relationship element:** An element that relates two RDA entities.
>
> RDA Glossary

The relationship elements have a definition and scope, element reference, and instructions for up to four recording methods. The relationship elements are an integral part of the standard. They are included in the list of elements associated with each entity. By changing the relationship designators into relationship elements, there are many more relationship elements in the new RDA Toolkit. The inverse relationships are also treated as separate relationship elements.

In the original RDA definition of a relationship designator such as *editor*, the three entities, *person, family*, and *corporate body*, were explicitly mentioned in the definition. In 2016, the phrase "person, family, or corporate body" was replaced with *agent*, as was done throughout the RDA text in 2016. It was more efficient to use the more general entity. But it underlines that the designator itself was general; it did not specify whether it was a relationship between a person and an expression, or between a family and an expression, or between a corporate body and an expression. A human could infer this information, for example, from the rest of the access point, but it is not sufficiently precise for machine processing.

When the relationship designators were changed into relationship elements, these elements were made more precise. If one looks at the term *editor*, the one relationship designator in the original Appendix I.3 becomes ten relationship elements in the new RDA Toolkit, each one associated with one particular entity and describing one precise relationship:

RDA in the original Toolkit **relationship designator in the appendix**
Appendix I.3 *editor/editor of*

RDA in the new Toolkit **ten relationship elements**
    Expression relationship elements
        editor agent
        editor collective agent
        editor corporate body
        editor family
        editor person
    Inverse relationships:
        Agent relationship element
            editor agent of
        Collective agent relationship element
            editor collective agent of
        Corporate body relationship element
            editor corporate body of
        Family relationship element
            editor family of
        Person relationship element
            editor person of

Although this level of detail may seem redundant to a human, it is more accurate for automated processing. There is no ambiguity for a computer that is processing the information. RDA focuses on the definition of a clear and unambiguous set of elements. Choices can be made later for mapping to user-friendly labels, but one starts with clearly defined elements.

The relationship designators that originated from Appendix I are noticeably more precise as relationship elements. The change for other designators is less noticeable. The names of some of the new relationship elements are quite close to the former relationship designator.

RDA in the original Toolkit   **relationship designators in the appendix**
dramatization of (work)
dramatized as (work)

RDA in the new Toolkit   **relationship elements**
dramatization of work
dramatized as work

The relationship elements add precise data about the nature of the relationship. This data can then be used to improve resource discovery. For example, a search on "Margaret Atwood" may return a set of results that includes resources where Atwood is an author, some where she is an editor, and perhaps also where her relationship is that of former owner. However, in current catalogs, the results are not usually sorted according to the type of relationship. By using relationship elements, the data is present and can support a more meaningful clustering of search results, for example, showing all the works where Atwood has as an "author person of" relationship, all the expressions where Atwood has an "editor person of" relationship, then the items where she has a "former owner person of" relationship.

For example:[26]

> Atwood, Margaret, 1939-
>   Author of *Alias Grace*
>   Author of *The blind assassin*
>   Author of *Negotiating with the dead*
>   Editor of *The new Oxford Book of Canadian verse*
>   Former owner of *Moodie, Susanna, 1803-1885. Roughing it in the bush.*
>   *New York : George P. Putnam, 1854. Library's copy 2.*

The use of precise elements means that automated processes can be programmed to pick up this information and cluster resources that share the same elements, possibly with the addition of labels, so that the user can quickly grasp the nature of the relationship and use this information to explore, and to find, identify, and select relevant resources.

RDA emphasizes relationships: recording relationships and giving precise information about the nature of the relationship. After alignment with IFLA LRM, RDA also has more relationships because of the changes in IFLA LRM. IFLA LRM introduced the *place* and *timespan* entities. As a result, long lists of attributes from the earlier models were eliminated in favor of relationships. Relationships between entities are a more fruitful way to record data for the linked data environment because links are based on the existence of relationships between entities. This LRM modelling change is brought into RDA. RDA in the new RDA Toolkit has fewer attribute elements and more relationship elements. But one still records essential information such as the date of publication. However, we no longer understand it to be an attribute element of a manifestation but rather see it as a relationship element between a manifestation and a timespan.

RDA in the original Toolkit

attributes
    date of distribution
    place of publication
    date of birth

RDA in the new Toolkit

relationship elements
    date of distribution
    relationship: manifestation – timespan
    or in RDA's element reference terminology:
        domain = manifestation
        range = timespan

    place of publication
    relationship: manifestation – place
    or in RDA's element reference terminology:
        domain = manifestation
        range = place

    date of birth
    relationship: person – timespan
    or in RDA's element reference terminology:
        domain = person
        range = timespan

When using a structured description to record a relationship, there are also data elements that can be used to construct an access point to identify the relationship clearly and uniquely. RDA in 2010 included instructions for the construction of authorized access points to identify works and expressions. These instructions were found in the original

RDA's chapter 6, "Identifying Works and Expressions." A significant step forward was the deliberate grouping together of instructions for formulating access points for expressions. For expressions, the basic instruction was to start with the authorized access point for the work that the expression realized, and to extend that access point with other data elements. RDA presented a list of data elements that could be used to identify the expression and to differentiate it from other expressions of the same work. The instructions were originally at RDA 6.27.3, and are now found at:

Entities > Expression > access point for expression

Additional elements and designations in access points for expression

The additional elements that can be used are *content type, date of expression, designation of version, language of expression,* plus there is a general instruction on using another designation that is a distinguishing characteristic for that expression, an appropriate characteristic that distinguishes the expression from other expressions of the same work. *Designation of version* in the new RDA Toolkit replaces the element in the original RDA Toolkit, *other distinguishing characteristic of expression.* The original element had a broad definition which also made it ambiguous. The new RDA element is defined more tightly. In the new RDA Toolkit, one still has the option to use yet another type of designation (RDA 41.33.40.14), but this is just a general instruction and is not presented as a data element.

The metadata creator chooses the element or elements that make the most sense for identification of a particular expression. For example, an audio recording of an English translation of the famous Babar story. This expression:

has authorized access point for expression

Brunhoff, Jean de, 1899-1937. Babar en famille. English. Spoken word

This access point uses the authorized access point for the work extended with two elements for identifying the expression. The access point relays a lot of information to the user, such as indicating that this expression is a translation into English, and that the form of expression is not text, but spoken word.

Formulating access points has always been an important part of RDA. RDA in the new RDA Toolkit goes further. There are now instructions for formulating access points for all the entities, including manifestations and items. Logically, there are times when one needs to reference a manifestation or item, not just a work or expression. The basis for an access point for a manifestation or an item is the title of the manifestation, as would be expected.[27]

5.5 AGGREGATES

In the bibliographic environment, an aggregate is a collection of resources issued together. When RDA was first published, it distinguished between a compilation and a collaborative work, with instructions specific for each one. With "compilation," RDA was beginning to provide some guidance for aggregates. But it is not until the alignment with IFLA LRM that RDA incorporates a full treatment of aggregates.

The description of collections, anthologies, compilations, and augmentations have posed problems for a long time. What are they? Is the aggregate itself a work? What are each of the components, works, expressions, manifestations? What entities are being brought together?

As mentioned in chapter 3, section 3.2.3.4, of this book, the modelling of aggregates had been a challenge. When FRBR was first published in 1998, there was criticism that it did not provide adequate modelling for aggregates. This issue was finally addressed during the development of the IFLA LRM. At first, the modelling seems a little complex, but it provides a way of understanding aggregates that is valid and consistent across all the different types of aggregates, including serials.

RDA follows the IFLA LRM model and places aggregation at the manifestation level:

> An *aggregate* is a manifestation that embodies an aggregating expression and one or more expressions that are aggregated.
>
> Guidance > Aggregates

An *aggregate* pulls together various expressions. Each of the components in the aggregate is a work realized in a particular expression, and these expressions are embodied in the aggregate. The aggregate is a single manifestation that embodies more than one expression. For example, an anthology of poems is an aggregate that embodies the expressions of poems; the poems are individual works and, in an anthology, usually by many different authors.

With an *aggregate*, there are two things happening at the same time. An *aggregate* is a single manifestation that usually embodies two or more expressions. The expressions were selected to be part of the same *aggregate* because there was a plan. For example, a person selects the poems to include in the anthology. The person who selects and arranges the poems did not write the poems. They simply created the plan. This plan is a special kind of work, called an aggregating work, and it is realized in an *aggregating expression*.

The aggregate embodies 1) two or more expressions and 2) the aggregating expression, the realization of the plan. For example, the anthology embodies the expressions of the poems selected and it embodies the expression of the plan for the anthology.

In figure 5.8, there are three works, poems A, B, and C. A person decides on a plan to create an anthology that includes these three poems. The plan is an aggregating work that is realized through an aggregating expression. The expressions of these poems and the expression of the plan result in the aggregate, a manifestation that embodies the three expressions of poems A, B and C, and also the expression of the plan for the anthology.

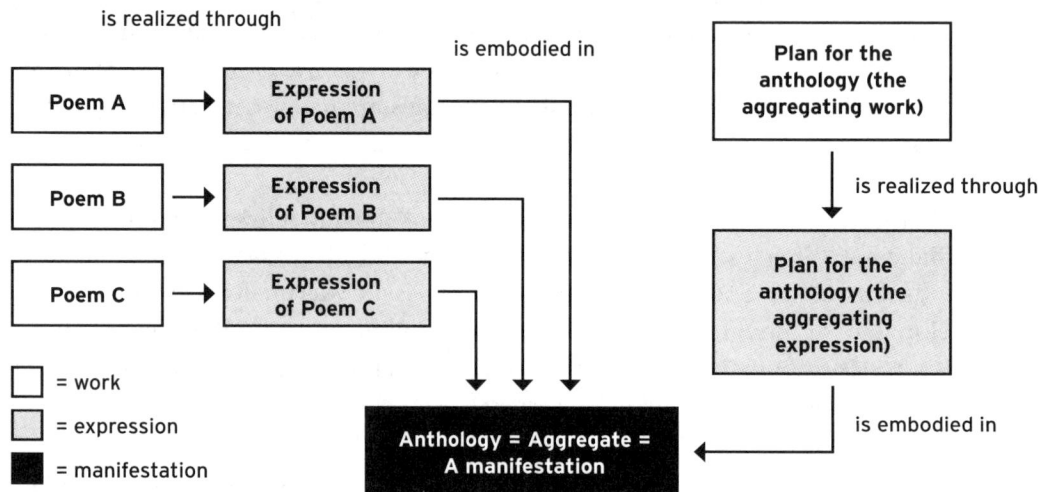

FIGURE 5.8
Aggregates modelling for an anthology with three poems

This modelling does not mean that a cataloger or a metadata creator must describe and give access to every poem in an anthology. It is simply a way of explaining and ensuring that the relationships are kept straight. When it is desirable to describe and give access to the components of an aggregate, there are clear instructions in RDA on how to proceed so that the relationships are valid and properly identified.

Likewise, the modelling does not mean that every plan needs to be recorded in a description. The cataloger can acknowledge and record the plan when that is desirable. If there is an anthology of poems selected and arranged by a famous literary person, such as Margaret Atwood, a cataloger may judge that it is important for the user to know who created the plan.

In the section on aggregates (Guidance > Aggregates), three categories of aggregates are described (the same categories as in IFLA LRM but with slightly changed names):

collection aggregate
such as, compilation of short stories by a single author, an album of folk songs by different performers, an issue of a periodical with multiple articles

augmentation aggregate

such as, a novel with a foreword, illustrations and index, an atlas with an introductory essay

parallel aggregate

such as, a volume with the English and French text of a government report, a website with text in all the languages of an international institution

Also, in this section, RDA points the metadata creator to relevant instructions for each entity; these instructions are found in different places in RDA depending on the entity:

Describing an aggregate:
> Describing a manifestation that embodies two or more expressions
>> Links to: *Guidance > Resource description > Describing a manifestation*
>
> Describing expressions of aggregating works and expressions that are aggregated
>> Links to: *Guidance > Resource description > Describing an expression*
>
> Describing aggregating works and works that are aggregated
>> Links to: *Guidance > Resource description > Describing a work*

It is critically important for the metadata creator to recognize when they are encountering an aggregate as opposed to a single work with parts. For example, *Dante's Inferno* is always part of *La divina commedia*, regardless of the manifestation in which it appears. *La divina commedia* is a work created in three parts. *Inferno* is sometimes published alone, such as in the 1985 manifestation published by Mondadori. It is often published with the other two parts, *Purgatorio* and *Paradiso*, as the complete *La divina commedia*, such as the 2011 manifestation published by L. S. Olschki. *Inferno* always has the same relationship to *La divina commedia*; it is the first part of the larger work. If *Inferno*, *Purgatorio*, and *Paradiso* are published together in a single manifestation, this is not an aggregate; it is a manifestation that embodies an Italian expression of the whole work.

A collection of children's stories is a good example of a collection aggregate. For example, the *Classics of children's literature* is a collection of short stories and novels, selected by John W. Griffith and Charles H. Frey, published by Macmillan in 1981. The *Classics of children's literature* is an aggregate, a manifestation that brings together *Treasure island*, *The adventures of Tom Sawyer*, *The wind in the willows*, and English expressions of other works written for children. Robert Louis Stevenson's *Treasure island* does not have a whole-part relationship to the *Classics of children's literature*. It appears in this collection because Griffith and Frey had a plan and selected it for inclusion in this aggregate. *Treasure island* is embodied in the aggregate planned by Griffith and Frey.

The English text of *Treasure island* can be embodied in many different manifestations. It can be embodied in manifestations, by itself. It can be embodied in different aggregate manifestations: it could be in a parallel aggregate with the French translation of *Treasure island*; it could be in an augmented aggregate with extensive notes and commentary; it could be in a different collection aggregate, such as a collection of pirate stories, a collection of Scottish children's literature, or a collection of nineteenth century literature.

Each aggregate embodies two types of expressions: a) the expressions of the works selected for inclusion in the aggregate and b) the aggregating expression of an aggregating work which is the plan for the aggregate. The plan to aggregate the original English text and a French translation is a different plan from the plan to single out and collect pirate stories or the plan to select the time-honored classics of children's literature.

RDA introduces elements specifically for aggregates. For example, there are two relationship elements: *aggregated by* and *aggregates*. This is the relationship between the plan (the aggregating expression) and the expressions that are being aggregated, arranged, and embodied together in the aggregate. The plan embodied in the manifestation *Classics of children's literature* aggregates *Treasure island*, *The adventures of Tom Sawyer*, *The wind in the willows*, etc.

There are also relationships between agents and manifestations that are specific for aggregates. For example, the contributor relationships, such as *contributor agent of text, contributor agent of still image, contributor agent of cartography*; these relationships have *manifestation* as the domain and *agent* as the range. These relationships also apply and are defined for all the subclasses of agent, such as *contributor person of still image, contributor corporate body of cartography*, etc. To demonstrate, one can look at an augmentation aggregate that brings together a novel with drawings. For example, in 2015, Princeton University Press in association with the National Museum of Mathematics published an aggregate, a manifestation that embodied an English expression of Lewis Carroll's *Alice's adventures in Wonderland*, augmented with illustrations by Salvador Dalí. Dalí has a relationship to this manifestation: this manifestation has Dalí as the *contributor person of still image*.

The RDA treatment of aggregates in the new RDA Toolkit may seem complex but the modelling has shown us that aggregates are complex. RDA provides a thorough treatment of aggregates and adds the elements required to support an accurate and valid description.

5.6 SHORTCUTS

RDA in the new RDA Toolkit has a section on relationship shortcuts as part of the guidance for data elements:

> A *shortcut* is a *relationship element* that directly relates two RDA entities that are indirectly related through one or more intermediary entities.
>
> This allows the two entities to be associated without recording any of the intermediary entities or relationships.
>
> Guidance > Introduction to RDA > Data elements.
Relationship shortcuts (RDA 00.93.23.44)

A shortcut offers a faster way to describe relationships. A shortcut acknowledges the full modelling of the relationships but allows for an efficient, shorter path that is still completely valid. When one uses a shortcut, it is understood that the intermediate steps still exist but do not have to be explicitly spelled out every time.

There was a first shortcut element in chapter 17 of RDA, in the original RDA Toolkit, although it was not labelled as a "shortcut": *work manifested/manifestation of work*:

> The relationship between a work and a manifestation that embodies that work may also be represented without explicitly identifying the expression through which the work is realized.
>
> RDA 17.4.1

The elements *work manifested* and *manifestation of work* are found in the new RDA Toolkit, and the shortcut aspect is explicitly mentioned. *Manifestation of work* is an element that is a shortcut for the full chain of relationships that is usually expected between work and manifestation:

Entities > Work > manifestation of work

full chain of relationships	*shortcut*
work	work
has expression of work	↓
has manifestation of expression	has manifestation of work

Instead of recording the intermediate part about the realization of the work in an expression, this element allows one to take a shortcut directly from work to manifestation. Shortcuts allow for an efficient implementation of the model. RDA explicitly created elements that were shortcuts to facilitate the work of resource description. If there is a shortcut, it is always mentioned in the prerecording section to underline that the model is being respected and that the relationships are understood to be there. But the element provides a shorthand way to record the data and support efficiency.

There are numerous shortcuts for *nomen* elements, such as *name of publisher*:

> Entities > Manifestation > name of publisher
>
> Prerecording
>
> This element is a *shortcut* for the following chain of relationships:
>
> 1. Manifestation: **publisher agent**
> 2. Agent: **name of agent**

In the underlying conceptual model, there is no direct relationship between a manifestation and the name of an agent who has an association with the manifestation. But there is a relationship between the manifestation and an agent, such as *publisher agent*. And there is a relationship between an agent and the name of an agent. So, one can have a shortcut element that is the relationship between the manifestation and a name for an associated agent. Thus, *name of publisher* is a valid element, it conforms with IFLA LRM, and it also offers an efficient way to record the name of the publisher.

full chain of relationships	*shortcut*
manifestation	manifestation
has publisher agent	↓
publisher agent has name	has name of publisher

Shortcuts also show up in a number of the aggregate relationship elements, especially the contributor elements, for example, *contributor person of still image*:

> Entities > Manifestation > contributor person of still image
>
> Prerecording
>
> This element is a shortcut for the following chain of relationships:
>
> 1. Manifestation: **expression manifested** for an expression of a *still image work* that is aggregated
> 2. Expression: **creator person of expression** for a person who is responsible for an expression that is aggregated

The aggregate is a manifestation. It embodies expressions of works, and one of these works is a still image work. A person created this still image work. This shortcut relationship element allows one to record directly the relationship between the aggregate and the contributor without explicitly mentioning the intervening step, the expression of the still image work that is embodied in the aggregate.

Certain elements are shortcuts. In terms of straightforward resource description, the element and the instructions for recording the element are sufficient for completing the description of a resource entity. However, it is good to be aware that some elements are shortcuts. Information about shortcuts is found in the prerecording area for the elements where a shortcut is used. The explanation of shortcuts provides justification for shortening the chain of relationships and proves that the element is still valid and aligned with IFLA LRM.

5.7 NOMEN

Nomen is a new entity in RDA. It seems to add complexity, but this new modelling is a more accurate reflection of what is happening when we record names and titles of entities. It is particularly useful in the area of identity management or authority control.

During the consolidation of the models, IFLA LRM followed the approach in FRAD and FRSAD where appellation data was modelled as separate entities rather than as attributes.[28] RDA had followed the FRBR approach and RDA's structure in the original RDA Toolkit mirrored that approach in every section and chapter. Introducing *nomen* does not fundamentally change the data produced by following RDA instructions. But it does represent a major change in thinking.

> title of work = relationship between work and *nomen*
>
> name of person = relationship between person and *nomen*

One can see the change of thinking in the wording of the instructions:

> **RDA in the original Toolkit**
>
> Record the name chosen as a preferred name for person by applying the general guidelines at . . .
>
> RDA 9.2.2.4
>
> **RDA in the new Toolkit**
>
> Record this element as a value of a Nomen: **nomen string** or as an instance of a **Nomen.**
>
> Entities > Person > preferred name of person

But all the specific instructions about choosing preferred names of person remain essentially the same.

Nomen is an umbrella entity. It can include: a name, a title, an access point, an identifier, a subject classification code or heading. The entity is broader than simply "name." Name, identifier, and access points are examples of types of *nomen*.

Nomen string is an attribute element, an attribute that describes a nomen. It is simply a combination of signs, characters, symbols, etc. It is the appellation associated with an entity. The *nomen string* can be any combination of signs, symbols, and notations but it only has meaning when it is associated with an "'instance" of that entity. For example, if the entity is *person*, an instance of that entity is an individual person. The string of characters "Chris Oliver" is a *nomen string*. It is only when the string of characters is associated with an individual person that it becomes a *nomen* for that person.

The *nomen string* has meaning only when it is associated with an entity, such as a particular person. *Nomen* is that association between the string and the entity to which it refers. *Nomen* is a puzzling entity because it is an entity that also has aspects that resemble a relationship. Pat Riva explained this well in the 2018 Lectio Magistralis she presented at the University of Florence:

> The *nomen* entity is certainly the most abstract of the IFLA LRM entities. Instances of the *nomen* entity are created as the result of applying the <has appellation> (LRM-R13) relationship to an instance of *res*. Once an association is created between the entity that is named and the name used for it, that relationship becomes the *nomen*.[29]

This aspect of associating a *nomen string* with an entity does resemble a relationship.[30] But *nomen* is defined as an entity. This means that *nomen* can have relationships—relationships to other *nomen* and relationships between nomen and all the RDA entities.

Appellation elements are the relationship elements between a *nomen* and any RDA entity, such as *appellation of person, appellation of work, appellation of timespan*. Every RDA entity has a relationship to a nomen. *Appellation* is the relationship between a *nomen* and an entity.

An example may help to unravel the connections between *nomens* and *nomen strings*. If one takes the example of the nineteenth century person who was both an author of children's literature and a mathematician, there is one person but many nomens:

Lewis Carroll

L. Carroll

Charles Lutwidge Dodgson

C. L. Dodgson

Charles L. Dodgson

The Reverend Charles Lutwidge Dodgson

Carroll, Lewis, 1832-1898

Dodgson, Charles Lutwidge, 1832-1898

In the first six examples, we have names used in different contexts and at different times. He may also have had nicknames used by the family, such as "Charlie" or "Uncle Charles." A cataloger or metadata creator may be transcribing these strings from title pages in manifestations or using these strings when referring to this person in an unstructured description, such as a note. There are also two access points that refer to this same person, one that is a preferred access point for the person as author of the Alice stories, and the second for his nonfiction work. Each *nomen* in this example has its own *nomen string*. One person can have many *nomens*. In this example, each of these *nomens* refers to the same person.

But what about the many authors who share an identical name, such as Thomas Brown? It is not their *nomens* that are identical, but their *nomen strings*. The *nomen string* "Thomas Brown" is identical. But the association between each of those authors and their *nomen* remains unique. In a library context, this is where authority work is done on authorized access points to create unique nomen strings so that users can easily distinguish between multiple authors whose *nomens* may share the same *nomen string*.

RDA introduces the entity *nomen*, the appellation relationships, and the attribute elements of *nomen*, such as *language of nomen, script of nomen, status of identification*. One very useful attribute element is *context of use*. For example, sometimes *nomens* are associated with an entity in particular contexts. "Carroll, Lewis, 1832-1898" may be used when cataloging his fiction for children, such as *Alice's adventures in Wonderland*, and "Dodgson, Charles Lutwidge, 1832-1898" when cataloging one of his mathematical treatises, such as *Euclid and his modern rivals*. RDA now has a precise data element to record the context of use for a particular *nomen*.

Nomen does introduce an added layer of complexity into RDA but it does not introduce radical changes. It is simply a more accurate reflection of what we do, and it allows us to record information that was challenging to record when name was treated as an attribute.

Nomen is a useful entity that helps to clarify bibliographic relationships and provides better modelling for bibliographic identities, for example, one person with many *nomens*. It provides accurate modelling when there are *nomen* equivalents in different languages and scripts, or *nomens* derived according to different cultural or linguistic conventions. It also provides greater accuracy by distinguishing between the *nomen* and the *nomen string*.[31]

The terms *nomen, nomen string,* and *appellation element* are new in RDA because of the alignment with IFLA LRM. A lot of the language for instructions about titles and names has changed. For example, the instructions always start with a reminder of the new modelling:

title proper — Record this element as a value of a Nomen: **nomen string** or as an instance of a **Nomen**.

access point for place — Record this element as a value of a Nomen: **nomen string** or as an instance of a **Nomen**.

identifier for corporate body — Record this element as a value of a Nomen: **nomen string** or as an instance of a **Nomen**.

variant title of work — Record this element as a value of a Nomen: **nomen string** or as an instance of a **Nomen**.

The change in phrasing is evident in the introductory instruction on recording the element (also evident in the element reference section). When one gets down to the detailed instructions, there is recognizable continuity with the RDA instructions in the original RDA Toolkit:

RDA in the original Toolkit

11.2.2   **Preferred Name for Corporate Body**

11.2.2.5.4 Conventional Name

Conventional name: a name other than the real or official name by which a corporate body has come to be known. If a body is frequently identified by a conventional name in reference sources in its own language, choose this conventional name as the preferred name.

RDA in the new Toolkit

Entities > Corporate Body > preferred name of corporate body

Recording

Record this element as a value of a Nomen: **nomen string** or as an instance of a **Nomen**.

Recording an unstructured description

...

Conventional name

CONDITION

A corporate body has a real or official name and a *conventional name*.

A corporate body is frequently identified by a *conventional name* in sources of information in a language of the corporate body.

OPTION

Record a conventional name.[32]

Preferred name of corporate body is recorded as a relationship between the corporate body and the *nomen* entity, so this is a change from RDA in the original RDA Toolkit because the instructions begin with an explicit reminder about the *nomen* entity and its attribute, the *nomen string*. But the instruction itself remains identical. The museum that has the official name Museo Nacional del Prado is frequently identified as Museo del Prado, even on its own website. The metadata creator is instructed to choose the conventional name as the preferred name and record "Museo del Prado."

This change in modelling is particularly of interest in the area of authority control.[33] The modelling exists in the background; the instructions conform to the modelling. A frontline cataloger is not required to have an in-depth understanding of *nomen* and the modelling of *nomen*, but it is useful to be aware of the changes. There are some new elements, such as *nomen string*. The instructions are organized and formulated differently to accommodate the use of the *nomen* entity. There are changes in vocabulary and there are new phrasings to align with the introduction of the *nomen* entity and the *appellation* relationships.

The use of *nomen* is also more in line with the modelling of other communities. For example, it is compatible with the museum community's model, the CIDOC Conceptual Reference Model.[34] This modelling of *nomen* is also more compatible with ontologies designed for the Semantic Web, such as SKOS, Simple Knowledge Organization System (a standard of the W3C, the World Wide Web Consortium).[35] Thus this change in modelling also makes it easier to use and reuse RDA data in a broader range of contexts.

5.8 NEW WAYS OF THINKING ABOUT RESOURCE DESCRIPTION

5.8.1 Fictitious and Non-Human Entities

IFLA LRM defines person as an individual human being, a real person who lives or is assumed to have lived. This definition is in line with the original FRBR definition. When RDA was originally developed, it had followed the FRAD definition of person which included fictitious entities and non-human entities. IFLA LRM made this definition invalid. Therefore, RDA's definition of person had to be amended to align with IFLA LRM.

The change in definition caused some alarm that one could no longer record the names of fictitious characters and non-human entities as authors, such as Snoopy, Miss Piggy, Doctor Watson, Geronimo Stilton.

RDA provides guidance when encountering the appellation of a fictitious or non-human entity in a statement of responsibility that appears on a manifestation. RDA includes a section of guidance: Guidance > Fictitious and non-human appellations.

For a fictitious character, it is important to note that the focus is on the name:

> **An appellation of a fictitious entity that is included in a statement in a manifestation that assigns responsibility to an agent is assumed to be a pseudonymous appellation of an** *Agent, Collective Agent, Corporate Body, Family,* **or** *Person.*
>
> Guidance > Fictitious and non-human appellations

RDA changes the definition of *person*, but it also introduces the entity *nomen*. *Nomen* as a separate entity is very useful when dealing with purported animal authors, or the creation of works by puppets or cartoon characters, etc.

For a fictitious entity, it is the name that is important to the user, not the entity with which the name purports to be associated. Agents created these works. Agents have *nomens*. The agents in these cases chose to use the names of fictitious characters. The relationship between a name and an agent who created the work remains, whether the agent is known or unknown. The RDA instructions on fictitious entities are divided into these two conditions: whether the agent is known or unknown.

If the agent is known, then this falls into the usual pattern for pseudonyms. For example, *Fantastic beasts and where to find them* is written by Newt Scamander, a fictitious character, and has a foreword by Albus Dumbledore, another fictitious character. It is well known that J. K. Rowling is the actual author. In this case, one can use the *nomen* "Newt Scamander" or "J.K. Rowling" as the *nomen* of the author person, depending on a cataloging community's practice for dealing with pseudonyms.

There are cases where the agent associated with a name is unknown, or at the time of cataloging, the agent is unknown. For example, *The autobiography of Sherlock Holmes* is ostensibly written by Sherlock Holmes; *Before you leap: a frog's eye view of life's greatest lessons* is ostensibly written by Kermit the Frog. In terms of resource description, the name "Sherlock Holmes" and "Kermit, the Frog" can still be recorded as the preferred name of the agent, whether or not one has information about the agent who actually created that work. It is understood that there is an agent that created the work, even if the real identity of the agent is unknown. The agent chose to use the name of a fictitious character. The association between the *nomen string* and the agent exists even if one knows nothing more about the agent. When creating the metadata, one can record that name.

For non-human entities, the approach is a little different. There are non-human entities who make contributions, especially animal performers. These entities are not covered by the *nomen-agent* relationship. They are also not a subclass of *agent* because an agent is either a person or two or more persons acting as a unit. If the use cases were compelling, they could be included in the IFLA LRM model through *res*, as a subclass that is not *agent*. But it would require the addition of new modelling. In RDA, the RDA entity is narrower than *res*, so it is not possible to model these non-human entities as a subclass of RDA entity. But there is the possibility of recording a relationship with an unspecified non-RDA entity:

> A non-human entity that is associated with a statement in a manifestation that assigns responsibility to an agent is treated as an entity that is external to RDA.
>
> Guidance > Fictitious and non-human appellations

There are instructions to cover these cases by using related entities: *related entity of work, related entity of expression, related entity of manifestation*, or *related entity of item*. These are basically non-RDA entities and no assumptions are made about these entities.[36] These entities are external to RDA. But they are entities associated with a work, expression, manifestation or item so they can be used to record information that is outside the RDA entities. RDA is providing a way to deal with these non-human entities when they are occasionally encountered.

5.8.2 Diachronic Works

> A static work is a work that is planned to be embodied by a manifestation that results from a single act of publication or production.
>
> RDA Glossary

> A diachronic work is a work planned to be embodied over time, rather than in a single "act of publication".
>
> Guidance > Diachronic works

Works issued over time have always needed extra attention. AACR2 had introduced the umbrella term "continuing resources" to encompass serials and integrating resources, bibliographic resources issued over time with no predetermined conclusion. These were the resources for which there were special instructions on how to deal with changes that happened over time.

RDA has never used the term "continuing resources" because it is not useful to group serials and integrating resources together considering that many of the instructions are different, even diametrically opposed. When RDA was originally published, there was a new element called *mode of issuance*, an attribute of the manifestation (RDA 2.13). There were four terms that could be used to record mode of issuance:

RDA in the original Toolkit (RDA 2.13.1.3)

> single unit
>
> multipart monograph
>
> serial
>
> integrating resource

Three of these modes of issuance could change over time. This was an important step forward because it separated serials and integrating resources and it acknowledged that multipart monographs had aspects resembling single unit publications and also serial publications. Sometimes the instructions for multipart monographs and serials had more in common with each other than with those for integrating resources.

RDA in the new RDA Toolkit further refines the treatment of works issued over time. The *mode of issuance* element is simplified and focuses on a single aspect of the manifestation: whether the manifestation is issued in one or more units. There are now only two terms:

RDA in the new Toolkit

Entities > Manifestation > mode of issuance

> multiple unit
>
> single unit

RDA introduces a new attribute element, an element that characterizes the work *extension plan*.

> Entities > Work > extension plan
>
> A categorization reflecting an intention to extend the content of a work

A work planned over time means that its content will be extended/changed over time. The extension can happen along two dimensions—the type of extension and the type of termination:

extension mode	successive *or* integrating
extension termination	determinate *or* indeterminate

This categorization is derived from the RDA/ONIX Framework and is described in the "Guidance" section (Guidance > Content and carrier > Extension plans).

In the new RDA Toolkit, there are five possibilities for *extension plan*:

Extension plan	Example and definition
successive determinate plan	a dictionary created over several years *content is accumulated at intervals and there is a definite end*
successive indeterminate plan	an academic journal *content is accumulated at intervals and there is no predetermined end*
integrating determinate plan	a website for a conference *content is replaced, updated, integrated and there is a definite end*
integrating indeterminate plan	an updating news website *content is replaced, updated, integrated and there is no predetermined end*
static plan	*content embodied simultaneously* a complete novel embodied as a single volume a history embodied in three volumes all issued at the same time

Mode of issuance is quite separate from *extension plan*. *Mode of issuance* is simply a manifestation attribute element. For example, both values, single and multiple units, can apply to the same extension plan. A static plan can result in a single act of publication, but the manifestation is issued as a single volume or as three volumes, either as a single unit or as a multiple unit. So, there is no correlation between *mode of issuance* and *extension plan*.

Extension plan is a work element and is a different categorization from *mode of issuance*. The use of two different elements results in a more precise separation of content and carrier.

The term *diachronic work* is new: a diachronic work is a work that is planned to be embodied over time, rather than as a single "act of publication."[37] What is revolutionary is the concept of the plan:

> The essence of a diachronic work is a plan for the change of content.
>
> An *extension plan* describes the intended method for extending the content of a work through time.
>
> Guidance > Diachronic works

For a work that changes over time, one cannot predict what the actual changes will be. All that one can describe is the plan for change.

Serials are a type of diachronic work with successive, indeterminate extension plans. The way of understanding a serial undergoes even more of a change. The IFLA LRM modelling of serials affects serials at several levels.

IFLA LRM introduced a new way of understanding serials (as described in chapter 3). In summary, the modelling of serials is a complex modelling at work, expression, and manifestation levels that also links to the new modelling of aggregates.

- Each article in a serial issue is an expression of a work. These expressions are embodied in the serial issue.
- Each serial issue is an aggregate: it is a manifestation that aggregates the expressions of different works (the articles) according to a plan (the aggregating expression for that issue).
- The serial work/expression is the plan, the collection of editorial concepts. The serial work is the aggregating work, the serial expression is the aggregating expression for the sequence of issues.
- There is a large sequence of issues. Each issue is an aggregate and an aggregate is a manifestation. A serial issue has a whole-part relationship at the manifestation level to the larger sequence of issues.

This new modelling for serials also answers questions about the relationship between serial works, expressions, and manifestations, questions that have been asked since FRBR was first published. Now, with the notion that the serial work is the plan, there can be only one expression, and only one manifestation (referred to as WEM lock in RDA). If the plan is for an online journal on biology with an editorial board following a set of policies about quality, scope, etc., the plan includes its online character. If there is a print equivalent of this journal, this is a slightly different plan. The editorial policy and selection criteria may be the same, but the plan is to publish print issues, so the plan is different. A difference in plan, no matter how slight, makes it a different work. The print and online journals are not manifestations of the same work. They are different works. However, they are closely related.

RDA introduces the new term "work group." This is not a new entity nor is it an element. It is a term for a group of works that are closely related, such as the print and online versions of journals with the same title.

> **work group** A group of two or more works that have a common appellation assigned from a vocabulary encoding scheme.
>
> RDA Glossary

"Work group" provides a way to identify serials, distinguish between them and cluster together the ones that have close relationships. It enables *work-nomen* relationships, supports collocation, and acknowledges that there is a very close relationship between certain works:

> **appellation of work group**   A nomen used within a given scheme or context to refer to a work as a member of a work group.
> RDA Glossary

There are are elements related to work group. The *appellation of work group* element is the mechanism for clustering these highly related works into a work group. An ISSN-L is an identifier from the ISSN vocabulary encoding scheme, so it is a *nomen* used within a given scheme. It refers to works that are members of the same work group. It can be considered an *appellation of work group*, or more specifically, an *identifier for work group*. Similarly, a preferred title in the LC/NACO authority file is also a *nomen* within a given scheme. For example, Spectator (London, England : 1828) is an appellation that applies to the print, microform, and online serials and can be considered an *appellation of work group*, or more specifically, an *authorized access point for work group*.

In time, this new understanding of the serial work will lead to more changes in the instructions, and possibly some far-reaching changes in the future. At this point, the new modelling has been introduced into RDA, but the instructions remain consistent with past instructions. RDA also has a longstanding commitment to consult with the ISSN and ISBD communities so that all three are in step with each other for the description of serials, to support consistency and data interoperability.

There are a few small changes. For example, RDA now makes a distinction between the recording of a *manifestation frequency statement* and the recording of the work element *frequency*. *Frequency* used to be considered a manifestation element. It is now separated into two elements because of the new understanding of the serial work as the plan. *Frequency* is now a work element because it implies a plan for the release of issues or updates. It is an element that describes the work, the plan for the serial. The manifestation frequency statement is an element where one records a statement that appears on the manifestation.

IFLA LRM's treatment of serials highlighted the need to reexamine the way we think about serials, but also about all works that change over time. IFLA's modelling of serials is the beginning. There will likely be further changes as the ISSN and ISBD communities reevaluate the treatment of serials in light of the IFLA LRM modelling. There are some changes in RDA with the introduction of new vocabulary, the development of new elements, and the careful categorization that separates content from carrier. The RDA Steering Committee will continue to monitor international developments with the aim of keeping RDA aligned as the international treatment of serials develops.

5.8.3 Representative Expression

RDA incorporates the IFLA LRM concept of the representative expression and defines it as:

> **representative expression**
>
> An expression that is considered a canonical source of data for identifying a work.
>
> RDA Glossary

It is very practical and efficient to have an additional set of elements that assist with the identification of a work. The slightly puzzling part is that expression elements are being used as work elements. The work is a very abstract entity and it has a strictly defined set of attribute elements. But because it is so abstract, some expression elements of an original or very well-known expression will get associated with a work that has been realized in many expressions.

Robert Maxwell presented a good example when he asked, "So what's the problem?" in his 2019 presentation on representative expressions. He took the example of *Alice's adventures in Wonderland*. If asked about identifying characteristics of this work, many people will respond with:

a novel	category of work = a work element
a text	content type = an expression element
in English	language of expression = an expression element
for children	intended audience of expression = an expression element[38]

Many of the ways people commonly identify a work are intertwined with some expression characteristics of the original or best-known expression.

The concept of a representative expression acknowledges that some expressions are considered more representative of the creator's original intention than others. *Hamlet* as a text in English may be considered a more representative expression than *Hamlet* as an audiobook in English or *Hamlet* as a text translated into French.

There are two sets of RDA elements related to the representative expression: the attribute elements and the relationship elements.

For the attribute elements, the purpose of these representative expression elements is to identify the work and distinguish it from other similar works. If one keeps the purpose in mind, it is easier to see why expression elements are being used in this work element.

IFLA LRM left it up to individual implementations to determine the list of attributes that could be used as representative expression attributes. RDA has identified many representative expression attribute elements. All these work-level data elements include the phrase "of representative expression," such as *content type of representative expression, intended audience of representative expression, scale of representative expression,* and *medium of performance of musical content of representative expression.* One can find a complete list of these at Guidance > Representative expressions.

The expression elements, such as *language of expression*, remain expression elements. They do not become work elements. But they can be collected and "parked" in the work elements of representative expression to assist with the identification of works. So, *language of expression* is an expression element. But *language of representative expression* is a work element.

RDA also defines two relationship elements: *representative expression* and *representative expression of*. Representative expression is the relationship between a work and an expression that has been judged to be representative. Kate James uses the example of the First Folio expression of Shakespeare's work *Hamlet*. This expression is regarded as a reliable, canonical text and may be considered a *representative expression* of the work *Hamlet*.[39] Therefore, some of the expression elements of the First Folio can also be recorded as work elements, as elements that describe a representative expression of the work *Hamlet*.

The representative expression data elements can be used to identify a work, to distinguish between similar works, and to construct access points. In a discovery interface, these elements could be used to guide a user first to the expression considered to be the one that best represents the creator's original intention, such as an English text of *Hamlet* rather than to a French translation.

5.8.4 Manifestation Statement

Manifestation statement is another practical idea. The definition is simple and mirrors the LRM definition of the manifestation statement attribute:

> **manifestation statement**
> A statement appearing in a manifestation and deemed to be significant for users to understand how the manifestation represents itself.
>
> RDA Glossary

In IFLA LRM, it was understood that individual implementations would subtype the manifestation statement according to the needs of their community of users.

In the new RDA Toolkit, RDA adds an element that matches the IFLA LRM attribute. This is a high-level, general element, *manifestation statement*. RDA also subtypes the general statement into narrower elements, for example, *manifestation edition statement, manifestation publication statement, manifestation title and responsibility statement*. But these statements are still considered to be "broad categories of information" (Guidance > Manifestation statements). Manifestation statements are unstructured descriptions that mirror how the manifestation presents itself: they mirror, as exactly as possible, the information that appears on the manifestation.

At the same time, RDA continues to include the more granular elements: for example, *place of publication, date of publication, name of publisher; designation of edition, statement of responsibility relating to edition*, etc. RDA carries forward the elements from the original RDA Toolkit's chapter 2.

RDA presents many options. One can continue to use the granular elements from the original RDA Toolkit. Or one can use the more general statements that are better suited for digital capture of manifestation information and that allow one to record this information without any intervention or manipulation. The general statements support the direct capture of data from a digital source, such as embedded metadata in a digital manifestation, or the reuse of electronically available publisher data.[40] They are valid RDA elements. The introduction of these general manifestation statements permits a workflow where the data is ingested without adjustments made by humans to fine-tune the data, to make it fit into the more granular data elements, or to normalize and structure it according to cataloging practices.

When recording manifestation statements, RDA has always offered multiple options for transcription. In the original RDA Toolkit, there were the transcription instructions accompanied by two alternatives (so essentially three options). In the new RDA Toolkit, transcription methods are presented as three options: basic, normalized, or using another set of transcription guidelines. RDA gives guidelines for basic and normalized.[41]

RDA distinguishes between basic and normalized transcription by referencing the degree of intervention required by a human. The basic guidelines require "a minimal degree of cataloguer intervention." Capitalization, punctuation, numerals, and diacritics are transcribed as they appear. There are a few simple instructions, such as transcribing in the order in which the information appears and using a mark of omission when something is not transcribed. These instructions support transcription without a lot of manipulation or arrangement of the data. Since there is some intervention, it is more than straight data capture, but it is much simpler than normalized transcription. The guidelines for normalized transcription require "additional cataloguer judgment." These are the traditional library transcription guidelines, with instructions about language and script, capitalization, spacing, acronyms, etc. With the third option, "apply any transcription guidelines," RDA can encompass a broad variety of practices when recording manifestation data, thus accommodating the needs of diverse communities, whether from different regions or different domains, and also accommodating different workflows.

With the manifestation statements and the options for transcription, RDA makes it clear that a) it is very important for the user to know how the manifestation represents itself and b) that there is not one single way of capturing this identifying data from the manifestation. Although it must be recorded, it can be recorded at different levels of granularity. It should be transcribed, but it can also be captured directly without human intervention. When it is transcribed, there is no single definitive set of guidelines. Metadata communities will guide their members on how the data from the manifestation will be recorded, the level of granularity and the recommended transcription guidelines. For example, those who have been using RDA since it was first published will probably continue to use the more granular manifestation elements and normalized transcription guidelines.

5.9 SUMMARY

When RDA was originally published, it introduced a new way of understanding bibliographic data and new ways of recording this data to ensure that the data is unambiguous, precisely parsed, and optimized for machine processing. But this data must also respond to user needs so that users are able to have a successful resource discovery experience and explore large amounts of bibliographic data to find, identify, select, and obtain the resources they need. RDA continues to adhere to these fundamental principles. As it develops, RDA goes further to refine elements and add elements that will make RDA data better optimized for machine processing and for use in the Semantic Web.

The IFLA bibliographic conceptual models have provided the underlying theoretical framework on which RDA is based. RDA has evolved as the IFLA models have evolved. The alignment with IFLA LRM has had a noticeable impact on the concepts used in RDA. IFLA LRM introduced new entities, attributes and relationships; it changed many attributes, generalizing some and changing other ones to relationships; it introduced new concepts such as the representative expression, manifestation statements and aggregates. During this alignment with IFLA LRM, RDA made the changes required to align with IFLA LRM.

Some key aspects of RDA, such as its structure, are a combination of incorporating IFLA LRM and adapting to a new technical infrastructure. The structure of RDA continues to be organized according to the entities identified in IFLA bibliographic conceptual models, now the IFLA LRM entities. But RDA has also evolved from a linear text to a set of data elements that can be used in a multiplicity of ways. RDA now also has a technical infrastructure that is responsive, flexible and able to support improved workflows for the current standard and its future development.

RDA in the new RDA Toolkit looks radically different because of the deconstruction of chapters into separate data elements. It also introduces more relationships and greater precision in the naming of elements to ensure a valid application of RDA in automated environments. Some changes, such as introducing the use of domain and range when defining an element, have been made so that RDA conforms to the syntax of linked open data and the Semantic Web. Data use and reuse in the wider web and as part of the Semantic Web is an important aspect of resource description in the twenty-first century.

By improving the data that is recorded, RDA sets the stage for improving the user experience of resource discovery, whether in traditional library environments or in web environments.

NOTES

1. Guidance > Introduction to RDA > Objectives and principles governing RDA (RDA 96.15.50.28); formerly 0.4.2.1 in the original RDA Toolkit.

2. For example, IFLA LRM 3.2, 15.

3. Guidance > User tasks (RDA 16.62.50.83).

4. There were instructions in one of the placeholder sections: chapter 16, "Identifying Places." These were an anomaly. As early as 2012, during the discussion of 6JSC/ALA19, there was recognition that the instructions related to *place* had to be reviewed and revised. The Steering Committee decided in 2013 to form a working group looking at the issue of how *place* was treated in RDA.

5. IFLA LRM, LRM-E1 scope note, 20.

6. Entities > RDA Entity, Definition and scope.

7. Guidance > Introduction to RDA > Data elements. RDA entities (RDA 08.86.06.25).

8. Kathy Glennan, "New Expression of RDA (Not RDA 2.0)" (presentation, Cataloging and Metadata Town Hall, Music Library Association Annual Meeting, St. Louis, Missouri, February 22, 2019), slide 3, https://dx.doi.org/10.17613/4g2w-qj31.

9. For more detail about navigation, see chapter 6, section 6.1.

10. Chapter 6 presents a more complete description of the new RDA Toolkit functionality.

11. Joint Steering Committee for Development of RDA, "Strategic Plan for RDA, 2005–2009" (5JSC/Strategic/1/Rev/2; November 1, 2007), www.rda-jsc.org/archivedsite/stratplan.html (last updated July 1, 2009).

12. See also chapter 4, section 4.2, "Deconstruction of AACR2;" Tom Delsey, "The Logical Structure of the Anglo-American Cataloguing Rules," 1998, www.rda-jsc.org/archivedsite/docs.html#logical (1998); and ALCTS CC:DA Task Force on Rule 0.24, "Overview and Recommendations Concerning Revision of Rule 0.24" (4JSC/ALA/30, August 16, 1999). https://www.libraries.psu.edu/tas/jca/ccda/docs/tf-024h.pdf.

13. IFLA LRM states that "for an implementation to be viewed as a faithful implementation of the model, the basic structure of the entities and the relationships among them (including the cardinality constraints), and the attachment of those attributes implemented, needs to be respected," IFLA LRM 2.2, 10.

14. "RDA/ONIX Framework for Resource Categorization" (5JSC/Chair/10, 3 August 2006), www.rda-jsc.org/archivedsite/docs/5chair10.pdf.

15. RDA in the new RDA Toolkit: Guidance > Content and carrier > RDA resource categorization; Guidance > Content and carrier > RDA resource category extension.

16. Thomas Brendorffer, "RDA-ONIX Framework: new content types and new carrier types" (presentation, ALA Midwinter Meeting, Seattle, Washington, January 28, 2019), www.rda-rsc.org/sites/all/files/Brenndorfer%20RDA-ONIX%20Framework%2028%20Jan.pdf.

17. Kate James outlined some criteria to consider when choosing a non-RDA vocabulary encoding scheme; see Kate James, "RDA Vocabulary Encoding Schemes" (presentation, RDA Linked Data Forum, ALA Midwinter, Philadelphia, Pennsylvania, February 4, 2020), www.rda-rsc.org/sites/all/files/James%20RDA%20Vocabulary%20Encoding%20Schemes.pdf.

18. RDA in the new RDA Toolkit also offers the options of using identifiers or IRIs as recording methods. Recording methods are explained in chapter 6, section 6.2.

19. Tom Delsey, "Categorization of Content and Carrier" (5JSC/RDA/Part A/Categorization, August 4, 2006): 3–4, www.rda-jsc.org/archivedsite/docs/5rda-parta-categorization.pdf.

20. In the new RDA Toolkit, RDA 13.51.54.04.

21. Tom Delsey, "Encoding RDA Data" (5JSC/Editor/3, May 31, 2007), www.rda-jsc.org/archivedsite/docs/5editor3.pdf.

22. It is also possible to customize one's view so that element reference is always open. This can be done through logging in to one's personal profile, then going to Views > Manage Views.

23. In an RDF triple, there is a subject, a predicate, and an object. The domain is the subject, the element is the predicate, and the range is the object. See also Kate James, "RDA Concepts: Domain and Range," YouTube video, April 23, 2020. https://www.youtube.com/watch?v=c8tlydXB_AA&t=29s.

24. For more details on this filtering feature, see chapter 6, section 6.1. The "Find Element" search box allows filtering for attribute elements or relationship elements. This search box appears on all the entity pages and can be used to search when one knows the name or part of the name of the element that one needs.

25. Kate James, "Relationship Elements" (presentation, ALA Midwinter Meeting, Seattle, Washington, January 28, 2019), www.rda-rsc.org/sites/all/files/James%20Relationship%20Elements%2028%20Jan.pdf.

26. This example uses some possible phrases that a community might use when it chooses labels to display the relationship elements to the user. The *former owner* part of the example is devised for the purpose of illustration.

27. Entities > Manifestation > Access point for manifestation (RDA 27.56.07.48); Entities > Items > Access point for item (RDA 75.89.55.28).

28. See chapter 3, section 3.2.2.

29. Pat Riva, "The IFLA Library Reference Model," Lectio Magistralis in Library Science, Florence, Italy, March 6, 2018 (Firenze: Casalini Libri, 2014), 15. Available online: http://digital.casalini.it/9788876560255.

30. This aspect was recognized during the development of IFLA LRM; Riva explains how *nomen* is an entity, yet has characteristics of a relationship: "In modelling terms, a *nomen*

is a reified relationship. Reification is used in models to allow an association to function as an entity so that it can in turn have attributes and participate in further relationships. This technique is a good fit for the entity *nomen*, as in the bibliographic universe we are very interested in recording attributes of instances of *nomens* and in the relationships among *nomens*. This is a large part of the function of our authority files, an essential component of bibliographic databases." see Riva, "IFLA Library Reference Model," 16. See also Gordon Dunsire, "A Deeper Dive into Nomen and Appellations" (presentation, ALA Midwinter Meeting, Seattle, Washington, January 28, 2019), www.rda-rsc.org/sites/all/files/Dunsire%20Deeper%20Dive%20into%20Nomens%2028%20Jan.pdf.

31. For a more detailed discussion of nomens and appellations, see Dunsire, "A Deeper Dive into Nomen and Appellations;" Robert L. Maxwell, "Nomens and Appellations" (ALA eLearning Solutions, RDA New Concepts series), July 17, 2019, https://www.slideshare.net/ALAeLearningSolutions/new-concepts-nomens-and-appellations.

32. In the new RDA Toolkit: RDA 97.42.71.40, RDA 29.20.39.93.

33. Dunsire, "A Deeper Dive into Nomen and Appellations," slide 5.

34. See chapter 3, section 3.3, for more information about CIDOC CRM. See also Definition of the CIDOC Conceptual Reference Model, especially E41, Appellation, www.cidoc-crm.org/.

35. Gordon Dunsire. "A Deeper Dive into Nomen and Appellations."

36. Guidance > Fictitious and non-human appellations (RDA 46.88.39.21). See Kathy Glennan and James Hennelly, "Getting a Handle on the New RDA Toolkit," (May 10, 2019), slide 15, www.rda-rsc.org/sites/all/files/Getting%20a%20Handle%20on%20the%20New%20RDA%20Toolkit%20rev.pdf; Gordon Dunsire, "The LRM and Its Impact on RDA and Related Standards" (presentation, ALCTS Bibliographic Conceptual Models Interest Group, ALA Midwinter Meeting, January 27, 2019, Seattle, Washington), slide 13, www.rda-rsc.org/sites/all/files/Dunsire%20LRM%20and%20its%20impact%2027%20Jan.pdf.

37. Guidance > Diachronic works. See also Ed Jones, "Diachronic Works in RDA" (presentation, Program for Cooperative Cataloging Operations Committee Conference, May 2, 2019), www.rda-rsc.org/sites/all/files/Diachronic%20works%20Jones%20PCC%20OpCo.pdf.

38. Robert L. Maxwell. "Representative Expressions and Manifestation Statements" (ALA eLearning Solutions, RDA New Concepts series), slide 14, https://www.slideshare.net/ALAeLearningSolutions/new-concepts-representative-expressions-and-manifestation-statements?qid=db0f2150-4c73-4a15-b8ff-42f89d519fad&v=&b=&from_search=3.

39. Kate James, "Representative Expressions" (presentation, RDA Preconference: RDA Toolkit Redesign Update and Preview, ALA Midwinter Meeting, Denver, Colorado, February 9, 2018), Slides 15-16, www.rda-rsc.org/sites/all/files/Representative%20expressions.pdf.

40. Another possible use case is the recording of manifestation information from early printed resources that often have grammatically complex statements. The general manifestation statement eliminates the need to parse information into distinct manifestation elements. Kathy Glennan, "Recording Methods, Transcription, and Manifestation Statements" (presentation, The Redesigned RDA Toolkit: What You Need To Know To Get Ready, Montréal, Québec, October 22, 2018), slide 26, www.rda-rsc.org/sites/all/files/Recording%20methods%20etc-EN.pdf.

41. RDA in the new RDA Toolkit: Guidance > Transcription guidelines.

6

USING RDA

RDA is a standard that is published within an online tool, RDA Toolkit. RDA Toolkit contains the full text of the standard accompanied by supporting documentation and tools to facilitate the resource description process. This chapter will look at the way the online tool is organized to support and facilitate the application of the standard.

The 3R Project included a major restructuring of RDA Toolkit. To rebuild the infrastructure, a new RDA Toolkit website was created, and during the development phased, it was referred to as the "beta" RDA Toolkit site. During the time of transition, there will be a period of time when RDA Toolkit subscribers have access to the original RDA Toolkit and to the redesigned RDA Toolkit. As the original RDA Toolkit will be phased out, this section will focus on RDA in the new RDA Toolkit, the only RDA Toolkit that will exist after the transition:

6.1 Navigation in the RDA Toolkit
6.2 Recording Methods
6.3 Element Reference
6.4 Condition/Option
6.5 Encoding Schemes: Vocabulary Encoding Schemes (VES) and String Encoding Schemes (SES)
6.6 Policy Statements and Application Profiles
6.7 Data Provenance
6.8 Examples
6.9 Glossary

6.1 NAVIGATION IN THE RDA TOOLKIT

This section focuses on navigation through the text of the standard.

6.1.1 Navigation and the Structure of RDA in the New RDA Toolkit

RDA in the new RDA Toolkit has a very different appearance because each element has its own page, and the elements are individual clusters of data, rather than being bundled together into traditional chapters. The underlying technical and intellectual structure of the standard has changed.

In the original RDA Toolkit, RDA was a linear text, with a beginning, middle, and an end. There was a table of contents that provided one of the navigation paths. The original RDA Toolkit was divided into sections and chapters. Several of the chapters were very long. When the chapters were originally published as single large segments of data, there were challenges with the speed of navigation. Therefore, the chapters, although still appearing as single chapters, were broken down into subsections to improve the speed of navigation.[1]

In the new RDA Toolkit, the original RDA chapters were deconstructed into individual data elements. The text was broken down into small clusters of information and instructions for each individual element. In the new RDA Toolkit, RDA has neither chapters nor a table of contents. These multiple small clusters of data are easier and more efficient to manipulate than large chapters. But it is necessary to become accustomed to new ways of navigating through the standard.

There are several tools to navigate through RDA:

- four tabs and their drop-down menus
- extensive links throughout RDA Toolkit, in the instructions, guidance, glossary, etc., links between related elements and broader and narrower elements
- searches and the filters available in the left pane of the results page
- bookmarks and notes
- documents: application profiles and community provided documents

6.1.1.1 The Four Tabs

The redesigned RDA Toolkit has four tabs, each with its own drop-down menu (see figure 6.1). The first two tabs are "Entities" and "Guidance"; these two constitute the main content of the standard. The "Entities" menu lists the thirteen RDA entities and leads to the complete set of RDA data elements associated with each entity, along with the instructions for recording data for each element. The "Guidance" menu expands on the instructions with additional context and background, and explanations of aspects that affect multiple data elements. The "Policies" menu leads to the policy statements from different national libraries and cataloging communities. The "Resources" menu leads to useful documentation that does not fall into the category of entities and their elements, nor in the category of guidance.

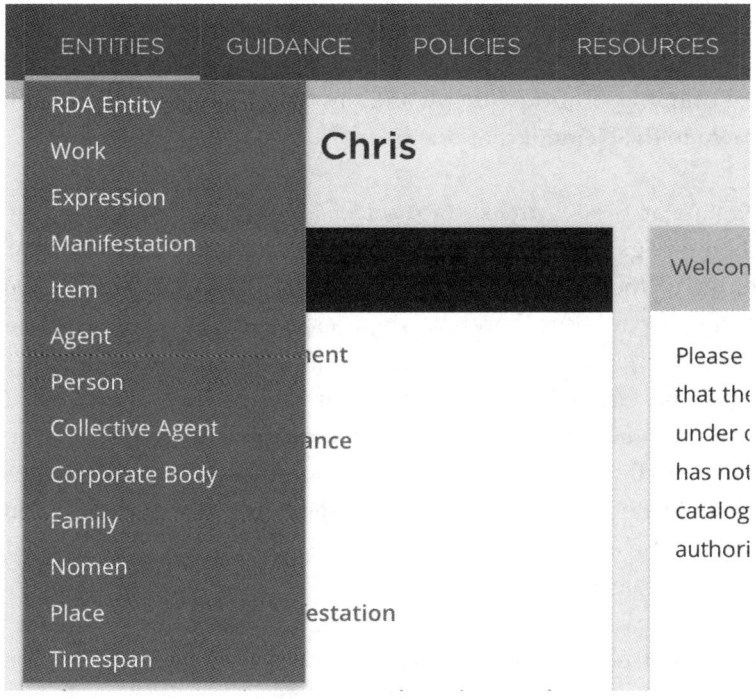

FIGURE 6.1
Navigating RDA Toolkit: the four main tabs with the Entities menu open

The Resources tab has a mix of content. Here one finds the link to the Glossary and to the list of all the RDA Vocabulary Encoding Schemes (VES). The Glossary and the VES are considered part of RDA and are searched as part of "RDA Only." The Resources tab also includes supplementary documentation related to RDA that is not part of the standard, such as RDA's revision history, the link to AACR2, and a section called "Community Resources." "Community Resources" contains the type of information that may be specific for particular communities or languages and not universally applicable. For example, lists of controlled names for the Books of the Bible. This used to be part of an RDA instruction in chapter 6 when RDA was first published. But the list represented one particular perspective on the Bible and in one particular language. The list was removed from the standard and placed on the Tools tab of the original RDA Toolkit to signal that each cataloguing community could develop and maintain their own lists. Three communities contributed their lists in the original RDA Toolkit. In the new RDA Toolkit, this kind of information is found in "Community Resources" as part of "Community vocabularies." Another example is some of the information that used to be in the appendices of the original RDA Toolkit such as initial articles in various languages and terms of rank; this information is now organized according to the language to which it applies within "Community vocabularies." "Community resources" offers the opportunity for communities to integrate within RDA Toolkit the resources, lists, vocabularies, etc. that they use. This section is expected to expand as communities around the globe contribute content.

6.1.1.2 Browsing and Searching

If one is well-acquainted with the RDA entities, one way to navigate is by selecting the relevant entity from the "Entities" menu and navigating to the appropriate instructions by drilling down to the element that one needs.

For example, start at the "Entities" tab, select "Manifestation" from the drop-down menu, and then navigate to "Title proper." At the "Manifestation" entity page, there is a complete list of the manifestation elements in alphabetical order. One can scroll through to "title proper." But there is also an efficient "Find Element" box above the list of elements. It has several useful features. First of all, one can start typing "title proper" and results start appearing after one or more letters are typed. On this page for "Manifestation," *title proper* is also mentioned in the general instructions under "Recording," so one could also use that link. The long list of elements can also be filtered to show only attribute elements or only relationship elements. The "Find Element" box above the list of elements can search all, only attributes, or only relationships. In addition, when one selects "Relationship Elements," one can also narrow down to the entity to which one wants to link. For example, a cataloger or metadata creator may need an element that relates their manifestation with a timespan, but is unsure what elements are available. They can select "Relationship Elements" and then specify the entity "Timespan" for a list of all the elements that relate a manifestation with timespan (see figure 6.2).

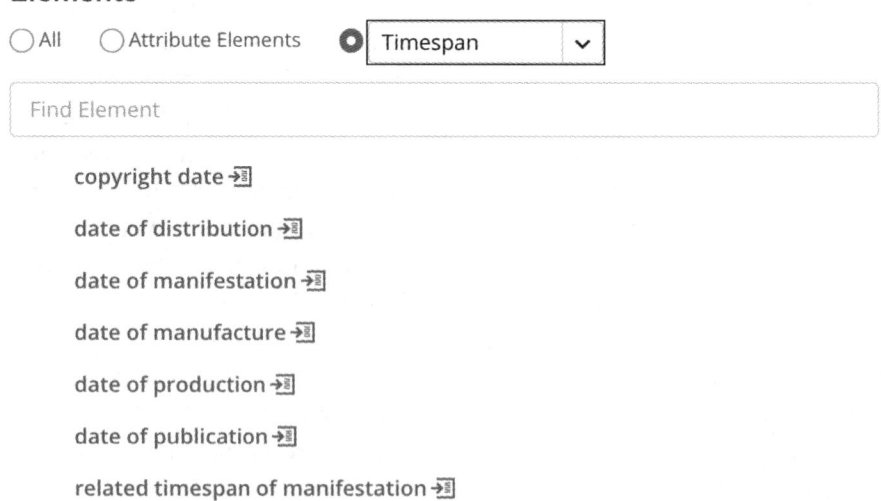

FIGURE 6.2
Filtering manifestation elements: relationship elements with a relationship to timespan

If one knows the name of the element, the "Search" box at the top of the page can also bring one to the relevant element(s). The results list is labelled with the type of document that is the source of the result, such as "Element" or "Glossary." When looking for instructions, one may well know the definition and want to go directly to the "Element" page that has all the instructions for recording this element (see figure 6.3).

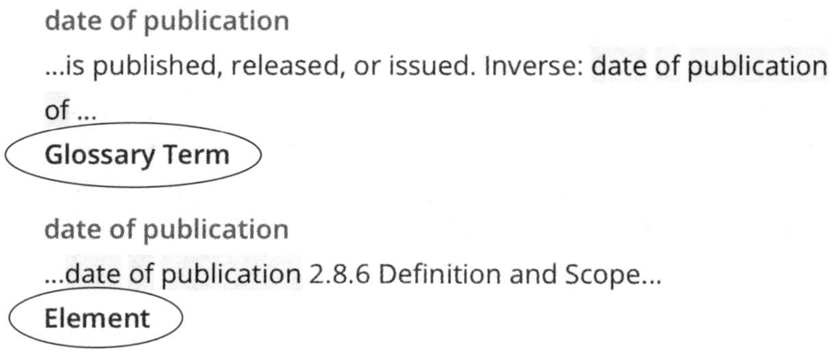

> date of publication
> ...is published, released, or issued. Inverse: date of publication of ...
> (Glossary Term)
>
> date of publication
> ...date of publication 2.8.6 Definition and Scope...
> (Element)

FIGURE 6.3
Search results for "date of publication" showing where the result is found

The "Search" box allows one to search everything in RDA Toolkit.[2] The "Search" box also has its own drop-down menu. "All" is the default search, but one can also limit a search to "RDA Only," only the policy statements (Policies), or only the glossary. There is also an "Exact Title" search if one knows the exact name of the element. This takes one directly to the data element. Searches return a set of results, and it is possible to refine the search from the results page using the filters in the left pane.

6.1.1.3 Signposts for Orientation

When following a series of links from page to page, it is helpful to know where one is within the structure of the standard. When RDA was first published, one used the table of contents to orient oneself. The chapter names also gave indications of how an element fit with the entities.

RDA in the new RDA Toolkit has a useful feature that appears at the top of the page, sometimes called "breadcrumbs" or a "breadcrumb trail" (see figure 6.4). It reveals one's location within the web tool by giving a summary indication of where one is.

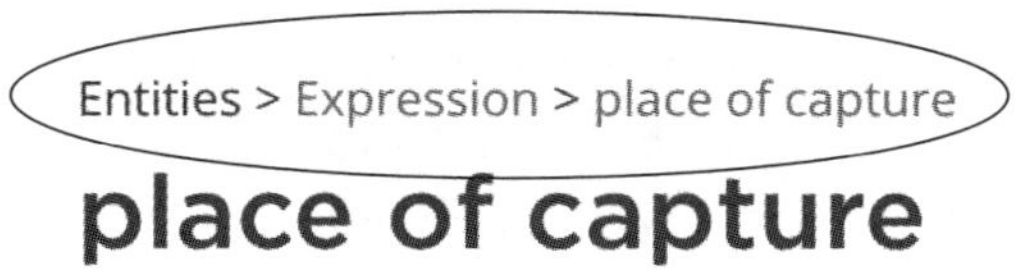

> (Entities > Expression > place of capture)
>
> **place of capture**

FIGURE 6.4
Breadcrumb trail

If one has found the element through the glossary, it may not be clear what kind of element it is. The breadcrumb trail, at a glance, shows that *place of capture* is an element for describing an expression. It summarizes the path to find this element from the "Entities" menu, to expression, and then through the list of elements associated with expression. It shows a path that can then be used again for future navigation.

Another thing to note is a construction that did not exist in the original RDA Toolkit. As mentioned in chapter 5 (5.2.3), when RDA refers to an element, the name of the element is preceded by the name of the entity to which it belongs (see figure 6.5). These references are active links. The presence of the name of the entity in front of the name of the element provides a clear indication of where the link will lead. For someone new to RDA, it provides a reinforcement of the underlying structure; it gives the metadata creator an opportunity to assess whether that link leads to an element that is valid for the entity they are describing.

Entities > Manifestation > title proper

Prerecording

A *title proper* does not include:

- Manifestation: other title information →
- Manifestation: parallel other title information →

A file name or data set name is not considered a *title proper* unless it is the only title appearing in the manifestation.

FIGURE 6.5
Example of links to two elements preceded by the name of the entity that they describe

6.1.1.4 Additional Search Features

There are some search features that may be especially useful for those accustomed to the original RDA Toolkit.

The element reference section includes MARC mapping. Due to this mapping, it is possible to search using a MARC 21 field (as long as that field has been mapped to an RDA element).

If one remembers the name of an element from the original RDA Toolkit, and that name has changed in the new RDA Toolkit, it is still possible to use the old name and navigate to the right element. For example, "form of work" was the element name in the original RDA Toolkit but the name is now *category of work*. The old names are retained as alternate labels. Thus, one can search "form of work" and get to the *category of work* element page.

It is also possible to search using instruction numbers from the original RDA Toolkit. However, not all the old instruction numbers will work: searches will work for some instruction numbers, for example, 2.14 and 9.3; a search will not work when information from the original instruction has moved to several places in RDA, such as 2.2.2, "Preferred sources of information."

6.1.1.5 *Personal Log-In*

The functionality described so far applies to the general subscription log-in for the institution. There are additional features when one logs in with a personal profile. First of all, the log-in process has been simplified. If one is signing in through the subscription account of one's library, it is no longer necessary to sign in twice, first to the library's account and then to one's personal account. The personal profile is associated with the subscription, and one can log in directly to one's personal account. Second, when logged in with a personal profile, there is more information on the home page. For example, one sees a list of recently viewed instructions. If one was interrupted during cataloging, one can quickly resume where one was.

Even the search options are a bit different when one is logged to a personal profile (see figure 6.6).

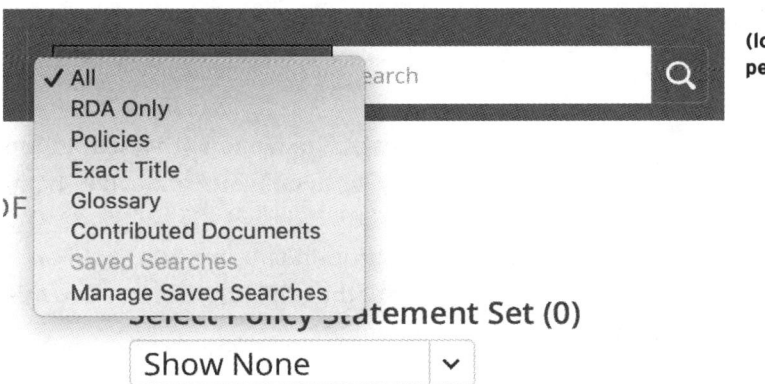

FIGURE 6.6
Search options

One also gains access to an expanded toolbar at the very top of the screen (see figure 6.7).

FIGURE 6.7
Toolbar when logged into personal profile

"Bookmarks and Notes," "Documents," and "Views" are only accessible after logging in to one's personal profile.

6.1.1.6 Bookmarks and Notes

Bookmarks and notes are accessed and organized from this toolbar. As in the original RDA Toolkit, one can create bookmarks and notes, but now there is more flexibility for organizing and sharing. Bookmarks and notes can not only be saved but also organized in folders. One can keep them private (only for the individual log-in) or local (shared with all the staff logged in to the same subscription). An administrator can also limit an institution's bookmarks so that the standard is not cluttered with unessential details that may be pertinent to only a few staff members.

Searches can also be saved and are managed through the "Search" menu. Again, they can only be saved and managed after logging in to a personal profile.

There is also the option to set views—to set a language preference, choose one's preferred policy statements, and other options for customizing one's view. A single log-in can have several saved views; for example, if one catalogs very different types of resources, or if one follows different policy statements depending on the type of resource being described.

6.1.1.7 Documents

The "Documents" section gives one access to user-created documents that can guide one's daily work. RDA Toolkit provides a place to create documents and save them, similar to the workflows and maps in the "Tools" tab of the original RDA Toolkit. The documents can be private, shared only within the institution/subscription, or shared widely (global or public). Building on the experience with the original RDA Toolkit, this functionality is improved, especially for shared documents.

In the original RDA Toolkit, the workflows and maps were powerful documents, but also became unwieldy because there was no way to filter and there was no control on authorship. It was possible to post documents with no indication of who wrote them and whether they were valid documents or experiments. Now the documents cannot be created unless one signs in with a personal log-in. But there is also greater flexibility to allow editing by several people, and also by people other than the original author, for example, by a new staff member who has just joined the department. There is also the option of deleting one's own documents when they become obsolete. There is greater rigor in the naming and identification of documents. A metadata form opens up as the first step in creating a new document so that there is consistency in the metadata associated with documents.

The categories of documents are also broader than in the original RDA Toolkit:

- application profile
- local policy
- map
- quick reference
- training material
- workflow

These documents assist metadata creators in their daily work.

Application profiles are one category. They provide a road map through RDA, guiding a metadata creator to the elements required for that profile. Different communities will design the profiles they prefer for their national, linguistic, or format-specific cataloging community. Decisions for the application profiles will depend on the type of content and carrier, the implementation scenario (e.g., linked data or MARC), and the requirements for data interoperability within that community.[3]

In the redesigned RDA Toolkit, there is more control over what one sees. All the openly shared documents are accessible and visible, but a metadata creator can choose what they see and access in their "documents collection." There is the option to "subscribe" to documents. For example, one can subscribe to individual documents or to all the documents created by one author, such as all documents created by one's own national library.

RDA allows a range of choices to accommodate data created in many different contexts, for different implementation scenarios, and within different communities of practice. Many metadata creators will rely not only on the official policy statements but also on application profiles and other shared community documentation to guide them to the options they need to follow.

Even without a "title page" for the standard, there are several ways to navigate the new RDA Toolkit.

6.1.2 Numbering of Instructions

When using an application profile or a workflow document contributed to RDA Toolkit, how will one be able to find the right place when there are no instruction numbers?

RDA is a standard that is constantly being revised. The revision process is an important strength of the standard. So, the standard continually evolves. The linear text and chapter structure were not-well suited to an evolving standard. The original Toolkit not only had chapters, but also a detailed numbering sequence for every instruction. Changes to instructions that impacted the sequence of numbering, such as moving an instruction to a more logical place, caused a ripple effect throughout the whole chapter, requiring editing work beyond the actual change in content. In addition to changing instruction numbers, all references to those numbers had to be changed as well. The effect of these kinds of changes also affected all documentation and training material that used that numbering. Even with small changes, the linear, numbered text was inefficient and inflexible.

The alignment of RDA with IFLA LRM introduced new entities. Adding these new entities to the original RDA Toolkit would have caused a large amount of renumbering and reorganization of instructions, such as introducing the *nomen* entity. The 3R Project was an opportunity to introduce a new approach to organizing the standard, an approach designed to support the continued evolution of RDA and to enable a streamlined integration of changes, whether small or large.

The instructions are not sequentially numbered. At first glance, there is no evidence of any numbering at all. But the instructions have tagging that can be used to reference instructions. The instructions can be found using URLs or citation numbers, so there are options for both online and print documentation. All the pages have unique URLs that can be easily copied for use in online documentation. Citation numbers were subsequently added for those creating print documentation. They are random but permanent numbers with the format XX.XX.XX.XX. These numbers can be used in the "Search" box to navigate to the relevant place in the standard.[4]

To find the link or citation number, one highlights the text one wants to cite, and a pop-up toolbar appears. One can choose either the link symbol or the citation number (#). In figure 6.8, the metadata creator has signed in and also has the option to create a bookmark or a note at that spot.

Further information on navigation, searching, and customization can be found in the "Help" menu in RDA Toolkit. Detailed information can also be found in videos and presentations through links at the RDA Toolkit site and at the RDA Steering Committee website.[5]

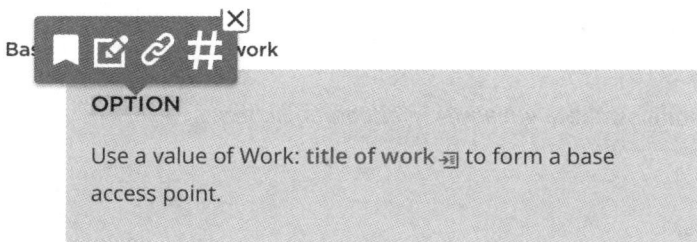

FIGURE 6.8
Pop-up toolbar for URLs and citation numbers (also bookmarks and notes)

6.2 RECORDING METHODS

The instructions for each entity and element include the option to choose the recording method.

There are instructions for up to four recording methods:

- Recording an unstructured description
- Recording a structured description
- Recording an identifier
- Recording an IRI

The recording methods make RDA in the new Toolkit look quite different from the original Toolkit. Compare the same element in the original and in the new RDA Toolkit:

RDA in the original Toolkit

9.16.1.3 Recording Profession or Occupation

Record a profession or occupation by recording a term indicating the class of persons engaged in the profession or occupation.

RDA in the new Toolkit

Entities > Person > profession or occupation

Recording an unstructured description

> **OPTION**
>
> Record an uncontrolled term or a term that is transcribed from a *source of information*
>
> ...

Recording a structured description

OPTION

Record a term from a suitable *vocabulary encoding scheme*.

...

Recording an identifier

OPTION

Record an identifier or notation for a term from a suitable *vocabulary encoding scheme*.

...

Recording an IRI

OPTION

Record an IRI for a term or concept as a *real-world object* selected from a suitable *vocabulary encoding scheme*.

In the original RDA Toolkit, the instruction simply said to record the information. In the new RDA Toolkit, the instructions are separated out into the four recording methods.[6] At first glance, it may seem overwhelming to see the headings for four recording methods at every element. The use of the four recording methods is a new way of presenting possible options, but the underlying idea that there are several ways to record data is not new. Before looking at the roots of these methods in the original RDA Toolkit, it is important to understand what the methods are and the differences between them.

In the new RDA Toolkit, there is a guidance section on recording methods. After listing the four methods, the "Guidance" section states:

> The methods are listed in order of increasing utility in general applications of RDA data, from low utility to high utility or smart data.
>
> For example, an unstructured description supports keyword indexing while an IRI supports Semantic Web and linked open data applications.
>
> Guidance > Recording methods (RDA 38.91.12.94)

Each method has its particular utility depending on the context in which the metadata is being used.

The four methods are carefully separated and explicitly defined in the new RDA Toolkit.[7] The pattern is always to list the four methods for every element, and then to specify which ones are or are not applicable. Existing and new RDA instructions are assigned to the appropriate method. Every element follows the basic pattern of the four methods.

Unstructured description includes transcribed data, free text notes, and uncontrolled terms, terms that are not part of a vocabulary encoding scheme. The main access is via keyword indexing.

Structured description includes data that is structured or controlled. It is often associated with a vocabulary encoding scheme or a string encoding scheme or both. Examples of structured descriptions are an access point, terms from a controlled vocabulary, names and titles from an authority control system (such as the NACO authority file), or even a note when the data elements are presented in a structured way, such as with ISBD punctuation to separate the elements.

An *identifier* can be assigned by an independent external agent, for example, ISBNs and ISSNs, or a number from an authority file. It can be an identifier assigned locally. It can also include notations from a controlled vocabulary, such as the notation 1007 for audiocassette in the RDA vocabulary encoding scheme for carrier types. These identifiers are unique within a specific context but are not necessarily universally unique. They are associated with a particular scheme or with an agency that assigns them.

An IRI (Internationalized Resource Identifier) is a unique identifier based on Semantic Web technologies. The IRI is a little bit different because it is not just another identifier. It is a machine-actionable link that is unique at the global level and designed for the Semantic Web environment.

At the element *language of expression*, there are instructions and examples given for each recording method. If one is recording the language of the expression as Chinese, this is what RDA instructs for each recording method, with the examples that are in RDA Toolkit:

> Entities > Expression > language of expression
>
> **Recording an unstructured description**
>
> > **OPTION**
> >
> > Record an uncontrolled term or a term that is transcribed from a *source of information*...
> >
> > > Example
> > >
> > > Chinese
>
> **Recording a structured description**
>
> > **OPTION**
> >
> > Record a term from a suitable *vocabulary encoding scheme*...
> >
> > > Example
> > >
> > > Chinese (language)
> > >
> > > > **VES source:** Getty AAT
> >
> > ...

Recording an identifier

OPTION

Record an identifier or notation for a term from a suitable *vocabulary encoding scheme*...

Example

300388113

VES source: Getty AAT

...

Recording an IRI

OPTION

Record an IRI for a term or concept as a *real-world object* selected from a suitable *vocabulary encoding scheme*.

Example

http://vocab.getty.edu/aat/300388113

In the new RDA Toolkit, the four recording methods are always listed for each entity and element.

Not all the recording methods are applicable to all data elements:

- parallel other title information

    the only applicable method is unstructured description
- file type

    all four methods are applicable
- ISSN

    the options are identifier or IRI
- authorized access point for person

    the options are structured description or IRI

When a method is not applicable, there is a clear statement at the method not to use it: "This recording method is not applicable to this element."

A recording method is applicable depending on the type of data element and the context in which one is creating the metadata. An ISSN by its very nature is an identifier, so it makes sense that structured and unstructured descriptions are irrelevant. But there is the possibility of recording the ISSN as an IRI; this would be essential for a linked open data implementation scenario.[8] Likewise, an authorized access point by its very nature is a structured description, and it can also be recorded as an IRI, the choice for a linked data implementation.

In the new RDA Toolkit, it is not the idea of multiple recording methods that is new. What is new is the way the recording methods are presented.

When one looks at the original RDA Toolkit, there is evidence of choices in recording methods, though not yet systematically worked out throughout the standard. The RDA relationship chapters in the original RDA Toolkit had introduced the notion of options for recording relationships, including the use of an identifier. They were called "techniques" rather than recording methods, but the germ of the idea was already there in chapters 17, 18, 24 and 29. RDA in the new RDA Toolkit takes the principle, expands it to all elements, and expands it also to include the unstructured description as a technique or method for recording the data.

The RDA chapters on recording attributes in the original RDA Toolkit describe the methods of unstructured description and structured description, When recording a free text description, one is recording an unstructured description. Similarly, instructions on transcribing information that appear on the manifestation are instructions for recording an unstructured description. Some instructions specified to record the element by using one or more terms from a list that was included in RDA, such as *form of tactile notation, carrier type,* or *production method*—in effect using a vocabulary encoding scheme, and thus recording a structured description. Instructions for access points led to the formulation of structured descriptions.

In the original RDA Toolkit, there were a few instructions on using the Uniform Resource Locator. These instructions were in chapter 4, "Providing Acquisition and Access Information." There were a couple of examples with URIs and URLs in other chapters. But there were no instructions on using the IRI, using the IRI as a recording method.

Of the four recording methods, one can see evidence of three methods in the original text of RDA. In the new RDA Toolkit, identifiers are given more prominence. Using IRIs as a formal recording method is new. The pattern of always listing four recording methods for every element is also new.

6.3 ELEMENT REFERENCE

When one lands on the page for an RDA element, the first thing one sees is "Definition and Scope." Immediately below is "Element Reference:"

👁 Element Reference

Clicking the button reveals information that may not be required every time one uses the element, but it is important information.[9] The content of the "Element Reference" box changes slightly depending on the element.

There is always domain information and there is often range information.[10] Domain is simply the entity with which the element is associated; it is the entity that the element describes. For example, *designation of edition* has the domain *manifestation*. *Designation of edition* is an element that describes a manifestation. In this case, there is only a domain, and no range, because *designation of edition* is an attribute element, not a relationship element (see figure 6.9).

Entities > Manifestation > designation of edition

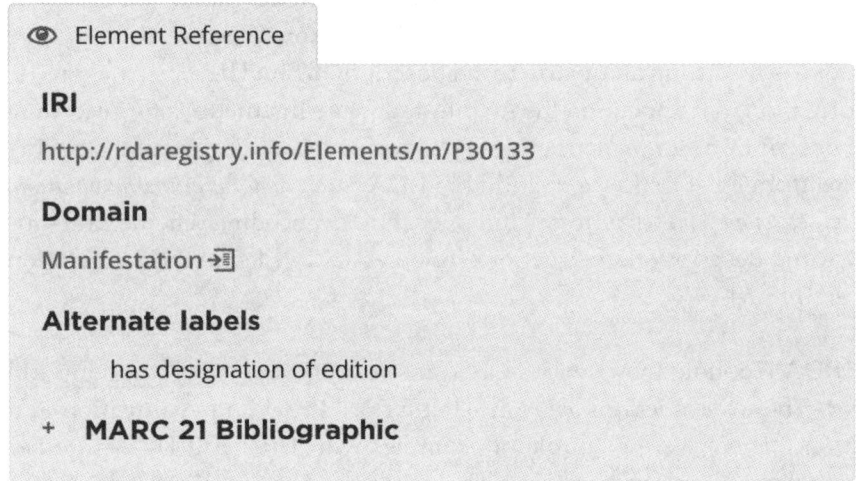

FIGURE 6.9
Element reference for *designation of edition*

In the case of *date of publication* (see figure 6.10), the domain of this element is manifestation but there is also a range. There is only a range when the element describes a relationship. In this case, the relationship is between manifestation and timespan. So, timespan is the range.[11] The relationship with timespan, *date of publication*, describes the manifestation.

The IRI always appears in the "Element Reference" box. This is the official IRI from the RDA Registry for this data element.[12] When working in a linked data context—using, for example, a RDF/XML application—then this IRI is data that one would need. It is the Semantic Web identifier for this data element.

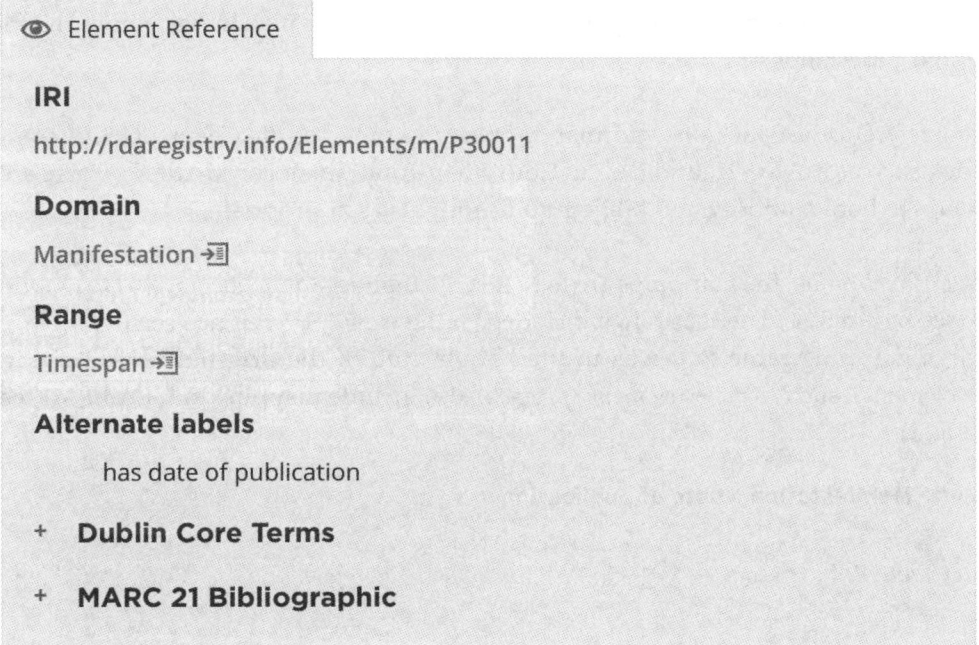

FIGURE 6.10
Element reference for *date of publication*

Every element has one or more alternate labels. One label is the "verbalized" label, a label that has a verb in it; a verbalized label fits well into a statement and can be easier to understand. For example, the manifestation *A better man* "has date of publication" 2019.

Other alternate labels are labels no longer used in RDA:

The alternate labels for *category of work:*

has category of work	verbalized label
form of work	alternate label (former label used in the original RDA Toolkit)

Since labels that existed in the original RDA Toolkit may still be used in applications, they were maintained as alternate labels.

The labels for elements were designed to be very precise, especially for use in automated environments. The labels remove any ambiguity that would cause problems when interpreted/mapped by a computer. These labels do not need to be the ones displayed to users. The expectation is that there can be one or more sets of user-friendly labels. Different communities may develop their own sets of labels to match their community's needs and expectations.[13]

Element reference also includes information about mapping the data element to different schemes, such as MARC 21 (and Dublin Core when applicable). For MARC 21, there are mappings to both authority and bibliographic formats as appropriate.

For *date of publication,* the mappings are to MARC 21 Bibliographic Format and to Dublin Core (see figure 6.11). The mappings included in the element reference section replace the large mapping table that was in the "Tools" tab of the original RDA Toolkit. Some elements, such as *preferred name of person,* also include mapping to IFLA LRM (see figure 6.12).

Entities > Manifestation > date of publication

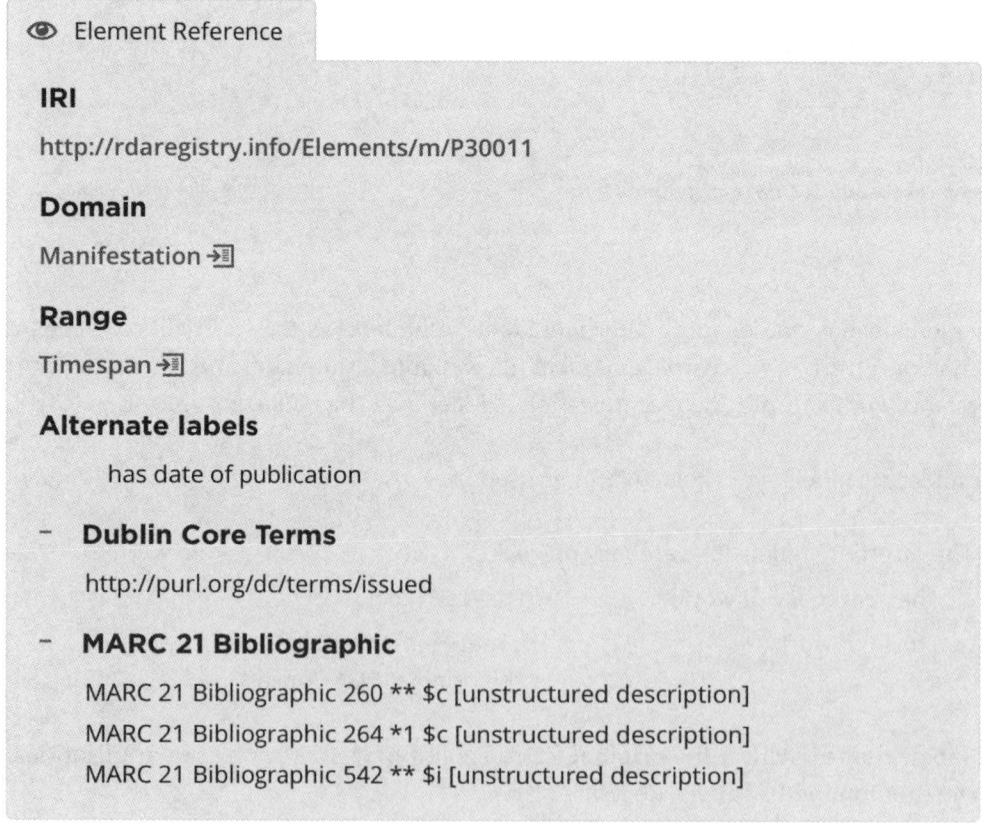

FIGURE 6.11
Mapping of RDA *date of publication* to Dublin Core and MARC 21 Bibliographic

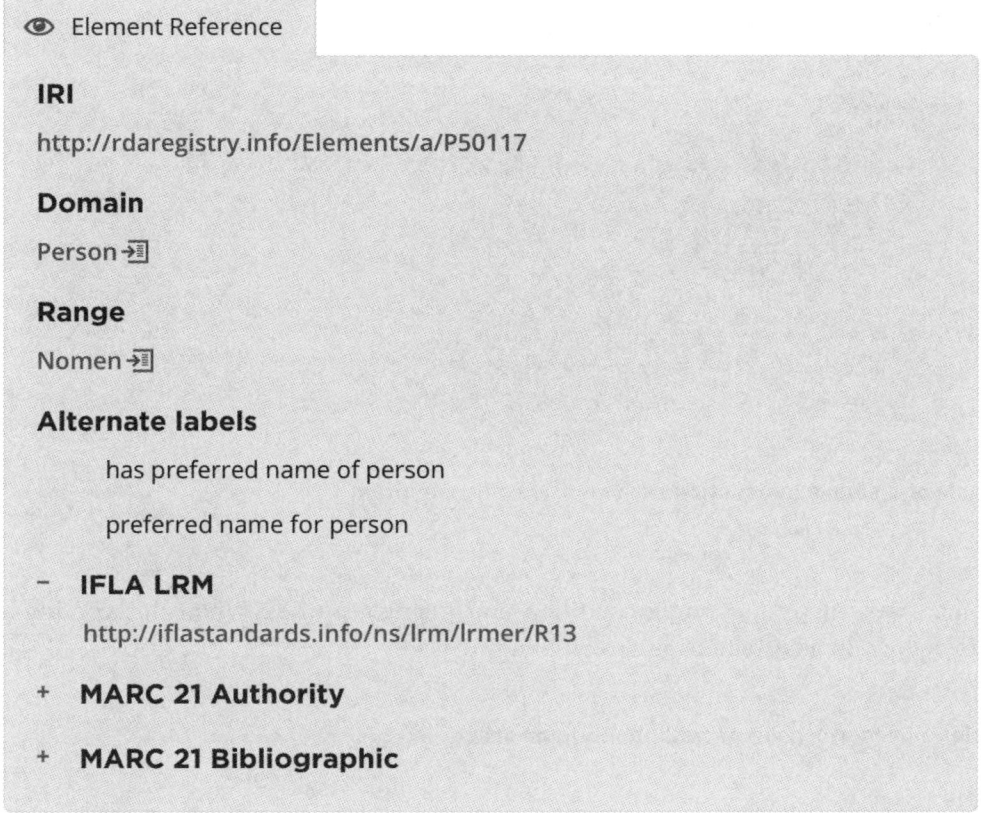

FIGURE 6.12
Mapping of RDA *preferred name of person* to IFLA LRM

6.4 CONDITION/OPTION

When one looks at the actual RDA instructions, there is a new format. The instructions are in boxes shaded in two colors to reinforce that there are two different types of information: conditions and options. At first glance, it may seem puzzling to see the word "Option" above every instruction. In effect, anything labelled "Option" is an instruction. And it is also usually optional because RDA is not a prescriptive standard. There are very few "requirements," but many options.[14]

Anything labelled *Option* is the instruction. *Condition* spells out when a particular instruction should be applied.

In the example shown in figure 6.13, there is simply the instruction. It applies in all cases. There are no special instructions for special conditions.

Entities > Expression > interactivity mode

Recording a structured description

> **OPTION**
>
> Record an appropriate term from the *RDA Interactivity Mode vocabulary encoding scheme*:
>
> > interactive
> >
> > non-interactive

FIGURE 6.13
Example of a simple instruction with no preceding condition

In some cases, there is a single condition and a single option. When this condition occurs, follow the instruction, as shown in figure 6.14.

Entities > Person > term of rank, honour, or office

Popes

> **CONDITION**
>
> A person is a pope.

> **OPTION**
>
> Record the term *Pope*.

FIGURE 6.14
Example of a single condition and a single option

In some cases, there is a single condition and multiple options. It will be the metadata creator who decides which option to follow, either on their own or following the policy statement or application profile mandated by their institution (see figure 6.15).

Entities > Expression > content type

Recording

CONDITION

An expression has two or more values of Expression: content type ⇥.

OPTION

Record all of the content types.

OPTION

Record only the predominant content type.

OPTION

Record only the content types that apply to the most substantial content of the expression.

FIGURE 6.15
Example of a single condition and multiple options

There are also examples with multiple conditions. The instruction applies when all the conditions in the box are met as shown in figure 6.16.

Entities > Person > preferred name of person
  Names of person in two or more languages

> **CONDITION**
>
> A value of a name does not appear in manifestations.
>
> A value of a name appears in two or more languages in sources of information.

> **OPTION**
>
> Record a value that appears most frequently in a *source of information* that is published in a place associated with a person.

FIGURE 6.16
Example of an instruction that is applied when the multiple conditions are met

This new formatting using the pattern of conditions and options is used consistently for all instructions, whether they have one condition, many conditions, or no conditions. The new pattern plus the use of the colored boxes gives a uniform look and feel to the text of the standard.

6.5 ENCODING SCHEMES: VOCABULARY ENCODING SCHEMES AND STRING ENCODING SCHEMES

Vocabulary encoding schemes (VES) and string encoding schemes (SES) are new ways of referring to conventions and practices that we have long used in the library. The terminology is new in RDA but the practices are not. RDA includes its own controlled vocabularies, called vocabulary encoding schemes, but also supports the use of external ones. RDA does not include string encoding schemes but expects that metadata creators will select and use the string encoding schemes that are appropriate and approved for their institution.

Constructing access points usually requires the use of both a vocabulary encoding scheme and a string encoding scheme. The definitions of access point for each entity are similar and they reference vocabulary encoding schemes and string encoding schemes:

> **access point for work**
>
> A nomen that is an appellation of work in natural language that is taken from a vocabulary encoding scheme or is constructed using a string encoding scheme.

When constructing an access point, one might use both a vocabulary encoding scheme and a string encoding scheme. For example:

> Olympic Games (31st : 2016 : Rio de Janeiro, Brazil)

The names of the corporate body and the place are the preferred forms of name in the LC/NACO authority file, which is a kind of vocabulary encoding scheme. The order of the data elements and the punctuation to separate them is a string encoding scheme. The string encoding scheme in this example is the one used in the LC/NACO authority file. It is not necessarily the only string encoding scheme that could be used, although it is the string encoding scheme used in many RDA examples.

6.5.1 Vocabulary Encoding Schemes (VES)

A common example of a vocabulary encoding scheme is a controlled vocabulary, such as the Art and Architecture Thesaurus or the Library of Congress genre/form terms. A vocabulary encoding scheme can also be a list of codes, such as the MARC 21 code list for countries or an ISO 3166 list of country codes:

> **vocabulary encoding scheme**
>
> A named structured list of representations of controlled values for elements.
>
> A vocabulary encoding scheme includes an RDA list of terms or their corresponding value vocabularies in the RDA Registry, an ISO code list, a standard terminology, an authority control system, etc. Simple keyword indexes are excluded.
>
> RDA Glossary

A vocabulary encoding scheme is a list of values that have been deliberately created and controlled. It is an identifiable scheme. The terms are structured in a particular way, as codes, other notations, preferred words, or strings of words.

From the beginning, RDA encouraged the use of controlled vocabularies and proposed lists of terms for many elements. In the new RDA Toolkit, this approach is made more consistent by expanding the number of lists. Wherever RDA originally suggested the use of particular terms, all these terms were extracted and put into formal lists called vocabulary encoding schemes. Each of the RDA vocabulary encoding schemes lists the terms and every term is now defined; each term has an RDA identifier (a notation tied to that term) and also its own unique IRI from the RDA registry.[15]

For example, from the vocabulary encoding scheme *RDA broadcast standard:*

HDTV	**term**
http://rdaregistry.info/termList/broadcastStand/1001	**IRI**
(Notation 1001)	**identifier**

A broadcast standard that is an encoding system for digital broadcast television, named after high-definition television.

Resources > Vocabulary Encoding Schemes > RDA Broadcast Standard

The definition is in the vocabulary encoding scheme list as well as in the glossary.

There is a complete list of the RDA vocabulary encoding schemes in the "Resources" tab (Resources > Vocabulary Encoding Schemes).

RDA instructions encourage the use of the RDA vocabulary encoding scheme appropriate for that data element, when recording a structured description, identifier, or IRI. But RDA is flexible, so it also offers the option of recording a term, identifier, or IRI from another suitable vocabulary encoding scheme.

Also, when RDA has no vocabulary encoding scheme, it is still possible to use the recording methods: structured description, identifier, or IRI. The metadata creator is encouraged to select a term from a suitable and identifiable vocabulary encoding scheme. The examples for *accessibility content* demonstrate the instructions (see figure 6.17).

Entities > Manifestation > accessibility content

Recording

> 👁 **Example**
>
> Open signed in American Sign language
> > **Recording method:** unstructured description
>
> Includes subtitles
> > **Recording method:** unstructured description
>
> Closed captioning available
> > **Recording method:** unstructured description
>
> synchronizedAudioText
> > **Recording method:** structured description
> >
> > **VES source:** W3C
>
> 300206232
> > **Recording method:** identifier
> >
> > **VES source:** AAT
>
> http://vocab.getty.edu/aat/300206232
> > **Recording method:** IRI

FIGURE 6.17
Examples for the four recording methods when recording *accessibility content* including use of VES sources that are not part of RDA

6.5.2 String Encoding Schemes (SES)

The string encoding scheme (SES) is a way of putting together data elements following a standardized pattern:

> A set of string values and an associated set of rules that describe a mapping between that set of strings and a value of an element.
>
> RDA Glossary

For example, a string encoding scheme indicates the order in which data elements are presented in an access point; it indicates how to use marks of punctuation (or other delimiters) in a specific way to separate data, such as the comma that precedes a date of birth in the access point for a person.

A string encoding scheme supports the recording of structured descriptions, such as the order and punctuation in an authorized access point or ISBD punctuation used when recording a publication statement. RDA instructs the metadata creator to apply a string encoding scheme in various places throughout the standard (see figures 6.18 and 6.19).

Entities > Place > authorized access point for place
    Recording a structured description

> **OPTION**
>
> Construct an access point by applying a *string encoding scheme* to the values of one or more other elements.

FIGURE 6.18
Example of an instruction to apply a *string encoding scheme* when constructing an access point

Entities > Work > dissertation or thesis information
    Recording a structured description

> **OPTION**
>
> Record a structured description by applying a *string encoding scheme* to select, sequence, and punctuate values of one or more sub-elements.

FIGURE 6.19
Example of an instruction to apply a *string encoding scheme* when recording an element

In the original RDA Toolkit, there were two appendixes, D and E, and they focused on the presentation of data and were called "record syntaxes": record syntaxes for descriptive data and record syntaxes for access point control. In the new RDA Toolkit, this "presentation of data" or "record syntax" is now called a *string encoding scheme*. String encoding schemes can vary between communities and the new RDA Toolkit continues and steps up the practice of putting guidance about string encoding schemes outside the text of the standard so that one particular scheme does not have special status. This is another example of the way RDA is designed for use by an international audience, with the emphasis on harmonization rather than on strict conformity for all details. The same RDA elements can be used in many contexts and by many communities; different communities may prefer a particular string encoding scheme. Metadata creators will be guided by the application profiles and/or policy statements that they follow.

There are references to string encoding scheme in RDA, and string encoding schemes are used in examples. But string encoding schemes are not part of the standard itself.

6.6 POLICY STATEMENTS AND APPLICATION PROFILES

There are several ways to provide guidance for frontline catalogers and metadata creators. In the new RDA Toolkit, two important ways to provide this guidance are through policy statements and application profiles.

RDA is designed to be an international standard that can be used in different technological and cultural contexts. In addition to choosing which options to follow, there are also other areas where choices need to be made:

a) There are choices about recording methods depending on the technological context in which the recorded data will be used and which encoding scheme will be used.

b) There are many elements that can be used. RDA aims to support data interoperability by offering a large set of precise data elements that are designed both for human understanding and computer exploitation but not every element needs to be used.

c) RDA also develops and maintains multiple controlled vocabularies to improve navigation and exploration through large collections of bibliographic data; RDA also offers the option to use other suitable vocabularies. There are many choices for vocabulary encoding schemes.

The wording of the RDA objective, internationalization, references the role of policy statements and application profiles, especially in a broad, international context:

> RDA is designed for an international audience, with the expectation that cataloguing agents will make application decisions when desirable. These decisions may be formally recorded in RDA toolkit as policy statements, or as separate documents such as an *application profile* issued by an agent.
>
> Guidance > Introduction to RDA > Objectives and principles governing RDA (RDA 94.23.91.09)

Policy statements and application profiles are important community documents that provide a road map for using RDA. Renate Behrens, a member of the RDA Steering Committee, summarized the difference succinctly: the application profile outlines *what to use*, the policy statements will provide more background and information on *how to use*.[16]

6.6.1 Policy Statements

When RDA was first published in 2010, there were many alternatives, optional additions, and optional omissions. Even then, RDA was aiming to be open to different metadata communities.

If there are choices to be made, how does a new cataloger maintain consistency with the practices of other catalogers in their institution or community? How does the cataloger know which options to follow? When RDA was first published, there was some uncertainty about how to work with the presence of alternatives, optional additions and optional omissions. There were also a large number of elements from which to choose, although a small number were designated as "core."

RDA implementation became a reality with the distribution of policy statements. Policy statements provide guidance on applying a particular instruction. The Library of Congress led the way (later joined by the Program for Cooperative Cataloging) and produced the first policy statements. The policy statements outlined which data elements to use, and what alternatives, optional omissions, and optional additions to follow. They also incorporated practices for the recording of data as had been done in the former Library of Congress Rule Interpretations. Other national libraries and cataloging communities followed this lead and produced their own policy statements. The availability of policy statements ensured a successful implementation of RDA because they guided frontline catalogers and resulted in consistent cataloging records. For example, the original Library of Congress-Program for Cooperative Cataloging (LC-PCC) policy statements specified which data elements had to be used in addition to RDA's core elements, such as *other title information* for monographs, and media type.

The policy statements stated when an alternative should be followed. The statements also included interpretation, detail, and examples for recording data, such as for the statement on extent. There were many policy statements in the original RDA Toolkit, from national libraries, such as the Kungliga Biblioteket of Sweden; from linguistic communities, such as the Anwendungsrichtlinien für den deutschsprachigen Raum; and from communities focused on a particular type of resource, such as the Music Library Association Best Practices.

Similarly, in the new RDA Toolkit, there are many elements, many options, many recording methods, and there are many choices for vocabulary and string encoding schemes. The policy statements will continue to be important guideposts for catalogers and metadata creators in national, regional, or linguistic communities and for communities focused on the description of specific types of works or manifestations, such as music scores and early printed books. In the new RDA Toolkit, the policy statements have their own tab and drop-down menu, immediately visible as one enters RDA Toolkit:

Policy statements run parallel with the data elements and the instructions. This is literally true because the new RDA Toolkit is designed to display policy statements and RDA instructions side by side.

Figure 6.20 is a view of one of the British Library policy statements at *content type*.

FIGURE 6.20
Example of an instruction and a policy statement displayed in parallel to each other

In "Views," metadata creators can choose the policy statements that are their preferred default and they can also choose whether to have these automatically displayed beside the instruction. The new RDA Toolkit offers a more integrated experience for those who rely on policy statements, by synchronizing the instruction and corresponding policy statement so that they display alongside each other. Policy statements created by all the libraries and associations will continue to be available. The side-by-side view is an efficient shortcut for metadata creators so that they can quickly consult their default policy statements at a single glance.

6.6.2 Application Profiles

An application profile indicates the metadata required for a particular application.

> An *application profile* specifies the entities, elements, and vocabulary encoding schemes that are expected in a set of metadata that meets the functions and requirements of an application that uses the metadata.
>
> Guidance > Application profiles

Policy statements will continue to provide interpretation and guidance for communities of users. But there is also the opportunity to create and use one or more application profiles. The application profile is a more technical approach to providing guidance. It specifies the RDA entities, elements, and vocabulary encoding schemes that should be used; it indicates which elements are required; and which elements are repeatable; it may also specify the recording methods, and the vocabulary and string encoding schemes.

For example, in the instructions for *type of binding* or *broadcast standard*, there is the option to use the RDA vocabulary encoding scheme for the element or another suitable vocabulary encoding scheme. Either the policy statements or the application profiles can specify the vocabulary encoding scheme to use. Similarly, either can specify the string encoding scheme to use when constructing an authorized access point for person. Policy statements are more closely integrated into RDA with their own tab in the RDA Toolkit and the possibility of viewing them in line with RDA instructions. Application profiles are supplementary documents. They can be stored and shared within the RDA Toolkit using the "Documents" section or they may be maintained outside RDA Toolkit.

In RDA Toolkit, there is one set of policy statements from each community. However, there can be multiple application profiles from each community. Application profiles can be specific, for example, for particular types of works, such as a musical work or a moving image work; for early printed manifestations; for serials; or for particular implementation scenarios, such as for a linked data RDF application.

Application profiles are not new. A well-known example is the application profile created and maintained by the Program for Cooperative Cataloguing, the BIBCO Standard Record (BSR) RDA Metadata Application Profile.[17] This profile specifies the elements to use, the fields to use in MARC 21, and references vocabulary encoding schemes such as the LC/NACO authority file and the Standard Citation Forms for Rare Materials Cataloging.

An application profile can specify which elements are mandatory and which ones are recommended, as well the elements that should not be used. Since an application profile specifies the elements that must be used, the profile takes the place of the "core element" designation that existed in the original RDA Toolkit.

To use RDA effectively, a community will define their needs and select the entities, elements, and options they will expect in a description or in a metadata description set (a set of metadata statements that describe one or more RDA entities). Application profiles support consistency across a metadata community; they could also potentially lead to the creation of data input forms or templates. They also provide a way to validate data and ensure that incoming data conforms to the institution's requirements.

There is likely to be some overlap between policy statements and application profiles. Different communities are free to choose how they write these documents. For example, a community may decide to put all its policy statements into application profiles. For another community, their application profile may resemble a workflow document.

RDA itself provides a vast array of data elements that produce well-structured or well-formed data, supporting the global interoperability of bibliographic data. RDA is designed to produce data that works in different types of implementations, from simple flat files to linked open data. RDA intentionally offers a wide range of possibilities so that metadata communities in very different circumstances can use the same structured element set, whether they are using a large number of the elements or a small subset. Each cataloging community will make its own choices, geared to the needs of their users, the ways in which their data will be used, their expectations for data reuse, and the capabilities of their technological environment. The policy statements and application profiles provide the means to communicate their decisions.

6.7   DATA PROVENANCE

RDA provides guidance on recording data provenance (Guidance > Data provenance). Data provenance is not an element. It is the use of existing elements to provide information about the data that is being recorded. For many years, there was recognition that some of the data we record is not describing an entity, but is information about the metadata that has been recorded.[18] For example, a source of title note does not record information about the title of the manifestation, but about the sources used by the metadata creator. It is information that can still be recorded in a general *note on manifestation*.[19] There is a methodical approach to identify data related to provenance. At the same time, the process of recording this data is brought into line with the process of describing any work/expression/manifestation/item.

6.7.1 Sources of Information

When RDA was originally published, it relaxed the stringency of the predecessor standard, AACR2, in terms of sources of information. There was still guidance, but RDA allowed more flexibility for sources of information. When one takes information from outside the manifestation, it is still important to indicate that the information comes from an external source. When choosing a *preferred name of person*, or *preferred title of work*, recording the source consulted remains important.

Recording sources of information continues to be important. But it is treated differently in the new RDA Toolkit. When data provenance began to be examined in a systematic way, the first recommendation was to provide a more uniform approach to data provenance. In the original RDA Toolkit, RDA had many types of notes related to data provenance scattered throughout the text: *note on title* (title source), *source consulted, cataloguer's note, date of usage, explanation of relationship, scope of usage, status of identification*. The information was important but there was the question of how these notes about the metadata fit into the underlying conceptual model.

In the new RDA Toolkit, some of the notes were mapped to more general notes, such as *cataloguer's note* and *explanation of relationship* becoming *note on metadata work*. Some became fully defined separate elements such as *status of identification*: it is an attribute element of *nomen*, and it has its own RDA vocabulary encoding scheme.

In the new RDA Toolkit, there is a more comprehensive approach for data provenance. *Data provenance* was added as a section that appears on several RDA element pages. The instruction to record a source of information is now followed by a reference to the special guidance section on recording a source of metadata. See figures 6.21 and 6.22 for examples.

Data provenance

> **OPTION**
>
> Record a *source of information*. For general guidance, see Guidance: Data provenance. Recording a source of metadata ⇥.

FIGURE 6.21
A recurring instruction about recording a source of information

Entities > Agent > name of agent

Data provenance

> **OPTION**
>
> Record the guidelines or scheme that is used for a transcription. For general guidance, see Guidance: Data provenance. Recording a transcription standard used for metadata →.

> **OPTION**
>
> Record a *source of information*. For general guidance, see Guidance: Data provenance. Recording a source of metadata →.

FIGURE 6.22
Data provenance instructions for *name of agent*

The instructions refer one to *Recording a source of metadata* (and also *Recording a transcription standard used for metadata*), found at Guidance > Data provenance. The instructions seem a little confusing at first because they keep referring to a "metadata work." The key to understanding this section is that a catalog record or any recorded metadata statement is a metadata work:

> **metadata work**
> A work that is a metadata statement or a metadata description set.
>
> RDA Glossary

> The catalogue record is a metadata work that is realized in a specific encoding scheme and embodied by a carrier such as a microfiche or online manifestation.
>
> Guidance > Data provenance (RDA 81.91.96.76)

RDA applies the same modelling to the resource and to the metadata about it. A metadata description set or a catalog record is a work. Any external "source" is also treated as a work in its own right. When one has been used to shorthand references to external sources, this is a change, but it is totally valid. The sources being consulted are works, realized in expressions that are embodied in manifestations, and we consult the exemplars of those manifestations. Therefore, one can use any appropriate RDA element and recording method to describe those sources. Likewise, a transcription standard is treated as a work. A cataloging standard is also treated as a work.

The instruction on recording a source of metadata shows up throughout RDA, for appellation elements such as *preferred name of person*; when supplying information, such as a date of publication (see also 6.7.2); also for recording an external VES. The instructions on data provenance are found in all the places where a metadata creator may be consulting external sources.

6.7.2 Sources of Information for the Manifestation

The data provenance section in "Guidance" is also where one now finds all the instructions on sources of information for the manifestation. It begins at "Recording a Source of Metadata," and starts off with this statement:

> A source of metadata may be a manifestation that is being described or another manifestation.
>
> Guidance > Data provenance. Recording a source of metadata
> (RDA 09.65.03.78)

Either the source of information is coming from the manifestation itself, the manifestation being described, or it is coming from an external source, another manifestation. The section then goes on to a brief summary of the original RDA instructions at 2.2 on sources of information (see figure 6.23).

Guidance > Data provenance

CONDITION
A manifestation that is being described does not provide a source of information for an element.

OPTION
Prefer the following external sources of information, in this order:

1. A published description of the manifestation
2. A container that is not issued with the manifestation itself
3. Any other available source

FIGURE 6.23
Instructions that were at 2.2.4 in the original RDA Toolkit (RDA 34.95.74.89, 26.32.80.93)

There are also enhancements, such as detailed instructions when recording a source of metadata (see figure 6.24) that are also consistent with the overall structure of RDA.

Guidance > Data provenance

Recording a source of metadata that is a manifestation that is being described

> **CONDITION**
> The source of a metadata work is a manifestation that is being described.

> **OPTION**
> Record the source of information as a Work: recording source ⤳.

FIGURE 6.24
General instruction on recording the source of information (RDA 25.29.25.23)

When one clicks through to *recording source*, it is an RDA element, with four recording methods. If choosing to record a structured description, identifier or IRI, RDA also provides a vocabulary encoding scheme for *recording source*:

caption
container
cover
embedded metadata
jacket
label
 [etc.]

Instructions on recording a source of metadata also show up when transcribing, and the data for an element is supplied, such as *edition statement* (see figure 6.25).

Entities > Manifestation > edition statement
    Recording an unstructured description

> **CONDITION**
>
> A manifestation lacks an edition statement but is known to contain significant changes from other editions.

> **OPTION**
>
> Record a supplied edition statement.
>
> Indicate that the information is taken from a source that is outside the manifestation that is being described. For general guidance, see Guidance: Data provenance. Recording a source of metadata →.

FIGURE 6.25
Instruction on recording a source of information when supplying information

Whenever the instructions guide a metadata creator to indicate that the information comes from a source outside the manifestation that is being described, one finds the same reference back to "Recording a source of metadata." And the source of metadata is treated in a way that is consistent with the treatment of any other resource.

6.8 EXAMPLES

Examples in the new RDA Toolkit are presented differently than in the original RDA Toolkit. In the original RDA Toolkit, all examples were presented in the same way. They illustrated the results of the instruction at a particular element.

In the new RDA Toolkit, there are four types of examples:

1. basic
2. view in context
3. view as relationship
4. recording methods

The basic example is very similar to the examples in the original RDA Toolkit. See figure 6.26 for basic examples at *profession or occupation*.

Entities > Person > profession or occupation

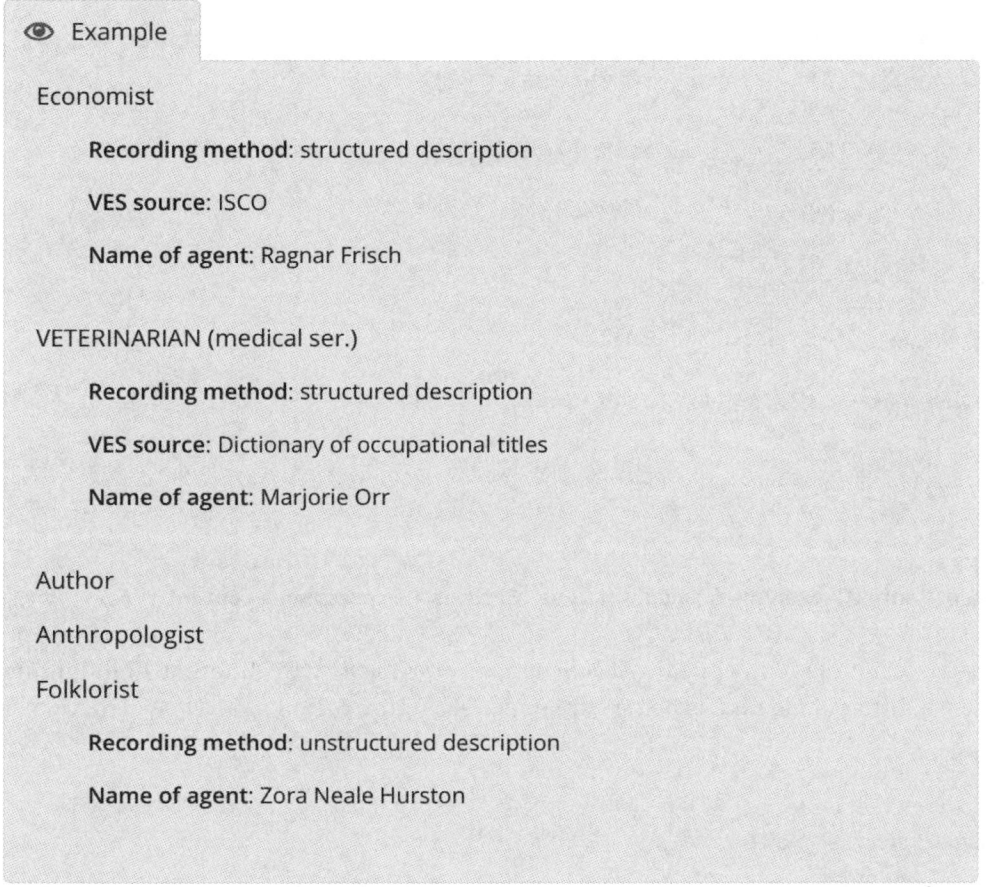

FIGURE 6.26
Basic examples for *profession or occupation*

A notable difference is that the examples are sorted according to recording method. For structured descriptions and identifiers, the source for the term is also given.

When RDA was published in the original RDA Toolkit, one complaint was the lack of full examples. The "View in Context" type of example shows a full set of metadata statements. The same example may show up in multiple data elements, but it changes slightly: the parts relevant for the particular element are highlighted.

Figure 6.27 shows the "View in Context" example that appears at the *content type* element. Blue highlighting in the RDA Toolkit (shown underlined in figure 6.27 and 6.28) shows the element being explained.

View in Context Example

> **Example**
>
> **Expression**
>
> | | |
> |---|---|
> | *has authorized access point for expression* | Brunhoff, Jean de, 1899–1937. Babar en famille. English. Spoken word |
> | *has content type* | **spoken word** |
> | *has place of capture* | New York, New York |
> | *has date of capture* | October 28, 1940 |
> | *has language of expression* | English |
> | *has date of expression* | 1940 |
> | *has narrator agent* | Luther, Frank, 1905–1980 |

FIGURE 6.27
"View in Context" example for *content type* (Entities > Expression > content type)

The same example also appears at *language of expression* with different highlighting because a different element is being explained (see figure 6.28).

> **Example**
>
> **Expression**
>
> | | |
> |---|---|
> | *has authorized access point for expression* | Brunhoff, Jean de, 1899–1937. Babar en famille. English. Spoken word |
> | *has content type* | **spoken word** |
> | *has place of capture* | New York, New York |
> | *has date of capture* | October 28, 1940 |
> | *has language of expression* | English |
> | *has date of expression* | 1940 |
> | *has narrator agent* | Luther, Frank, 1905–1980 |

FIGURE 6.28
"View in Context" example for *language of expression* (Entities > Expression > language of expression)

Relationships continue to be a central focus for resource description. The new RDA Toolkit includes a type of example called "View as Relationship." These examples demonstrate how RDA is optimized for a linked data environment.

A "View as Relationship" example appears at the *country associated with person* element (see figure 6.29).

Entities > Person > country associated with person

View as Relationship Example

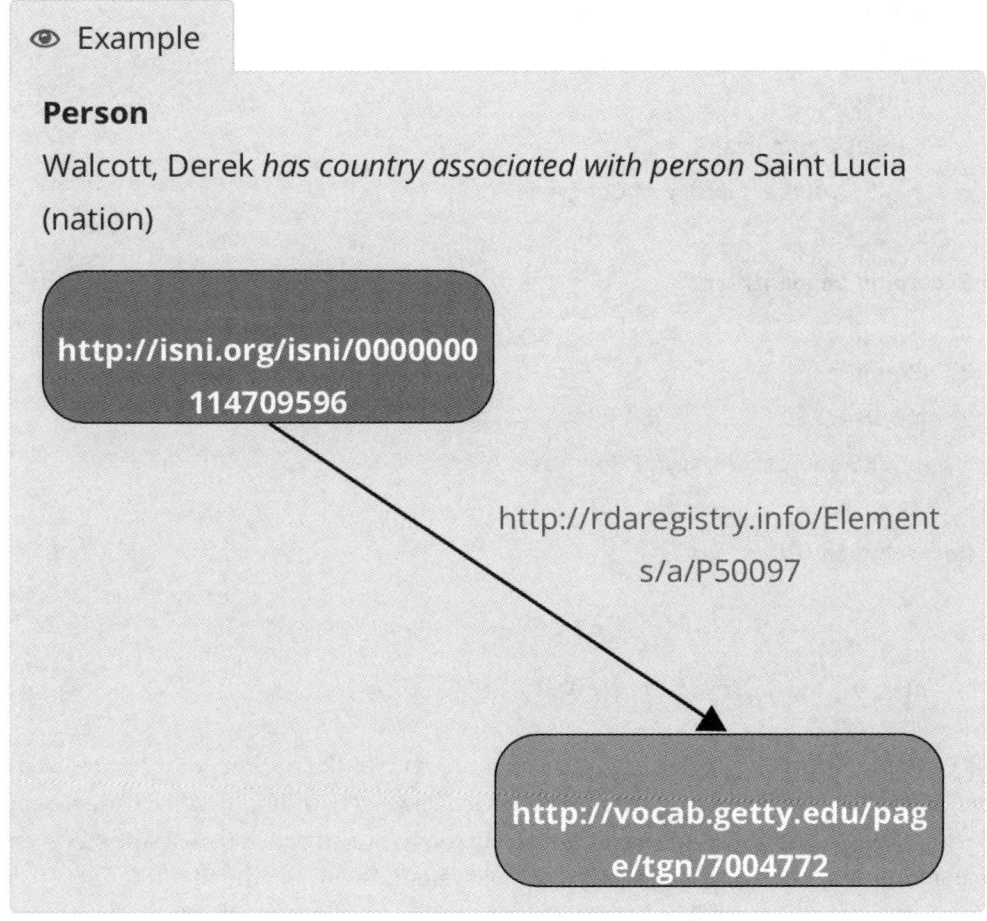

FIGURE 6.29
"View as Relationship" example for *country associated with person*

In this "View as Relationship" example, the person and the place are recorded as IRIs, using an ISNI IRI for the person and an IRI from the *Getty Thesaurus of Geographic Names Online* for the place. The relationship between the two is recorded using the IRI from the RDA Registry for *country associated with person*.

The fourth type of example is called "Recording Methods." It takes a single example and shows how it is recorded in different ways for each of the recording methods:

Entities > Work > creator agent of work

Recording an unstructured description

...

Example

Kansas Geological Survey

...

Recording a structured description

...

Example

Kansas Geological Survey

> VES source: Library of Congress

...

Recording an identifier

...

Example

n 86847709

> VES source: Library of Congress

...

Recording an IRI

...

Example

http://id.loc.gov/rwo/agents/n86847709

In this example, the name of the agent (unstructured) and the access point (structured) happen to look the same. However, for the structured description, there is a source for the vocabulary encoding scheme to demonstrate that it is a structured description taken from an identified scheme, an authority control system. Likewise, the identifier also has the source recorded because it only makes sense when associated with the domain from which it comes.

The use of four different types of examples helps clarify the instructions and gives a fuller picture of how the standard works in different contexts.

Examples continue to be added to RDA Toolkit.

6.9 GLOSSARY

The RDA Glossary in the new RDA Toolkit is much longer than in the original RDA Toolkit. A thorough effort was made to have a comprehensive list of terms and their definitions included in RDA Toolkit. The glossary includes all the entities and elements; it includes the inverse elements and alternate labels with see references; it also includes all the terms used in the RDA vocabulary encoding schemes.

The Glossary also acts as an aid to navigation because one can use the glossary element name to click through to the element instructions.

However, the glossary is also notable because it is not "handcrafted." It is part of the new automated infrastructure that was designed to improve efficiency when making revisions and changes. This technical infrastructure employs the principle of reusing data. The infrastructure has two registries, the RDA Staff Registry for back-end work that feeds into GitHub, and the RDA Registry that is the public-facing registry for use in linked data applications (at www.rdaregistry.info). Figure 6.30, a diagram from James Hennelly's 2020 presentation[20] illustrates how the RDA Toolkit glossary is populated by data that is pushed out of the RDA Staff Registry into GitHub and then out of GitHub to several applications, including the RDA Toolkit glossary:

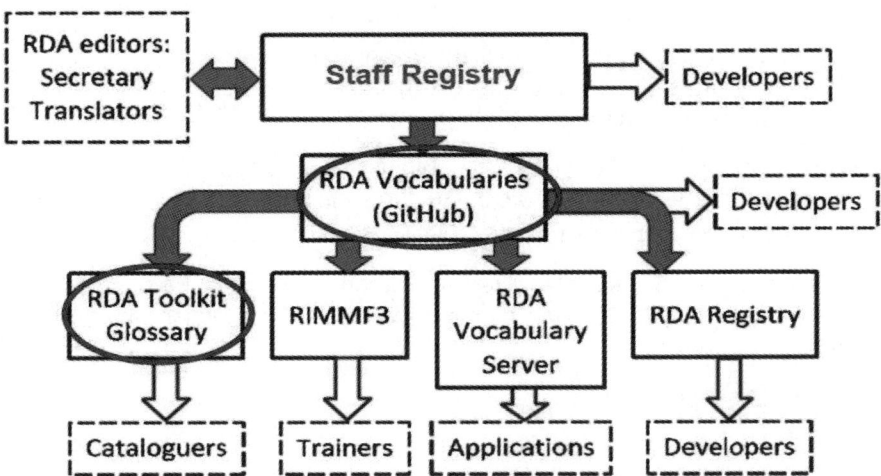

FIGURE 6.30
Automated reuse of data in the RDA infrastructure (The solid arrows show the automated data flow out of the Staff Registry for use in multiple places.)

RDA Reference includes the names, definitions, and scope notes for all the RDA entities and elements. It also includes all the RDA vocabulary encoding schemes and the definitions of those terms. RDA Reference is maintained in the Staff Registry. The Staff Registry holds all the source data, and the glossary is created automatically by populating it with this data from the Registry. The goal is to make a change in one place only, in the Staff Registry—and have that change automatically occur in all the places where that data is found. This is one example of the ways in which RDA's new infrastructure reuses data. RDA promotes the creation of data that can be efficiently reused, and the same principle is also applied to its own infrastructure.

NOTES

1. See Figure 5.3 in chapter 5.
2. For more detailed information on the search function, see the videos created by Kate James on the YouTube RDA Toolkit channel, https://www.youtube.com/channel/UCd5pa3AoQIr17wESE9YHcnw/videos.
3. Application profiles are discussed in more detail in section 6.6 of this chapter.
4. RDA Steering Committee, Beta Toolkit/3R Project "Frequently Asked Questions," http://rda-rsc.org/node/551; "Citation Numbering Arrives," News and Information, May 22, 2019, RDA Toolkit: https://www.rdatoolkit.org/node/190.
5. See RDA Toolkit Learning Resources, https://www.rdatoolkit.org/index.php/learning; RDA Toolkit You Tube channel, https://www.youtube.com/channel/UCd5pa3AoQIr17wESE9YHcnw (link is also on the Learning Resources page). See also recent RSC presentations at the RSC website: www.rda-rsc.org/rscpresentations, for example, Kate James, "RDA Beta Toolkit Basics" (presentation, RDA Toolkit Workshop, January 24, 2020, ALA Midwinter Preconference), https://www.rdatoolkit.org/sites/default/files/2020-01/RDA%20Beta%20Toolkit%20Basics%20Midwinter%202020_final.pdf.
6. When the four methods of recording were initially introduced in 2015, they were called the "four-fold path." See "RDA Accommodation of Relationship Data" (6JSC/TechnicalWG/6) August 3, 2015. www.rda-jsc.org/sites/all/files/6JSC-TechnicalWG-6.pdf.
7. Kathy Glennan, "RDA Toolkit 3R Project: Incorporating the 4-Fold Path (presentation for ALCTS Exchange, May 2017), www.rda-rsc.org/sites/all/files/Glennan%203R-4fold%20path.pdf.
8. Guidance > RDA implementation scenarios.
9. If logged into a personal profile, one can also customize display so that element reference always opens as you arrive at a page.
10. See chapter 5, section 5.4.2, for a more detailed description of domain and range.
11. If one is ever unsure whether a data element is a relationship element or not, one can check element reference to see if there is a range.
12. RDA Registry, www.rdaregistry.info.

13. More detail and examples for element labels can be found in Dominique Bourrassa, "A Quickstart Guide to RDA Terminology: Element, SES, and VES" (presentation, RDA Toolkit Workshop, January 24, 2020, ALA Midwinter Preconference 2020, https://www.rdatoolkit.org/sites/default/files/2020-01/ALA-Midwinter-Preconference-Bourassa.pdf.

14. The only place where you see "requirements" is in the information about "well-formed data." RDA in the new RDA Toolkit provides guidance on constructing a well-formed description of an information resource and this information is important when creating application profiles, templates or other workflow documents. It is found in two places. In Guidance > Resource description, there are guidelines on constructing coherent, minimum and effective descriptions. In Guidance > Well-formed RDA, there is additional information on the ways in which these three types of description follow RDA principles and objectives. Here there is also a section on what constitutes conformance with RDA.

15. This may seem like a great amount of work, but with the automated processes in the new RDA Toolkit, the data can be pushed to many places, and it always remains consistent and up to date. See chapter 6, section 6.9, for more detail.

16. Renate Behrens, "RDA and Application Profiles" (presentation, IFLA Satellite RDA 2019, Thessaloniki, Greece, August 21, 2019), www.rda-rsc.org/sites/all/files/Application%20Profiles_behrens_animiert.pdf.

17. Program for Cooperative Cataloging, BIBCO Standard Record (BSR) Metadata Application Profiles (MAPs), https://www.loc.gov/aba/pcc/bibco/bsr-maps.html; BIBCO Standard Record (BSR) RDA metadata application profile (January 21, 2020 revision), https://www.loc.gov/aba/pcc/bibco/documents/PCC-RDA-BSR.pdf.

18. The concern had been discussed for years preceding 2016. In 2016, the RDA Steering Committee discussion paper, "RDA models for provenance data," was the beginning of a formalized approach to data provenance. See "RDA Models for Provenance Data" (RSC/Technical WG/1, August 8, 2016), www.rda-rsc.org/RSC/TechnicalWG/1.

19. The *note on manifestation* was in the original RDA Toolkit's chapter 2 (2.17) and in the new RDA Toolkit is found at Entities > Manifestation > note on manifestation.

20. James Hennelly, "Deliverance: A Journey through the RDA Workflow" (presentation, RDA Linked Data Forum, ALA Midwinter Meeting, January 27, 2020) slide 6, www.rda-rsc.org/sites/all/files/Hennelly%20Deliverance%20RDA%20Workflow.pdf.

7
RDA AFTER THE 3R PROJECT

RDA in the new RDA Toolkit has a different look. It is organized differently. There is new vocabulary. There is new functionality. At first glance, it is hard to recognize the RDA that was in the original RDA Toolkit.

However, RDA remains essentially the same standard. The purpose of RDA is and has always been to produce metadata that supports "the discovery and identification of resources in library and other cultural heritage collections."[1] It has continued to evolve in response to changes in the environment. RDA in the new RDA Toolkit follows the same objectives as RDA did when it was first being developed. It moves in the same direction. One can think of it as a more complete realization of the original vision for RDA.

There are five simple objectives that have guided the development of the standard:

> **Responsiveness to user needs:** The metadata should meet functional requirements for the support of user tasks.
>
> **Cost efficiency:** The metadata should meet functional requirements of an application in a cost-efficient manner to produce standardized data allowing for broad data exchange.
>
> **Flexibility:** The metadata should function independently of the format, medium, or systems used to store or communicate metadata. They should be amenable to use in a variety of environments.
>
> **Continuity:** The metadata should be amenable to integration into existing databases.
>
> **Internationalization:** RDA is designed for an international audience . . . Given the flexibility of the guidance and recording methods, the metadata provided by different agents will not necessarily be identical, but as well-formed data, it will be understood by any agent when shared. The emphasis is on data harmonization rather than strict compatibility.
>
> Guidance > Introduction to RDA > Objectives and principles governing RDA

The objectives are reminders of some key aspects of RDA.

When using RDA, the goal is to record and create data that helps the user. This goes beyond a general well-meaning intention to help the user. The orientation to user needs and user tasks is grounded in the IFLA bibliographic conceptual models. Starting with FRBR, and following through to IFLA LRM, the models orient our perspective in two key ways: to look at bibliographic information as data, and to look at bibliographic information from the perspective of the user navigating through large catalogs, databases, or the web. In aligning with the IFLA models, RDA adheres to these same two fundamental principles: treat bibliographic information as data and create data that responds to user needs.

The objective of cost efficiency is to produce standardized data that can be easily shared. Cost efficiency is not about cutting corners or delineating minimum level records. It is about producing well-formed data that conforms to a recognizable pattern, as defined in a conceptual model. When data is well-formed, it has an explicit and identifiable structure. Data with a consistent and evident structure can be shared and reused reliably. Data reuse streamlines the data creation process and supports a sustainable landscape for bibliographic information. It allows for efficiency in a traditional cataloging environment as well as in a linked data environment.

The objective of flexibility enables a wide-ranging use of data. RDA is a set of elements. It is not tied to any encoding standard nor is it tied to being used or stored in any one particular system. The set of RDA elements is deliberately designed for use in various contexts, from simple flat files to linked data for the Semantic Web.[2] The introduction of the four recording methods underscores this flexibility. RDA is a set of data elements that can be shared among libraries that are functioning in very diverse technological environments. RDA also has the potential to be a set of data elements that can be used, wholly or in part, by institutions outside the library domain.

Libraries have large amounts of legacy data and continuity is an important consideration. It has been an RDA objective from the start. RDA is optimized for use in a linked data environment, for example, with the option to record data using IRIs. But it also has the recording methods to match traditional cataloging environments, specifically the unstructured and structured methods. It is a standard that has been expanded to accommodate the newly emerging linked data environment, but it is still a standard that can be used to create data for a traditional MARC 21 catalog within a library management system. It is conceivable that one could use RDA elements and instructions even for bibliographic information stored in a card catalog or a printed bibliography.

The first four objectives remain the same. The fifth objective, internationalization, was added in the new RDA Toolkit. It is an expansion of an aspiration in the Introduction chapter in the original RDA Toolkit (0.11). This is an important addition to the objectives and shapes the design and development of RDA.

When RDA was first published, the emphasis in its vision statement was on a standard designed for the digital world, a major difference from its predecessor, AACR2. It continues to be a standard designed for the digital world, designed to produce data that can be used in many environments, from simple text files to the structured data required for the Semantic Web. The vision statement for RDA now focuses on its place as a global standard for use in cataloging and metadata communities around the world. While AACR2 was used in countries around the world, it was a standard designed and controlled by a limited number of author countries for their own use; other countries adopted AACR2 and it became a standard that was used internationally. But it was not designed to be an international standard. From the start of RDA development, there was a conscious decision to ensure that RDA would be a standard for use in countries around the world, and that the former Anglo-American perspective would not dominate the standard. The changes evident when RDA was first published were small steps that confirmed this commitment and marked the beginning of the process of internationalization.

Alignment with the IFLA bibliographic conceptual models has an obvious advantage in terms of structuring RDA data. But this alignment also contributes to internationalization. The models provide a shared understanding of bibliographic data in the library domain throughout the world, they provide a starting point for building compatible standards, and they focus on the common ground that different cataloging communities share. The concepts and terms of IFLA LRM are a shared understanding of the bibliographic domain that acts as a shared language.

RDA has adopted the structure of data that is defined in IFLA LRM. The alignment means that, at a fundamental level, RDA is compatible with any other descriptive standard that also aligns with IFLA LRM. Both would be using the same starting point and sharing the same theoretical framework. There may be different extensions and refinements, but the core remains compatible because they reference the same internationally approved bibliographic conceptual model.

Alignment with the current IFLA model, IFLA LRM, means that the cataloging community within the library has an explicit conceptual model for bibliographic information. With an explicit model, the library community can explain how its data fits together and describe the relationships between data elements. This model can then be the start of developing a data model for use in specific applications. It can also be the start for developing interoperability with data coming from other cultural heritage domains, such as publishing or museum domains. It also provides a common reference point for cataloging communities around the globe.

The IFLA models achieved international approval relatively easily, in part because the models focus on a high-level definition of the structure of bibliographic data. When one examines the detailed data produced by different cataloging traditions, there are variations . How can one accommodate variations? The nature of RDA is that it was not designed to be "rules," but rather a set of instructions and guidelines that also include choices to accommodate differing environments, cultures and traditions. The focus of RDA is harmonization based on one shared element set. RDA allows choices and the new RDA Toolkit makes these choices more consistently explicit and visible across all elements.[3]

The last part of RDA's internationalization objective contains an important insight about the usability of bibliographic data in a range of different technological and geographical contexts:

> **Given the flexibility of the guidance and recording methods, the metadata provded by different agents will not necessarily be identical, but as well-formed data, it will be understood by any agent when shared. The emphasis is on data harmonization rather than strict compatibility.**

The focus of RDA is using a shared set of elements.

RDA, as an implementation of IFLA LRM, extends and refines the basic high-level structure of IFLA LRM. The core structure of the data provides fundamental consistency and conformity even if different recording methods are applied, different vocabulary encoding schemes are chosen, or different string encoding schemes are used to present the data. The fundamental harmonization comes from the shared use of the same set of elements that describe the same thirteen entities. This focus on the common ground, on data harmonization rather than strict compliance, is a defining aspect of RDA. RDA removes instructions about string encoding schemes that it inherited from AACR2; it never prescribes only one vocabulary encoding scheme; it does not prioritize one transcription guideline as "the main instruction" with others presented as alternatives.[4] The basis for internationalization is not rigid adherence to a single way of doing things but building on common ground and achieving harmonization.

Internationalization of RDA is also reinforced by the changes in governance structure. RDA is intended to be a standard for use in countries around the world—countries with different cataloging traditions, countries with different technological capacities. There is also the intention that RDA will be developed by representatives from around the globe.

RDA continues to follow the same objectives. But RDA looks very different in the new RDA Toolkit. There are some changes in content as a result of the alignment with IFLA LRM. The alignment required an expansion of RDA to incorporate the new entities and the elements associated with these new entities, such as the introduction of *nomen*. There are also some new concepts introduced by IFLA LRM, such as aggregates, representative expressions and manifestation statements. The changes caused by the alignment with IFLA LRM are not disruptive. IFLA LRM consolidated the earlier models FRBR, FRAD, and FRSAD. It evolved from the three earlier models. It carries forward the essence of those earlier models while also developing more nuanced modelling in areas that had been left out, such as aggregates. RDA's alignment with IFLA LRM is not disruptive to the content of RDA but it does perceptibly expand the content of RDA.

The radical redesign of RDA Toolkit changed the appearance and organization of RDA. As a web tool, RDA Toolkit is subject to the same pressures as all web products: inevitably, the software needs to be renewed, interfaces modernized, and functionality brought in line with current expectations.

RDA after the 3R Project is still the same standard even if it looks different in the new RDA Toolkit. RDA in the new RDA Toolkit is much more flexible because the basic unit is the element. Each element has its own page with all the relevant information, instructions, and links together in one place. The new design allows for easier manipulation of RDA content and more efficient integration of changes; it is more readily adaptable in case further reorganization is required in the future. RDA is an integrating resource; it is a standard that is constantly evolving. One of its strengths is the fact that it is constantly being reviewed and revised to keep in step with new developments.

Parts of RDA have been expanded to ensure that RDA is a standard that produces data for use in the Semantic Web. But RDA retains all the parts that support the production of data in more traditional environments, such as for library catalogs of MARC records.[5] RDA is intended for use by communities around the globe, in a range of different technological, linguistic, and cultural contexts. The main purpose of RDA is to support the user in the completion of their tasks of exploring, finding, identifying, selecting, and obtaining the resource they need, wherever they are looking for that resource. That user may be in a library or surfing on the web.

From the start, RDA has presented a new way of thinking about bibliographic data. RDA is designed to produce data that supports the user in their process of resource discovery, data that is well structured to promote interoperability, data that is well-suited for online environments and machine processing. Even while we function in traditional catalogue environments, RDA orients our thinking so that we are prepared for the forthcoming environments in which libraries will function.

NOTES

1. RDA in the new RDA Toolkit > Introduction to RDA (RDA 84.74.84.88).
2. Guidance > RDA implementation scenarios.
3. For example, there are choices about transcription guidelines; choices about which elements to use and which instructions to follow (in the cases where there are multiple options); choices about the inclusion and order of additional elements in access points; choices of recording methods; choices of vocabulary encoding schemes and string encoding schemes. Communities develop policy statements, application profiles, or other documents to guide the practices within their communities.

4. For communities of library catalogers, especially those accustomed to working in MARC formats, the application profiles and policy statements will create the conditions for strict compatibility as required.

5. An instructive example of using the new RDA Toolkit to produce data for a traditional MARC 21 catalogue is Kathy Glennan's video showing how to catalog a book. See Kathy Glennan, "Practical Implications: A Look at Cataloguing a Book Using New RDA" (video presentation, IFLA Satellite on RDA: Resource Description and Access, Aristotle University, Thessalonki, Greece, August 21, 2019 (42:27 minutes). Listed on the RSC web page "RDA Presentations 2019," www.rda-rsc.org/node/589. Available on the RDA Toolkit YouTube channel: https://www.youtube.com/watch?v=olo5uFVv3Ks.

SOURCES FOR FURTHER INFORMATION

This section lists authoritative starting points for keeping up to date with RDA developments and checking on the latest documents and presentations. It also provides a reference to a useful visualization tool, RIMMF.

RDA

RDA: Resource Description and Access. Chicago: American Library Association; Ottawa: Canadian Federation of Library Associations; London: Chartered Institute of Library and Information Professionals (CILIP), 2010– . RDA Toolkit is available at *https://access.rdatoolkit.org/*. There is also a general website about RDA and RDA Toolkit at *https://www.rdatoolkit.org/*.

RDA IN THE NEW TOOLKIT

Presentations from the RDA Steering Committee Website

http://www.rda-rsc.org/rscpresentations
Selected presentations on RDA mainly by RSC members and others closely involved with RDA development.

RDA YouTube Channel

https://www.youtube.com/c/RDAToolkitVideo
Instructional videos. One can also subscribe to this channel.

RDA Toolkit Learning Resources

https://www.rdatoolkit.org/index.php/learning
A centralized list with links to three sources of information: the RSC presentations site (also above); the YouTube channel (also above); and News & Information.

RDA STEERING COMMITTEE WEBSITE

http://www.rda-rsc.org/
The website includes all the current RSC work as well as historical documents and a link to the archived website of the Joint Steering Committee for Development of RDA. The RDA Board also shares space at this website.

FAQs

RDA FAQ
http://rda-rsc.org/content/about-rda

Beta Toolkit/3R Project FAQ
http://rda-rsc.org/node/551

Outcomes of RSC Meetings
http://rda-rsc.org/RSCmeetingoutcomes
RSC provides summaries of important decisions taken during its meetings.

http://rda-rsc.org/RSCminutes
For those interested in more detailed accounts of the decision-making, the minutes are also available.

Documents
http://rda-rsc.org/documents
The documents on the RSC website have varying levels of complexity because some are providing information and background, and some are discussing development proposals.

THE 3R PROJECT

RDA Toolkit 3R Project
https://www.rdatoolkit.org/3RProject

RIMMF

http://www.marcofquality.com/wiki/rimmf3/doku.php
RIMMF, RDA in Many Metadata Formats, is a software tool that expands one's understanding of RDA. It can be summarized as "RDA in action." RIMMF is a visualization and training tool. It allows one to practice recording RDA data without the constraints of encoding formats, especially the constraints of the MARC format.

RIMMF also provides a prototype for a cataloguing interface that complies with RDA. The software is freely available for download subject to its Creative Commons license. RIMMF4 is the version that incorporates changes resulting from the 3R Project and RDA's alignment with IFLA LRM.

INDEX

A

abbreviations, 87–88
access points, formulating, 120
accessibility content, 168–169
agent entity, 53, 82, 111
agents, 45, 132–133
aggregates, 121–124, 126
aggregating expression, 63–66, 121–124
aggregating work, 63–66
aggregation relationship, 62–67
Anglo-American Cataloguing Rules, 2nd edition (AACR2)
  adoption of, 19
  building on foundations of, 15, 73–74
  comparison with, 5
  continuing resources and, 133
  continuity with, 79–87
  deconstruction of, 74–79
  instructions derived from, 80–84
  limitations of, 6, 103
  limited perspective of, 9, 191
  moving away from, 87–91
  Paris Principles and, 16
  as precursor, 1
  translations and, 24
Anglo-American Cataloguing Rules (AACR), 15, 74
appellation elements, 128, 129, 131
appellation of work group, 137
appellation relationship, 48, 56–57
application profiles, 171–172, 174–175
association relationship, 55
attributes of entities, 38, 45–47, 58–60
augmentation aggregate, 123

B

base material, 83–84
Behrens, Renate, 172
Berners-Lee, Tim, 7
BIBCO Standard Record (BSR) RDA Metadata Application Profile, 174
BIBFRAME (Bibliographic Framework Initiative), 6
Bible, 84–85
bibliographic conceptual models
  alignment with, 3–4, 82, 103–104, 191
  introduction to, 33–34
  role of, 67–71
  user tasks in, 93
  . *See also* IFLA Library Reference Model (IFLA LRM)
bibliographic information, as data, 5–6

"Bookmarks," 152
breadcrumbs/breadcrumb trail, 149–150
browsing, 148–149

C

carrier data, 44, 75–76, 77, 103–108
carrier type, 107–108
cataloger judgment, 94–95
"Categorization of Content and Carrier," 108
characteristics of entities. *See* attributes of entities
CIDOC CRM (CIDOC Conceptual Reference Model), 68, 131
citation numbers, 154
class of materials concept, 75–76, 77–78
collection aggregate, 122
collective agent entity, 53–54, 97, 98–99
Committee of Principals (CoP), 26, 27, 77–78, 79
Committee on Cataloging: Description and Access (CC:DA), 77
"Community Resources," 147
"Community vocabularies," 147
Condition/Option, 163–166
content data, 44, 75–76, 77, 103–108
content type, 104–106, 107–108, 181–182
contextualize task, 37
continuing resources, 133
continuity, 189, 190
contributor person of still image, 126
controlled vocabularies, 167
Co-Publishers, 79
Copyright Holders, 79
corporate body, 97, 98–99
cost efficiency, 189, 190
country associated with person, 183
Cutter, Charles A., 38

D

data provenance, 175–180
date of publication, 160–162
Delsey, Tom, 75, 76, 108
designation of edition, 160
Deutsche Nationalbibliothek (DNB), 26–27
diachronic works, 133–137
"Documents," 152–153, 174
domain, 112–114, 160
Dublin Core, 18–19, 162

E

edition statement, 180
Element Reference, 159–163

197

elements, 89–90, 101–103, 109–120
encoding schemes, 5–6, 10–11, 21–24, 166–171
entities, 38–45, 51–58, 95–99. *See also* hierarchical structure for entities; relationships between entities; *individual elements*
"Entities" menu, 146–147, 148
entity-relationship models, 35, 38, 68
EURIG (the European RDA Interest Group), 29
examples, 180–184
explore task, 37, 50
expression entity, 40–44, 47–48, 62–63
extensibility, 6
extension plan, 134–136
extent of manifestation, 107

F

family, 97, 98–99
fictitious entities, 131–133
find task, 36–37, 50–51
Five Laws of Library Science, The (Ranganathan), 38
flexibility, 189, 190
format variation problem, 77
FRAD (Functional Requirements for Authority Data), 3, 17–18, 33–50, 82, 131
FRBR (Functional Requirements for Bibliographic Records), 3, 17–18, 33–50, 76, 95–96, 100, 121, 131
FRBR$_{oo}$, 68
frequency, 137
FRSAD (Functional Requirements for Subject Authority Data), 3, 17–18, 33–50
Functional Requirements for Authority Data (FRAD), 3, 17–18, 33–50, 82, 131
Functional Requirements for Bibliographic Records: Final Report, 34
Functional Requirements for Bibliographic Records (FRBR), 3, 17–18, 33–50, 76, 95–96, 100, 121, 131
Functional Requirements for Subject Authority Data (FRSAD), 3, 17–18, 33–50
Fund Committee, 79

G

general material designations (GMDs), 104
GitHub, 185
Glennan, Kathy, 80
Glossary, 147, 185–186
GMDs, 78
governance, 26–29, 79–80, 192
"Guidance" menu, 146–147, 178

H

Hennelly, James, 185
hierarchical structure for entities, 52–53, 59–60, 98–99

I

identifiers, 22–23, 86, 157–158, 184
identify task, 36–37, 50
IFLA Library Reference Model (IFLA LRM)
 aggregates and, 121
 alignment with, 2, 3–4, 78
 bibliographic conceptual models and, 108, 141
 definition of person and, 131
 entity-relationship models in, 17–18
 hierarchy of entities and, 98–99
 internationalization and, 191–193
 linearity and, 100
 manifestation statement and, 139–140
 organization according to entities and, 95–97
 overview of, 33–34
 relationships and, 119
 representative expression and, 138–139
 Semantic Web and, 68–69
 serials and, 136, 137
 user tasks and, 93–95
 WEMI (work, expression, manifestation, item) and, 42
inaccuracies, 88
inspiration relationship, 60
instructions, numbering of, 154–155
International Cataloguing Principles (ICP), 17
International Conference on Cataloguing Principles, 15
International Conference on the Principles and Future Development of AACR, 19, 75
International Council of Museums (ICOM), 68
International Federation of Library Associations and Institutions (IFLA), 16–17, 34–35. *See also* IFLA Library Reference Model (IFLA LRM)
International Standard Bibliographic Description (ISBD), 16, 18, 76
internationalization, 9–10, 15–31, 172, 189, 190–192
interoperability, 6, 8, 11, 18–19, 67
IRIs (Internationalized Resource Identifiers), 8, 86–87, 111, 157–158, 160, 168, 183, 184
ISBD (International Standard Bibliographic Description), 5
ISSN, 158

J

James, Kate, 139
Johnson, Bruce, 76
Joint Steering Committee for Development of RDA (JSC), 26, 27, 75, 77–78, 79–80, 84, 85–86
justify task, 37, 51

L

language of expression, 139, 157–158, 182
layout, 111
Library of Congress Rule Interpretations, 172
Library of Congress-Program for Cooperative Cataloging (LC-PCC), 172, 174
linear text, move away from, 100–103
linked data environment, 7–9
Logical Structure of the Anglo-American Cataloguing Rules, The, 75, 76
log-in, personal, 151–152
LRM$_{oo}$, 68

M

manifestation entity, 63–66

manifestation frequency statement, 137
manifestation of work, 125–126
manifestation statement, 60, 61–62, 139–141
MARC 21, 5, 18–19, 162, 167, 174, 190
MARC mapping/records, 84–87, 111–112, 150, 162
Maxwell, Robert, 138
media type, 104–105, 106, 107–108
metadata elements, 108–109
metadata works, 177
mode of issuance, 133–135
museum community, 68

N

name entity, 39–40, 48
name of person, 162–163
NARDAC (the North American RDA Committee), 29
navigation, 145–155
nomen, 40, 47, 49, 54, 56–57, 127–131, 132
nomen string, 128–131
non-human entities, 131–133
note on manifestation, 175
"Notes," 152
numbering of instructions, 154–155

O

obtain task, 36, 50
ONIX, 18–19, 104
ORDAC (the Oceania RDA Committee), 29

P

parallel aggregate, 123
Paris Principles, 15–16, 74
person entity, 55–57, 111
personal log-in, 151–152
place entity, 54–55, 58, 119
"Policies" menu, 146–147, 173
policy statements, 171–174
preferred name, 130–131
production method, 111
Program for Cooperative Cataloging (PCC), 85

R

Ranganathan, S. R., 38
range, 112–114
RDA (Resource Description and Access)
    after 3R Project, 189–194
    aggregates in, 121–124
    background of, 73–92
    bibliographic conceptual models and, 33–71
    content and carrier in, 103–108
    digital environment and, 3–9
    elements in, 109–120
    as global standard, 9–11
    impact of, 11
    as international standard, 15–31
    key aspects of, 93–144
    nomen in, 127–131
    overview of, 1–14
    principles governing, 16–17
    purpose of, 3
    resource description and, 131–141
    shortcuts in, 125–127
    standards related to, 17–19
    structure of, 95–103
    theoretical framework for, 3–4
    user focus of, 93–95
    using, 145–187
RDA Board, 26–29, 79
RDA entity, 97
RDA Reference, 8, 186
RDA Registry, 7, 8, 20, 25, 185
RDA Staff Registry, 185–186
RDA Steering Committee (RSC), 26–29, 79, 80, 84
RDA Toolkit
    application profiles, 171–172, 174–175
    Condition/Option, 163–166
    data provenance, 175–180
    Element Reference, 159–163
    encoding schemes, 166–171
    examples, 180–184
    Glossary, 185–186
    internationalization and, 20
    navigation, 145–155
    organization of, 100–103
    policy statements, 171–174
    recording methods, 155–159
    3R Project and, 1–3
    translations and, 24–25
    as web tool, 6–7
RDA/ONIX Framework for Resource Categorization (ROF), 104
RDF (Resource Description Framework), 5, 8, 19
RDFS (Resource Description Framework Schema), 113
record syntaxes, 171
"Recording Methods," 184
recording methods, 155–159, 190
recording source, 179–180
regional representation, 27–29
related entities, 133
relationship designator, 115–118
relationship elements, 116–118
relationships between entities, 38–39, 47–49, 58–60, 88–89, 114–120. *See also* entities
representative expression, 60–61, 138–139
res entity, 52, 53, 58, 97, 133
resource description, 131–141
"Resources" menu, 146–147
Riva, Pat, 50
Rules for a Printed Dictionary Catalog (Cutter), 38

S

scope note attribute, 46–47
searching/search features, 148–149, 150–151
select task, 36–37, 50
Semantic Web, 6, 7–8, 11, 68–69, 113, 157, 190, 191
serials, 65–67, 134, 136, 137
shared governance, 26–29. *See also* governance
shortcuts, 125–127
signposts for orientation, 149–150
Simple Knowledge Organization System, 131

SKOS, 131
spelling mistakes, 88
string encoding schemes (SES), 21–24, 166–167, 170–171, 174, 192
structured description, 157–159, 184, 190
subclasses, 45, 52–54, 58–60, 97–99, 124, 132–133
subject relationship, 49
subjects, 45
superclasses, 40, 45, 46, 50, 52–53, 58–60, 82, 97–99

T
tabs, in RDA Toolkit, 146–147
tactile resources, 111
thema entity, 40, 45, 46–47, 49
3R Project, description of, 1–2
timespan entity, 54–55, 58, 111, 119
transcription, 140–141, 177, 180
translations and translation workflow, 24–25, 26–27
Translations Team Liaison Officer, 29
Trustees, 79
type attribute, 46–47

U
Uniform Resource Locator, 159

unstructured description, 157–159, 180, 184, 190
user, focus on, 35–38, 93–95, 189–190
user tasks, 35–37, 50–51, 93–95

V
verbalized labels, 161
"View as Relationship," 183
"View in Context," 181–182
Virtual International Authority File (VIAF), 86
vision statement, 191
vocabulary encoding schemes (VES), 21–24, 147, 166–169, 174, 192

W
WEMI (work, expression, manifestation, item), 40–43, 44, 47–48, 53
Wider Community Engagement Officer, 29
work entity, 40–44, 47–48
work group, 136–137

Z
Žumer, Maja, 53

A000023176232